The European Union: Annual Review 2004/2005

Edited by

Lee Miles

General Editors: William Paterson and Jim Rollo

Blackwell
Publishing

First published 2005 by Blackwell Publishing Ltd

British Library Cataloguing-in-Publication Data applied for
ISBN 1 4051 2986 7

Set in the United Kingdom by Photoscript, Deddington, Oxon
Printed and bound in the United Kingdom by Page Bros, Norwich

The publisher's policy is to use permanent paper from mills
that operate a sustainable forestry policy, and which has been
manufactured from pulp processed using acid-free and
elementary chlorine-free practices.
Furthermore, the publisher ensures that the text paper and cover board
used have met acceptable environmental accreditation standards.

For further information on Blackwell Publishing, visit our website:
http://www.blackwellpublishing.com

CONTENTS

Editorial: A Fusing Europe in a Confusing World?

LEE MILES
University of Liverpool

Introduction

It seems highly appropriate to begin my last editorial as editor of the *Annual Review* by pondering several themes that are also highly pertinent in my other capacity as Director of the Europe in the World Centre (EWC) at the University of Liverpool: namely to reflect upon the present position and future capabilities of the European Union (EU) and its continual search to become 'a superpower without a superstate' (Regelsberger and Wessels, 2005, p. 116).

The year 2004 was a rather demanding one for the European Union. As Cameron (2004, p. 149) comments, the state of the EU at the end of 2003 could be 'best described as uncertain', something that was in many ways reflected in the previous edition of the *Annual Review*. Nevertheless, 2004 was to be a year when the Union made some positive inroads into dealing with such uncertainty.

As Wessels and Dinan illustrate in this *Annual Review*, the Union completed a number of important tasks that are compatible with an ongoing trend of a 'fusing Europe'. First, May 2004 saw the completion of the next phase in the enlargement of the Union, with the EU absorbing its largest influx of (ten) new members to date; expanding from an EU-15 to an EU-25. 2004 therefore represents a formal step in an ongoing process in which yet more European states are accepting the *acquis* of the Union with its mix of intergovernmental and supranational features. Nevertheless, as Smith in this *Annual Review* highlights, the year was also important since the Union did not shut the door to further enlargement in the future either. Progress was made on proposed

Bulgarian and Romanian accession in 2007, and other candidate countries where full membership is a longer-term prospect. Given the growing interest in EU membership from Balkan states as well as the Union making important decisions in 2004 on opening accession negotiations with Turkey, the Union is increasingly faced with ever more complicated demands in the near future on its external relations policy. Moreover, as Dannreuther (2004a, p. 2) comments, the impact of the 2004 enlargement is 'not limited to the accession of new members, but involves the definition of new borders and the creation of new neighbours with their particular demands and interests'. Pre-accession strategies as well as, for instance, the continued development of the European neighbourhood policy (ENP) that are designed to handle the demands of the Union's closest neighbours – and especially those where full membership is a longer-term prospect or not even on offer – will continue to be a source of attention for the Union.

Second, the Union was able to overcome the lack of agreement in December 2003 on an EU Constitutional Treaty, and the governments of the Member States finalized and signed that document in 2004. According to Wessels in his keynote article, there is some evidence of a continued shift of political attention as well as resources in the EU to the Brussels arena without always implying a direct communitarization in strict legal terms (see also Regelsberger and Wessels, 2004, p. 94). The 2004 EU Constitutional Treaty, if ever ratified given events in 2005, goes some way to making the Union 'easier to navigate' (Crum, 2005, p. 217). However, for the most part the Union will continue to develop under the influence of 'fusion dynamics' of mutually reinforcing learning (the so-called 'living' constitution) and legal treaty-making (the legal evolution) of the Union. As Wessels concludes, the Constitutional Treaty has gone further along the path of creating shared, pooled responsibility between the EU and national levels.

The EU Constitutional Treaty is not too rigid and, if approved, would create a stable, if complicated, system of governance, which may actually be the best the Union could achieve in 2004. At the very least, the 2004 Treaty should alleviate some of the concerns of Skach (2005, pp. 154–5) that any substantial 'strait-jacketing' of political actors that restricts their room for diplomatic manœuvre by having too detailed constitutional articles in a rigid constitution must be avoided. This, Skach believes, may actually undermine the Union's search for greater efficacy and efficiency.

Third, the Union, as Allen and Smith as well as Monar illustrate in this *Annual Review*, furthered its efforts to develop EU capabilities in handling external and internal security threats. The Union continued to implement its ongoing plans for civil and military crisis management capabilities and paid further attention to developing co-ordination between the Member States in the field of justice and home affairs. As Wessels and Monar show, the EU Constitutional Treaty will also include some important changes in the number of EU competences addressing internal security matters, not least because questions of terrorism, migration and transnational organized crime were all major issues discussed, rightly or wrongly, in connection with the discourse on the new Treaty and further enlargement.

Regardless of whether the 2004 Treaty is ratified, a more detailed examination of the Union's external policy may be especially relevant for this notion of a 'fusing Europe', especially since the 2004 Treaty envisages significant changes to the CFSP/ESDP operation and institutional apparatus. Certainly, an assessment of the Union's external policy 'may be considered the ultimate test case of whether member governments not only recognise the merits of co-operation ... but are willing to actually match their words with the provisions of common powers' (Crum, 2005, p. 208). It is also, as Wessels notes, the provisions of the EU Constitutional Treaty pertaining to EU external relations and, in particular, the creation of an EU minister for foreign affairs, where there is clearest evidence of 'fusion'. He regards the creation of such an EU foreign minister as not only a notable innovation, but one that can be seen as 'a ideal-typical case of fusion' and certainly consistent with the ongoing creation of a fusing Europe given that the new post merges the roles of high representative for the CFSP and a vice-president of the European Commission. Even if the Constitutional Treaty is not ratified, it is likely that the Member State governments will seek to introduce such important innovations in the future.

External relations policy and the CFSP/ESDP are clearly the policy fields where the Union will also be sending its clearest message to third countries, especially in the year in which the Iraq conflict continued to fuel tensions between the leading Member States, on how committed a 'fusing' Union is to acting constructively and with an assertive common European voice to both immediate and longer-term global problems. In effect, the changes to the EU external relations portfolio and capabilities as envisaged in the 2004 Treaty continue to reflect the Union's ambition to act as a more coherent and consistent international player and resolve, through fusion, to ensure that the Union can be a more forceful international actor even with an enlarged membership of 25.

This brings us to a further theme of 2004: that the Union continued to be faced with a 'confusing world' that makes ever growing demands on the Union's time, diplomatically, economically and even, if rather tentatively, militarily. As Dannreuther (2004a, pp. 2–3) recognizes, third countries are interested in EU developments since there are implications for them as the Union adapts to post-cold war geo-political challenges and 9/11, defines its new borders after the 2004 enlargement, seeks through a new Treaty to promote deeper political integration in Europe, and develops an EU internal and external security crisis management capability. After all, not only did the Union continue to expand its array of ongoing commitments, for instance, taking on larger peace-keeping roles from Nato and further developing its existing multilateral policies such as the Barcelona process and the ENP (mentioned above); but the Union is also clearly aware that third countries will not wait to see whether the EU Constitutional Treaty will come into play and thus enhance EU external policy co-ordination.

One of the problems is that the Union is having to respond to a large number of external pressures coming from other international organizations, third countries and, put simply, reacting to international events in differing regions that are sometimes confusing and often contradictory. Take one specific region, say the Middle East, where discussion appears regularly on the agendas of Member State governments. Here, Member States are faced with a multitude of issues, dealing with a wide variety of diplomatic contacts between the Member States themselves, and between the Member States and relevant third countries. In 2004 alone, the Member States were handling, amongst other things, responses to the continued Muslim insurgency in Iraq, and the desire for common EU support for democratization there. In addition, they were managing the implications of the evolving dialogue between Britain, France and Germany (EU-3) with Iran over its nuclear weapons programme.

Nevertheless, if a fusing European Union is to develop coherent external policy stances efficiently in order to respond to the demands of countries and regions in a confusing world then, as Peterson (2004) highlighted, relations between the EU Member States and the United States led by President George W. Bush, now elected for a second-term in 2004, will be central. The divisions between the governments of the Member States were an important backdrop to their response to the demands of a more assertive US fighting a 'war on terrorism', and the Madrid bombings in early 2004 brought the implications of such policies even closer in the minds of European policy-makers. The Member States also continued to fret about President Bush's limited enthusiasm for utilizing Nato as the premier crisis-management organization.

Indications by late 2004 were that the EU states of so-called 'old Europe', particularly Chirac's France and Schröder's Germany, continued to repair the diplomatic bridges with Bush's US and the 'new Europe' that included Blair's UK. This was, of course, only to be expected for, as Cameron (2004, p. 159) correctly identifies, the governments of both the EU and the US recognize that 'the bottom line is that when the EU and US work together, they get things done'. Perhaps what is sometimes less clear, yet remains equally important, is that unity between the US and Europe in handling the demands of a confused world are also facilitated when the EU states are more unified. Thus, a fusing Europe may also be a key, at least in the European context, to handling a confusing world. Rather than viewing two portraits – a fusing Europe and a confusing world – it is probably better for the painter to see them as two images in the same picture.

Returning to one theme of this editorial mentioned earlier, it is of some importance to third countries of a confusing world that a fusing Europe did not also agree a too rigid Constitutional Treaty in 2004. In simple terms, an EU Constitutional Treaty – if finally ratified in 2005–06 – that enhances the ability of the Union to speak with a coherent voice but not, at the same time, paying the cost by only allowing for slow or weak EU action – may be 'good' for a confusing world. For third countries, any assessments of the Union's external relations policy are driven largely by an analysis of the Union's capacity to deliver results. Any legitimacy and credence that they bestow on the Union's CFSP/ESDP come as much from evaluations of the Union's positive perform- ance in such fields as crisis management, as from any confidence or attention placed by them on the legal or constitutional basis on which the Member State governments take such action.

Hence, for a confusing world, as well as a fusing Europe, it could be argued that it is beneficial that the 2004 EU Constitutional Treaty allows for notions of 'flexibility' in the CFSP and ESDP domains that would also seem to be compatible with the concept of a 'hub and spokes Europe' (Miles, 2003) that this editor outlined in the *Annual Review* two issues ago. Certainly, there are articles in the EU Constitutional Treaty that enable the Union still to undertake CFSP-related actions led by 'coalitions of willing' EU Member States. Irrespec- tive of the fate of the Constitutional Treaty, the focus of the CFSP/ESDP will still be on enhancing the Union's capacity for action that will achieve positive and speedy results. Equally, and as part of 'fusion', the Member States will continue to recognize the benefits of enabling the Union to utilize and merge national and EU instruments and pool actors – as part of the Union's 'living constitution' – without always having first clearly defined their overall com- petences. At least in the field of EU external relations, it remains important that the proposed EU Constitutional Treaty enhances the stability of a fusing European Union without becoming too legalistic or rigid that its effectiveness or efficiency in handling a confusing world is restricted.

Closing Thoughts – 'No' to a Constitutional Europe, 'Yes' to a Fusing Europe?

In 2005, the future of the 2004 EU Constitutional Treaty was cast into doubt. On 29 May, the French public overwhelmingly rejected the proposed EU Constitutional Treaty (54.9 per cent against, 45.1 per cent for, on a turnout of 69.3 per cent) – a winning margin of almost 10 percentage points. This was followed a few days later when the Dutch population (1 June 2005) sent an even more categorical message to EU leaders. They too rejected the Constitutional Treaty (by 61.6 per cent against, to 38.4 per cent for, on a turnout of 62.8 per cent) with an even greater winning majority (24 percentage points); that also laid the ground for the UK's Prime Minister Tony Blair to express major doubts in early 2005 about plans for holding a British plebiscite previously scheduled for 2006. At the time of writing, the future of the proposed new Treaty remains very unclear.

Many differing reasons have been identified as to why the French and Dutch electorates voted against the proposed Treaty: some are common to both countries, such as public concerns over future EU enlargement; some are not, for example, French concerns that the Treaty would undermine the French 'social model'; yet others are purely domestic-oriented, for instance, public discontent in France with the performance of President Jacques Chirac. Equally, many of the motives for rejection had little to do with the actual content of the Treaty. However, at first glance some important preliminary and tentative conclusions can be drawn.

The conduct of the French and Dutch publics does seem to reflect the dynamics of the 'Paradox of a Popular Europe' that this author alluded to in last year's issue of the *Annual Review* (Miles, 2004). While there are many in France and the Netherlands who remained concerned about the democratic accountability of the existing Union, and thus support EU measures that aim to improve this, the message from the two electorates also seemed to include a common rejection of a Treaty that sought to give the Union a formal constitution that was construed as impacting too much on their own domestic political systems and nationally-derived constitutional rights. Hence, the peoples of France and the Netherlands may have been rejecting what they saw as too much of an interfering 'constitutional Europe'. They were voting 'no' to a perceived constitutional Europe even if, as argued earlier, the proposed Treaty did not actually envisage, or could be regarded in reality as, a fully-fledged European constitution.

Yet, can we regard this as a similar rejection of a fusing Europe? Are we looking at a scenario where the peoples of two of the founding EU Member States are calling for 'de-fusion' whereby national and EU competences should be clarified and ultimately power should be returned to the national level? The most probable answers to these two questions are an equally resolute 'no'. Neither vote should be taken as implying that the French or Dutch want to leave the Union or unwind the agreements made up to Nice in 2000. Rather, it would seem that, while many do not like the concept of a 'constitutional Europe', they are still happy to belong to a Union that represents a fused mix of intergovernmental and supranational features, although this may be with the proviso that the Union continues to produce outputs that have discernible economic and political benefits in the eyes of the electorates (so-called 'performance fusion', see Miles, 2005).

More specifically, improving foreign policy co-operation is universally perceived, and enjoys broad public support, as an area where the Union will need to make further reforms in order to enhance its effectiveness and will continue to be a basis for further EU innovation. Although there remains controversy over EU agreements that seek to create a symbolic European constitution, it is likely that the Member State governments will seek to repackage most of the treaty-based provisions relating to practical CFSP/ESDP co-operation and want to see them in place one day in the future. In many instances, it is unlikely that they will be resisted by the European populations. Hence, it may be the case that the future of a constitutional Europe may be in doubt, but the ongoing demands of a confusing world continue to provide broader rationales for a fusing Europe that represents a pragmatic compromise and a practical balance of intergovernmental and supranational features. Just as the demands of a confused world are better served by a fusing Europe, it remains the case that the pressures on Europe from a confusing world may help to steer the Union through a difficult period post-2004 as it seeks to resolve the future of the EU Constitutional Treaty.

Acknowledgements

During my three years as editor of this publication, I have been fortunate to enjoy the benefits accruing from the knowledge that the *Annual Review* has regularly brought together a healthy mix of established and emerging experts as contributors. Its strength has always lain as much in the professionalism of the respective contributors in meeting highly demanding deadlines as in the individual capabilities of any particular editor. In addition, there has been a strong consistency in the line-up of the contributors during my period as editor so that part of the remit – to provide annual authoritative assessments that readers can compile and read over different areas to chart the Union's evolution and meet their respective expert needs – has been, for the most part, achievable. My sincere thanks to Desmond Dinan, David Allen and Michael Smith, Julie Smith, Jörg Monar and Nigel Grimwade, who have stayed the course and remained regular contributors during my three years at the helm.

Furthermore, it also gives me great delight to see that the new additions to the list of contributors brought in over the last few years – David Howarth, David G. Mayes, Michael Dougan, Michael Bruter, Karen Henderson and Debra Johnson – have settled into their new roles with comparative ease. They continue to uphold the reputation of this publication as a premier contribution to the academic study of the European Union.

It also gives me a great pleasure to thank Wolfgang Wessels for writing the keynote article for this year, and to show my appreciation to Nicholas Rees and Peter van Ham for providing expert insights into the Council Presidencies of 2004. In particular, it has given me personal satisfaction to see that the keynote article continues to be viewed as one of the most important places for leading scholars to provide contemporary insights and make an academic contribution to assessing the evolution of the Union in a particular year. The keynote article on the EU Constitutional Treaty by Wessels continues this tradition in providing not just a detailed assessment of the proposed new Treaty, but also weaving in theoretical evaluations that academics and practitioners alike will, in my view, find of great relevance. As departing editor, I look forward to reading future contributions from the sidelines.

One further clarification should be added at this point. Due to the yearly production schedule of the *Annual Review*, contributors are regularly confronted with challenge of commenting on key aspects pertaining to the immediate future of the Union when things are rather uncertain. There is always an element of ongoing adaptation to contributions as later, often unpredictable, developments unfold that are of relevance and have to be incorporated at the last minute. Hence, contributing to this publication is a demanding task where writing chapters translates into an ongoing commitment with less focus on the early delivery of a finished package. In this year's issue there is, quite correctly, a strong focus on the process culminating in, and actual design of, the Constitutional Treaty. As events in 2005 have illustrated, the future of the Treaty, as agreed in 2004, is questionable. This *Annual Review* still fulfils an important task in outlining how the 2004 Constitutional Treaty arrived at its final stages, even if the fate of the Treaty hangs in the balance. Readers should keep this in mind when reading key chapters.

It is now time to hand over the mantle of *Annual Review* editorship to Ulrich Sedelmeier and Alasdair Young. May I take this opportunity to wish them well in their new roles, and hope that they will find editing this prestigious publication as rewarding an experience as I have done.

References

Cameron, F. (2004) 'Europe's Future'. In Cameron, F. (ed.) *The Future of Europe: Integration and Enlargement* (London/New York: Routledge).

Crum, B. (2005) 'Towards Finality? An Assessment of the Achievements of the European Convention'. In Verdun, A. and Croci, O. (eds) *The European Union in the Wake of Eastern Enlargement* (Manchester/New York: Manchester University Press).

Dannreuther, R. (2004a) 'Introduction: Setting the Framework'. In Dannreuther, R. (ed.) *European Union Foreign and Security Policy: Towards a Neighbourhood Strategy* (London/New York: Routledge).

Dannreuther, R. (2004b) 'Conclusion: Towards a Neighbourhood Strategy?'. In Dannreuther, R. (ed.) *European Union Foreign and Security Policy: Towards a Neighbourhood Strategy* (London/New York: Routledge).

Miles, L. (2003) 'Editorial: Moving Towards a "Hub and Spokes Europe"?'. In Miles, L. (ed.) *The European Union: Annual Review 2002/2003,* Vol. 41, pp. 1–11.

Miles, L. (2004) 'Editorial: The Paradox of a Popular Europe'. In Miles, L. (ed.) *The European Union: Annual Review 2003/2004*, Vol. 42, pp. 1–8.

Miles, L. (2005) *Fusing with Europe? Sweden in the European Union* (Aldershot: Ashgate).

Peterson, J. (2004) 'Europe, America, Iraq: Worst Ever, Ever Worsening?' In Miles, L. (ed.) *The European Union: Annual Review 2003/2004,* Vol. 42, pp. 9–26.

Regelsberger, E. and Wessels, W. (2005) 'The Evolution of the Common Foreign and Security Policy: A Case of an Imperfect Ratchet Fusion'. In Verdun, A. and Croci, O. (eds) *The European Union in the Wake of Eastern Enlargement* (Manchester/New York: Manchester University Press).

Skach, C. (2005) 'We, the Peoples? Constitutionalizing the European Union'. *Journal of Common Market Studies,* Vol. 43, No. 1, pp. 149–70.

Keynote Article: The Constitutional Treaty – Three Readings from a Fusion Perspective

WOLFGANG WESSELS
University of Cologne

'L'esprit humain invente plus facilement les choses que les mots: de là
vient l'usage de tant de termes impropres et d'expressions incomplètes'
Alexis de Tocqueville, *De la Démocratie en Amérique*

I. A Key Document in the Theoretical Spotlight

Challenges: A Variety of Perspectives

The 'Treaty establishing a Constitution for Europe' (TCE) poses a challenge:
just as politicians face considerable difficulty in explaining the merits of the
text to their respective peoples, so academics also need to consider how to
evaluate this document. The Treaty invites us to apply a set of stimulating
perspectives and thereby test the key assumptions of our *acquis académique*.
Notwithstanding the present uncertainty about its ratification, the text of the
Constitutional Treaty already comprises a central component in the analysis
of the European construction. Even if the Constitutional Treaty does not enter
into force, it will continue to serve to describe a certain state in the evolution
of the EU system, as well as to identify options for shaping the constitutional
architecture. In terms of EU 'constitutionalization' (see, e.g., Weiler, 1999;
Hobe, 2003), this treaty revision can be regarded as an 'historic milestone'
(Ahern, 2004, p. 1), a 'history making decision' (Peterson, 1995) at a 'critical
juncture' (Bulmer and Burch, 1998, p. 604), or as 'a choice for Europe' (see
Moravcsik, 1998). Each text of a 'legal' constitution (Olsen, 2000, p. 7; March
and Olsen, 2004, p. 8) is, however, open to, or even demands, numerous, often
controversial, readings and interpretations (see, e.g., Quermonne, 1992).

As a starting point, it is suggested that the TCE provisions are explored by applying three different time perspectives. The methodological assumption of this exercise stresses that the process of integration needs to be analysed in dynamic, and not static, terms. Catchwords such as 'fédération d'Etats-nations' (Chirac, 2004; Delors, 2004, p. 455; Constantinesco, 2002, pp. 120–31) or 'Staatenverbund' (association of states) (Bundesverfassungsgericht, 1994) merely represent analytical 'snapshots'. However, to understand fully the evolution of the Union, a 'film' focusing on constitutional changes over time appears to be the more appropriate route.

Thus, we may wish to direct the analytical spotlight on to the longer-term historical trends influencing the transformation of European states, i.e. in a 'longue durée' (Braudel, 1990, p.15) over the last five centuries. From this perspective, the Constitutional Treaty might signify a 'saut qualitatif' or a 'constitutional moment' (see Ackermann, 2000, p. 2; Nicolaïdis, 2004. p. 9) towards a European state writ large, which possesses all those functions and defining characteristics of a state in the conventional sense of the word. The labels 'United States of Europe' (Churchill, 1946; Monnet, 1975, p. 475; Kohl, 1994, p. 511) or 'europäischer Bundesstaat' (Hallstein, 1972) were employed in describing such a step. While thinking in terms of linking and comparing the Union to a nation-state might be considered outdated – reflecting somewhat a 'methodological nationalism' (Beck and Grande, 2004), or a biased state-centric perspective – it offers a helpful point of reference.

If a 'middle range' perspective (Merton, 1968, p. 52) concentrating on the evolution of the EU system throughout the last decades is employed, the Constitutional Treaty should be seen as consistent with the general trends influencing the European institutional architecture since the early 1950s. With this view, the TCE might be understood as a further step forward for 'a Europe of the third generation', which introduced a new quasi-constitutional approach after a period of limited piecemeal engineering. The debate over the principal features of these trends represents a further wave of decades-long political and theoretical controversies over the *finalité* and major characteristics of the European construction, which revolves around the key terms of 'Europe fédérale', on the one hand, and 'fédération d'Etats-nations' on the other (Constantinesco, 2002, pp. 120–31), as well as Community versus intergovernmental methods (see, *inter alia*, Giscard d'Estaing, 2003, p. 24). Hence, interpretations already differ after a first reading of the TCE: will the provisions of the institutional architecture strengthen a more intergovernmental (see, e.g. Bogdanor, 2004, p. 6), a supranational (see, e.g., Hughes, 2004, p. 12) or a federal (see Pinder, 2004, p. 7) orientation of the Union?

The third time horizon is more short term: taking a micro-perspective of the institutional architecture. We should ask if and how national and European actors might make use of the new, proposed, 'legal' constitution in order to create a durable and lasting pattern of 'living' institutions (Olsen, 2000, p. 6; March and Olsen, 2004, p. 8).

In this keynote article, all three perspectives are taken up, including discussions as to whether and how the Constitutional Treaty, if ratified, maps out a new step towards a further level of integration, in line with the logic of fusion (see Figure 1).

Figure 1 uses two dimensions: the vertical axis represents the allocation of competences and uses the terminology of the Constitutional Treaty; the horizontal axis applies conventional terminology, and looks at the modes of decision-making, especially the powers of the EP together with the provisions for voting in the Council, as indicators (see also Figures 5a, b, below).

In line with fusion theory (see Wessels, 1997; Miles, 2003), the Constitutional Treaty demonstrates that the EU is constructed by European states to

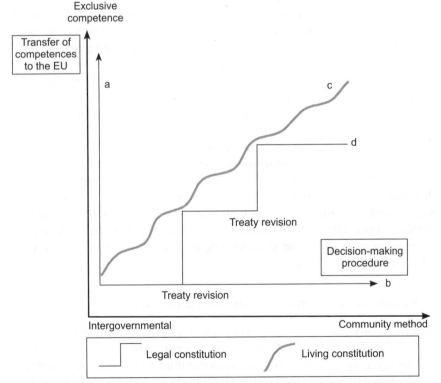

Figure 1: Trends of Integration by Transfer of Competences and Procedures of Decision-making
Source: Jean Monnet Chair, 2005.

serve their own objectives – in effect, not replacing but supporting them. The thesis claims that beyond the 'rescue of the nation-state' (Milward, 2000), the EU countries as 'masters of the Treaty' (Bundesverfassungsgericht, 1994) used the opportunity of the Intergovernmental Conference (IGC) to improve the efficiency and effectiveness of the Union's actions, so as to reinforce the functions of the nation-state that developed over the last centuries, and thereby moving upwards on the integration ladder (see line a) and towards the Community without, however, relinquishing their say altogether. By reinforcing their own channels of participation, Member States strengthen their 'voice'.

In this view, the Constitutional Treaty forms part of a 'multi-level constitutionalism' (Pernice, 1999) intertwining the national and EU level. Public policies pursued and operating at several levels complement each other and create a complex division of labour, whilst also seeking to achieve the primary objectives of the constituent states. This intensive interdependence reinforces the EU's long-term stability, as well as being a source of ever increasing criticism about the Union's lack of transparency and accountability.

With respect to traditional controversies over intergovernmental, supranational or federal features, the fusion argument claims that the concurrence of different trends within one and the same constitutional architecture is no mere coincidence, but a fundamental pattern of the EU construction. Ambiguities in the written text that indicate intra- and inter-institutional tensions are no accidental by-product of EU summitry; rather, they illustrate the basic logic of increasing the efficiency of EU institutions, while also preserving a high degree of national participation.

In order to test this thesis, the wording of the main chapters of the proposed Constitutional Treaty is examined. We expect, at the same time, that actors in the 'living' constitution (line c) will, in practice, promote further initiatives that will be incorporated into the next history-making revision of the EU's legal foundation (line d). In line with 'meta-theoretical approaches of social constructivism' (Risse, 2004, p.160) these readings are, in themselves, part of an ongoing process of 'constructing' one or several 'narratives' on the evolution of European integration.

II. Visions and Missions: Constructing an Identity

A deeper analysis finds its point of departure with the exact wording of the title of the TCE. The very term 'Constitution' refers to an established terminology commonly associated with state formation, although this label need not imply the existence of a state (see Weiler, 1997; Pernice, 2000: p.160; Hobe, 2003). From the perspective of fusion, the TCE reflects the attitudes of the constitution-makers to give the Union a specific legal nature: as states are transferring core policy areas to the EU, a 'Constitution' is perceived to be a must also for this level of the European constitutional set-up. Yet, at the same time, the term 'Treaty' reiterates the conventional state-based method and represents an international agreement between the EU countries.

The Preamble places the Constitutional Treaty within a long historical context 'drawing inspiration from the cultural, religious and humanist inheritance of Europe' (Preamble, para. 1), and also within a middle range evolution 'ensuring the continuity of the Community acquis' (Preamble, para. 5). What is more, these formulations of the TCE draw lessons from the past for visions of the future: 'remaining proud of their own national identities and history, the peoples of Europe are determined to transcend their former divisions and, united ever more closely, to forge a common destiny'. This vision leads to an ambitious mission: 'Europe offers … the best chance of pursuing … in awareness of their responsibilities towards future generations and the Earth, the great venture which makes of it a special area of human hope' (Preamble, para. 4); this is taken up in the formulation of the Preamble of the Charter (Part II TCE) and of the principles for 'external action' (see especially Art. III-292 (1)). These objectives go far beyond a community confined to functional economic tasks. In effect, the wording of the TCE resembles the 'creeds' of nation-states.

Such 'a canon of values [might] create a strong bond between the Union's citizens' (European Parliament, 2005) and might eventually lead to a 'constitutional patriotism' (Habermas, 1996), creating a special kind of legitimacy as the basis for an ever stronger 'transfer of loyalty' (see Haas, 1958, p. 16) of its 'citizens' (Art. I-1). Increasing moral support for the Union is thus driven by 'post-materialistic' (Inglehart, 1977, pp. 27–8) values, quite different from the expectation of economic benefits or a benign neglect of a 'permissive consensus' (Inglehardt, 1970, p.773).

A further, yet different, line of identity-building consists of fostering emotional support through the propagation of 'symbols of the Union' (Art I-8), which comprise its flag, anthem, motto ('united in diversity'), currency and the Union-wide holiday (9 May). Their inclusion in the constitutional document is reminiscent of the strategies followed by nation-states in the nineteenth century that sought to gain legitimacy and secure loyalty through the creation of visible forms of identification. The reference to solidarity, which appears no fewer than 18 times throughout the text of the TCE, for example in the 'Solidarity Clause' (Art. I-43), and some kind of delimited clause for mutual defence (Art. I-41 (7)), might also help in constructing a sense of 'imagined community' (Anderson, 1983).

There are also a substantial number of references to notions that reflect the ideal type of what constitutes a typical democratic and constitutional state. The choice to call legal acts 'laws' (Art. I-33 (1)) and to rename the co-decision procedure as the 'ordinary legislative procedure' (Art. I-34) reflect such notions, as do the references to 'democratic life', 'democratic equality' (Art. I-45), 'representative' and 'participatory democracy' (Art. I-46 and Art. I-47).

It is not surprising also to find formulations that lean towards an alternative interpretation of identity, demos and state characteristics. Supporting an intergovernmental reading that stresses the legal nature of a treaty, we find the term 'peoples' (in the plural) as opposed to simply European people (in the singular) in the Preamble of the Constitutional Treaty and that of the Charter of Fundamental Rights. On several occasions, the document derives the legitimacy of the EU and its Constitutional Treaty from the Member States in their role as 'masters of the Treaty' (Bundesverfassungsgericht, 1994) and as 'principals' (see Pollack, 1997; Kassim and Menon, 2003): 'Member States confer competences to attain objectives they have in common [to the European Union]' (Art. I-1 (1)). Also, only Member States (and not the EP, for example) are authorized to decide on the revision of the Constitutional Treaty (see Art. IV-443 and 445). The founding generation of the TCE has also erected firewalls in several places to guard against the erosion of the nation-state by a 'centralised, all powerful superstate' (European Parliament, 2005); for example, to 'respect … national identities … and their essential state functions' (Art. I-5 (1)). Another important indicator, or symbol, for this nation-state oriented reading is the article allowing the 'voluntary withdrawal from the Union' (Art. I-60). For the 'souverainistes', this option signals that the founding text is still a treaty between a 'group of nations' (Blair, 2004) resembling some kind of temporary alliance that also includes an authorized escape from the 'prison' of the EU (see Louis and Ronse, 2005, p. 121). This provision is seen as an essential threshold between a 'fédération d'Etats-nations' on the one side, and a federal Europe on the other (Moreau Defarges, 2004, p. 73). One possible use of this article also constitutes a test case for the fusion process.

To proponents of a rational choice approach, such a survey of rather general formulations may seem a somewhat unnecessary exercise, as these treaty articles may be perceived as shallow declarations that will, even if the Treaty is ratified, have no measurable impact on preference formation and interest representation in the Union's living constitution. This keynote article argues, however, that the wording of the TCE may reflect fundamental attitudes that influence the use of given opportunities and frame preferences affecting interpretations of the Treaty in real life.

III. The Union's Competences: Towards a State-like Agenda

The provisions specifying the 'Union competences' attempt to provide a coherent set of plausible criteria for the allocation of policy fields to the EU. A more detailed examination reveals ambiguities that are significant for the transfer and merging of competences in line with the thesis of this article. The fundamental principles of the TCE clearly state that it is the prerogative of Member States to 'confer competences' on the Union (Art. I-1 (1); Art. I-11 (2)). Those not conferred to the Union in the Treaty remain under the authority of the Member States. When viewed together with the revision procedures (Art. IV-443), the Constitutional Treaty does not allocate the 'Kompetenzkompetenz' (the competence to transfer competences) to the Union (Louis and Ronse, 2005, p. 3; Müller-Graff, 2003, p. 306). In this respect, the provisions affirm constitutional continuity (Louis and Ronse, 2005, p. 3). In reaffirming the principles of subsidiarity (Art. I-11 (3)) and proportionality (Art. I-11 (4)), the founding generation has reinforced intergovernmental efforts to restrict potential spillover. Moreover, a specific procedure creating an 'early warning system' has been added (Protocol on the Application of the Principles of Subsidiarity and Proportionality) so that national parliaments 'shall ensure the compliance with that principle' (Art. I-11 (3)).

With these principles in mind, it is astonishing that the Constitutional Treaty again – just as its predecessors – continues to enlarge the scope of policy fields of the EU, representing a movement towards a state-like catalogue of tasks and functions (see Lindberg and Scheingold, 1970, p. 71). This trend becomes obvious when we add up all the policy fields mentioned in the 'areas of exclusive …' (Art. I-13 (1)), of 'shared …' (Art. I-14 (2)) and of 'supporting competences' (Art. I-17), as well as those in the areas covered by the 'coordination of economic and employment policies', which also mentions the 'coordination of member states' social policies' (Art. I-16), and in 'the common foreign and security policy', which takes up a 'common defence policy' and a 'common defence' as future tasks (Art. I-16). New policy areas such as 'space' (Art. I-14) and 'sport' (Art. I-17) are included in the list, too.

To turn around this argument of enlargement of scope: there are few policy sectors associated with the conventional features of states that remain untouched by the provisions of the Constitutional Treaty. While the degree of EU regulation and intervention differs significantly from one field to another, it is noticeable that the last strongholds of the nation-state's exclusive competences – the *domaines reservés* – are increasingly restricted.

In these enumerations of the Constitutional Treaty, the origins of each phase of the European state's development during the last centuries can be traced, starting from the 'territorial (Westphalian)' and the 'nation-state', via the 'constitutional' and 'democratic state' up to the 'social' or 'welfare state' (see Tilly, 1975; Benz, 2001).

The above analogy should not conceal essential differences in the present-day functions of European states. If we take the budgetary spending of states as a major indicator of their activities and salience for the citizens, then the EU – with few 'own resources' (between 1 and 1.27 per cent of the EU's GNP) – is not involved in major areas of social and military spending (see Moravcsik, 2002, p. 608). If the modern state is not only characterized by regulatory agencies (Majone, 1994) but equally by budgetary interventions (to the sum of 45–60 per cent of national GNP), then the EU will continue to lack crucial aspects of a state's activities as commonly understood in the early twenty-first century. As the proposed Constitutional Treaty retains the criterion of unanimity in the Council as well as the requirement of national ratification for revising the provisions relating to the system of 'own resources' (Art. I-54 (3)), a substantial number of Member States, if the Treaty is ratified, are expected to make use of these rules to prevent the EU making many inroads into these core areas of state activity.

The assumptions of fusion theory, however, expect further pressures promoting the transfer of instruments to EU bodies. Through the provisions of the 'flexibility clause' (Art. I -18), the Council has the power to adopt appropriate measures to attain objectives, for which the Constitutional Treaty has not provided the necessary powers. When compared to the intention of the present Art. 308 TEC, the scope will be broader, as it is applicable to all objectives of the Constitutional Treaty and to all of Part III (including, for example, the CFSP) and not only to those of the internal market (see Art. 308 TEC, ex. 235). The new provisions set a high threshold by demanding unanimity in the Council and prohibiting the harmonization of Member States' laws in those cases where the Constitution excludes such harmonization (Art. I-18). Past experience tells us that Member States collectively have found such a clause repeatedly useful for extending the activities of the Union into territory so far unclaimed. Despite its restrictive formulation, this 'small Treaty amendment' will enable future generations of politicians to react flexibly to unforeseen challenges through the EU institutions, thereby opening new doors for a 'cultivated spillover' strategy (Tranholm-Mikkelsen, 1991, p. 15).

Furthermore, 'escalator effects' can be analysed: following experiences with concurrent competences (see Hesse, 1962) the extensive application of 'shared competences' – while not changing their legal nature – might turn them through use into 'exclusive competences' (Louis and Ronse, 2005, p. 32). If the TCE is ratified, Member States could widely use the opportunities afforded by the legal constitution to pursue a proactive EU policy, disregarding centralizing effects. The thesis of this article expects that the potential restraining power of national parliaments via the subsidiarity clause and the early warning system mentioned above will prove less strong in the 'living constitution' than the force of government preferences to involve the Union in problem-solving across vital areas of state functions.

IV. The Institutional Architecture: Balancing on a Higher Level

Turning to the EU's institutional configuration, the logic of fusion theory expects that the Constitutional Treaty will again strengthen each body of the Union's institutional architecture: built-in ambiguities will reinforce tensions between and within institutions in the living constitution. Increased transparency and accountability cannot be expected.

The analysis here starts from the dual principle of representation and legitimacy, as laid out by the Constitutional Treaty itself: 'Citizens are directly represented … in the European Parliament. Member States are represented in the European Council by their Heads of State or Government and in the Council by their government' (Art. I-46 (2)).

The European Parliament: Towards a Bicameral System

As in previous rounds of treaty revisions, this Intergovernmental Conference has reaffirmed the position of the European Parliament (EP) and extended its legislative, budgetary, control, and electoral functions (see Art. I-20 (1)). The Constitutional Treaty, if ratified, thereby enhances the role of an institution that is commonly associated with the federal orientation of the Union's institutional architecture (see Pinder, 2000). The extension of legislative rights is of particular importance: the 'co-decision' procedure has been relabelled the 'ordinary legislative procedure' (Art. I-34) for 'European Laws and European Framework Laws' (Art. I-33). In addition, the TCE proposes introducing the ordinary legislative procedure to an additional 47 cases (see Figure 2) and further extends it to include new central policy fields within justice and home affairs (JHA). The Treaty also extends the consent procedure to fundamental decisions, such as approving the 'multi-annual financial framework' (Art. I-55 (2)) and the 'simplified revision procedure' (Art. IV-444). The planned increase in EP powers includes the annual budgetary procedure (Art. III-404). The cases in which the EP is not involved will decrease, if the Treaty is ratified, from 47 per cent (Nice) to 26 per cent (TCE).

The European Parliament's electoral prerogative is also reinforced: it 'shall elect [NB not just approve] the President of the Commission' (Art. I-20 (1)) by the 'majority of its component members' (Art. I-27 (1)). It is also in accordance with the pattern anticipated by fusion theory (see Wessels, 1997; Miles, 2003) that envisages the Union evolving in a kind of 'hybrid' between an intergovernmental and federal Europe since the proposed Constitutional Treaty reserves the right of initiative for this procedure to the European Council. Taken together, these modifications of the Constitutional Treaty amplify a trend towards a 'bicameral system' (see Hix, 2001; Maurer and Wessels, 2003a).

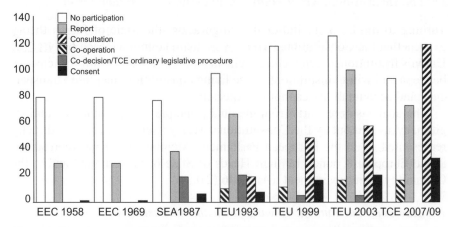

Figure 2: Development of Participatory Rights in Enacting Legislation for the European Parliament as Specified in the Treaties 1958–2006 (in absolute numbers)
Source: Maurer and Wessels (2003b). Figures for Nice and TCE added by Funda Tekin, Jean Monnet Chair.

The extension of the EP's role should not gloss over the remaining differences in comparison with constitutional powers held by national parliaments. Member States, as masters of the Treaty, have not granted the EP any powers of taxation over the citizens they represent. More specifically, there is no requirement of gaining EP consent when deciding on matters of 'own resources' – merely consultation is envisaged (Art. I-54 (2)).

As regards constitution-making powers, the EP will be granted specified opportunities for initiating and preparing IGCs (Art. IV-443 (1)). Final decision-making will, however, rest in the hands of the IGC (Art. I-443 (2)), and hence – *de facto* – with the European Council.

The European Council: Reinforcing the Principal Decision-maker

In balancing the increased powers of the EP, the Constitutional Treaty, as agreed, has not only reconfirmed but also further expanded the list of tasks of the European Council, thereby strengthening *prima facie* intergovernmental features.

The European Council is now classified as an institution of the Union (Art. I-19 (1)); it is supposed to 'provide the Union with the necessary impetus for developments and shall define the general political directions and priorities thereof. It shall not exercise legislative function' (Art. I-21 (1)). Given the observed performance of the EU over past decades, as well as the new articles in the Constitutional Treaty, this description is an understatement, hiding the

part played by heads of government as the principal EU actors in key procedures (de Schoutheete and Wallace, 2002; Ludlow, 2004, pp. 5–15). One major
role of the European Council is that of framing policies through the setting
of guidelines. Such a role is referred to in several cases, such as Art. III-258
and Art. III-295.

The European Council's role as a 'constitutional architect' has also been
reconfirmed: the European Council can – as it did, *de facto*, over past decades
– convene a 'conference of representatives of the governments of the Member
States' (Art. III-443 (3)). While it is not explicitly mentioned in the specific
treaty article, it is expected that the heads of governments will continue taking
final decisions on any treaty revision.

Another constitutional function has been bestowed on the European Council
by the so-called 'bridging clauses'. In one form of this 'passerelle', the heads
of government may adopt a European decision to replace the unanimity requirement by a qualified majority vote in the Council (see Art. I-40 (7)), or
transform a 'special' into an 'ordinary legislative procedure' (see, e.g., Art.
III-210 (3)). In order to constrain uncontrollable dynamics, the provision ties
this harder form of the bridging clause to the goodwill of national parliaments,
allowing each one of them a veto (Art. IV-444 (3)).

In a softer version of the 'bridging clause', the European Council may also
take a European decision on certain issues regarding the institutional architecture without facing a veto power – such as the distribution of seats in the
EP (Art. I-20 (2)), or the configurations (Art. I-24 (4)) and presidency of the
Council of Ministers (Art. I-24 (7)).

The functions of the European Council also include electoral powers.
Besides proposing the Commission President (Art. I-27 (1)) and appointing
the President of the European Central Bank (Art. III-382 (2)), this institution
will also elect its full-time President (Art. I-22 (1)) and, in co-responsibility
with the President of the Commission and the EP, it shall appoint the Union
Minister for Foreign Affairs (Art. I-28 (1)).

The powers of the European Council will also formally extend as far as its
role as final decision-maker in appeals: under the threat of a possible qualified
majority decision in certain specified cases (see below), a Member State may
request that the draft be referred to the European Council. This formulation in
the TCE highlights an important aspect of practical, real-life policy-making in
the EU today, namely that heads of governments interfere in Council business
whenever they feel that there is an important issue at stake.

Given their pivotal role in the governments of the Member States, the
decision-making procedures of the European Council deserve closer attention.
On electoral acts, the European Council can decide by qualified majority;
generally, however, decisions shall be taken by consensus (Art. I-21 (4)). Of

special interest is the new regulation for its Presidency: the Constitutional Treaty replaces the system of rotation by a full-time President of the European Council (Art. I-22), to be elected by the heads of government for a period of two-and-a-half years. In contrast to the current system of six-month rotating presidencies, the future President is supposed to professionalize the work of this institution and facilitate consensual decision-making. A further task of the President will encompass heading and managing the external representation of the Union for CFSP matters 'at his or her level and in that capacity ... without prejudice to the responsibilities of the Union Minister for Foreign Affairs' (Art. I-21 (2)). This formulation hints at potential conflicts between these two offices, yet leaves the resolution of it to the practical realm of the living constitution.

The job profile of the President of the European Council is only vaguely sketched out. There are no special procedural prerogatives for the President; the office-holder will serve as the 'face' and 'voice' of the European Council. Thus, in line with an intergovernmental reading of the TCE, the main function of this President could be interpreted as an 'agent' of the 'principal' watching over the other EU institutions – especially the Council, the Foreign Minister and the Commission.

Though less conventional, this author would suggest an alternative scenario for the Union's evolution if the TCE is ratified: from ignorance of the treaty provisions, the elected office-holder might be attributed with the reputation of 'President of the Union' or even 'of Europe' more generally (and not just the European Council): and the agent might emancipate himself from the mandates of national governments and, over time, might then lead to some kind of a federal-style leadership.

The Council of Ministers: Accelerators and Emergency Brakes

The Constitutional Treaty incorporates several revisions to the Council that represent a trade-off between a search for more efficient decision-making for this key institution at European level against that of retaining the influence of national voices in differentiated forms of participation and including the retention of national veto powers in some instances as 'emergency brakes'.

Significant indicators reflecting the dilemma of a 'balancing act' are the criteria for, and the usage of, qualified majority voting. In line with past revisions, this generation of constitutional architects has extended the opportunities for decisions by qualified majority (see Figure 3).

Nevertheless, Member States again showed risk aversion in areas central to national politics: foreign and defence policy (Art. III-300 (1)), social and tax policy (Art. III-210 (3)), as well as fundamental decisions on 'own resources'

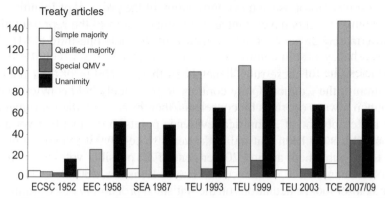

Figure 3: Development of QMV as Mode of Decision-making in the Council 1952–2007

Source: Maurer and Wessels (2003b). Figures for Nice and TCE added by Funda Tekin, Jean Monnet Chair.

Notes: [a] Special qualified majority includes: QMV with 72 per cent of the members and 65 per cent of the population, if decisions are not made upon proposal of the Commission or the Foreign Minister according to Art. I-25; qualified majority decisions excluding the affected Member State (QMV minus 1); qualified majority decisions with only a group of participating states, e.g. 'enhanced co-operation' or decisions of the euro group.

(Art. I-54 (3)) and the 'multi-annual financial framework' (Art. I-55) will remain subject to unanimity voting. In the latter case, the European Council can authorize the Council to act by qualified majority (Art. I-55 (4)). Following specific calls for retaining the national veto in a few cases of majority voting on issues relating to the common foreign and security policy (CFSP) (Art. III-300 (2)), the Constitutional Treaty includes 'emergency brakes' for each Member State as a last resort to cover sensitive policy fields where 'fundamental aspects of the (national) social security system' (Art. III-136 (2)), or of the 'criminal justice system' of a member are concerned (Art. III-271 (3)).

The new rules for qualified majority voting in the European Council (Art. I-22) and the Council (Art. I-25) are based on two sources of legitimacy (Art. I-1 (1)), i.e. 'citizens' for the population criterion, and 'Members' for the state criterion; both are needed for passing the threshold and are merged in their effect. The revised system of 'double majority' asks for '55 per cent of the members of the Council comprising at least 15 of them and representing at least 65 per cent of the population of the Union. A blocking minority must include at least four Council members' (Art. I-25 (1)). By abolishing the weighted votes as a criterion so far used in the treaties, these provisions are likely to increase efficiency in the Council as compared to the current rules of the Nice Treaty (see Figure 4).

Minority interests are protected by an additional declaration, which might, in practice, play a major role in the living constitution. In the spirit of the

Luxembourg compromise and in continuation of the protocol of Ioannina, the heads of governments have granted a suspensive veto to the representatives of approximately 25 per cent of Union citizens, or about one-third of Member States.

The relevance of these rules depends on the probability of their real-life application in the Council. Quite contrary to the widely held conviction that the Council always operates by consensus, thereby making the instrument of voting an 'empty threat', empirical evidence points to the fact that voting in the Council has not been unusual in the years since 1999 when voting results began to be published: around 20 per cent of all possible votes are actually taken (see Council, 2005; Wallace and Hayes-Renshaw, 2005).

For a closer look, calculations on the statistical probability of a Commission proposal being accepted by qualified majority in the Council can be considered (see Figure 4). Given that relevant negotiations in the Council are under the shadow of the vote, politicians and officials might seek a predictable long-term strategy to establish coalitions for a blocking minority or qualified majorities (see Table 1). This enumeration of coalitions illustrates that majority decisions are not easily reached.

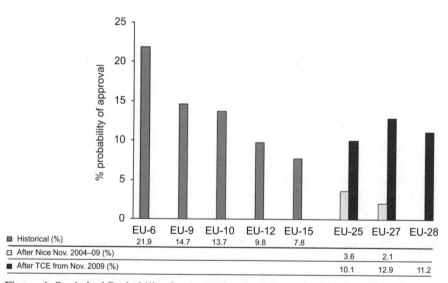

	EU-6	EU-9	EU-10	EU-12	EU-15	EU-25	EU-27	EU-28
■ Historical (%)	21.9	14.7	13.7	9.8	7.8			
□ After Nice Nov. 2004–09 (%)						3.6	2.1	
■ After TCE from Nov. 2009 (%)						10.1	12.9	11.2

Figure 4: Statistical Probability for Accepting Decisions in the Council
Source: Baldwin and Widgrén: Council voting in the Constitutional Treaty, p. 5.
Notes: The figure represents the probability with which a randomly chosen issue will be approved by the Council of Ministers. In the EU-25, there are more than 33 million possible combinations of 'yes' and 'no' votes. In a Union of 27, there will be more than 134 million; see Baldwin and Widgrén (2004), p. 3, note 2.

Table 1: Coalitions for Qualified Majorities and Blocking Minorities in the Council (EU-27 after TCE)

	No. of States	% of EU-27	% Share of EU-27 Total Population	Constructive Majority	Blocking Minority
EU-6	6	22.22	46.87	No	Yes
EU-9	9	33.33	61.10	No	Yes
EU-12	12	44.44	74.00	No	Yes
EU-15	15	55.56	78.60	Yes	Yes
EU-25	25	92.59	93.90	Yes	Yes
EU-27	27	100.00	100.00	Yes	Yes
Nato states	21	77.78	94.34	Yes	Yes
Three biggest MS (D, UK, F)	3	11.11	41.69 (no fourth MS)	No	No
Mediterranean (P, E, F, I, EL, CY, M)	7	25.93	37.37	No	Yes
Baltic states (D, DK, S, FIN, EST, LT, LV)	7	25.93	29.35	No	No
MS with soc. governments[a] (D, UK, E, PL, CZ, B, HU, S, LT, SK, CY, RO)	12	44.44	57.47	No	Yes
MS with con. governments[a] (F, I, NL, EL, P, A, SL, DK, FIN, IRL, LV, EST, L, M, BU)	15	55.56	42.53	No	Yes
'New' Europe[b] (UK, I, PL, NL, BU, DK, CZ, HU, RO, LT, P, SL, EST)	13	48.15	51.06	No	Yes
'Old' Europe[b] (D, F, E, EL, B, S, A, FIN, IRL, LV, SK, CZ, L, M)	14	51.85	48.94	No	Yes
Old net payers (D, F, UK, NL, A, S)	6	22.22	38.45	No	Yes
Net receivers	21	77.78	61.55	No	Yes
Central Europe (D, A, PL, CZ, SR, HU, LT, LV, EST)	9	33.33	33.37	No	No

Source: Compilation based on calculations by Ingo Linsenmann and Thomas Latschan, Jean Monnet Chair, Cologne, 2005.
Notes: [a] (as of July 2004). [b] 'New Europe' refers to the definition of US Secretary of Defense Donald Rumsfeld, i.e. those states that had participated in the Iraq war; as indicator for foreign policy changes. 'Old Europe' refers to the states that did not participate in the Iraq war. While such an enumeration, as for the party composition, is subject to change, it serves to discuss different potential cleavages.
Key: A = Austria; B = Belgium; BU = Bulgaria; CY = Cyprus; CZ = Czech Republic; D = Germany; DK = Denmark; E = Spain; EL = Greece; EST = Estonia; F = France; FIN = Finland; HU = Hungary; IRL = Ireland; I= Italy; L = Luxembourg; LT = Lithuania; LV = Latvia; M = Malta; NL = Netherlands; P = Portugal; PL = Poland; RO = Romania; S = Sweden; SK = Slovakia; SL = Slovenia; UK = United Kingdom.

The Commission: Representation and Efficiency

The mixed strategy of increasing efficiency and preserving national participation can also be observed in the TCE provisions relating to the Commission. As in previous revisions, the Constitutional Treaty again extends the scope of action for the Commission. Following fierce controversy during the negotiations on the TCE, the Treaty lays down rules relating to the composition of the Commission that give each Member State the power to nominate one candidate. The compromise inherent in the Treaty lies somewhere between the two poles of, on the one hand, a grand body with 'representative' character (one member per state) and a smaller, yet more efficient, institution on the other. The Constitutional Treaty reflects the popular tactics of some of its architects (Magnette and Nicolaïdis, 2004) and opts to keep the *status quo* by delaying a final decision: not before 2014 will the composition be reduced to two-thirds of the total number of Member States, to be selected by a system of equal rotation. The European Council may, however, change this procedure by unanimous agreement.

The expansion of the Commission to become a large collegiate body is also influenced by a fundamental attempt to bolster its efficiency. In a basic triangle of competing principles that has to consider the demands of running an institution as a collegiate body, the claim to leadership of the President and the responsibility of each Commissioner for his or her dossier, the Constitutional Treaty will once more strengthen the position of the President by including the possibility of dismissing single 'colleagues' (Art. I-27 (3)). At the same time, the power of leadership promotion is not matched by the possibility of censuring the President alone, through a 'vote of no confidence' passed by the EP. The present rule, by which a censure motion can target only the entire collegiate, is carried over into the Constitutional Treaty (Art. I-26 (8) and Art. III-340).

The Union Minister for Foreign Affairs: An Ideal-Typical Case for Fusion

The creation of the office of a 'Union Minister for Foreign Affairs' (Art. I-28) stands out as the most notable innovation to the Union's proposed institutional architecture included in the TCE. It is a continuation of past proposals that seek to increase the efficiency of the 'external action of the Union' (Title V Part III, especially Art. III-292 and Art. III-294), while simultaneously not reducing the dominant position of the Member States in the CFSP. For such a task, a merger of the posts of the High Representative for External Relations and the Vice-President of the Commission to create a 'double hat' position has been envisaged. When conducting his/her affairs, the Union Minister for Foreign Affairs shall be supported by the 'European external action service'

(Art. III-296 (3)), which should imply – in line with fusion theory – a pooling of national and community administrative resources.

Indeed, the combination of the electoral process and the description of the role envisaged for the Foreign Minister represent an almost ideal and/or typical instance of the trends predicted by fusion theory: legitimacy and functions are merged, while the officeholder is supposed to integrate several instruments and various procedures in a kind of hybrid function. As a result, supranational and intergovernmental elements are mixed in a complex set of provisions, while the proactive instruments at the Minister's disposal are rather limited in practice. The constitutional set-up envisaged in the TCE thus places the office-holder in the middle of a vortex of strong inter- and intra-institutional tensions and pressures (Wessels, 2004).

The ECJ and National Parliaments: Strengthening Community and National Players

In the search for institutional balance, the Constitutional Treaty will also strengthen the role of the European Court of Justice (ECJ). The jurisdiction of the ECJ will be extended to further policy fields – especially in questions of justice and home affairs (JHA).

In line with the expectations and trends of fusion theory, another group of national actors has been incorporated into the Union's institutional architecture. While Members of national Parliaments have hitherto been the 'losers' (Maurer and Wessels, 2001, p. 429) in the European integration construction, the Constitutional Treaty earmarks a role for them as guardians of subsidiarity in the areas of shared competence and for vetoing treaty amendments under the simplified revision procedure (Art. IV-444 (3)). With the extension of the participatory powers of these national actors, procedural complexity will be increased while at the same time transparency and accountability are reduced.

Overall, the revisions to the Union's institutional architecture point to an exercise of balancing intergovernmental and supranational features, as viewed from the perspective of fusion, in what has been described as a 'third way' (Miles, 2003, 2005). It also reflects the traditional equilibrium, although on a higher level on the fusion ladder (see Figure 1).

V. Procedural Profiles: Complexity and Shift

The Convention and the IGC (see Dinan in this *Annual Review*) set out to reduce procedural complexity to a few key procedures (Declaration of Laeken, 2001, pp. 19–26), as did previous rounds of treaty revisions. The 'ordinary legislative procedure' coupled with the modalities of QMV in the Council have become a leading, but not yet exclusive mode of EU decision-making. Compared to the presently operational Nice Treaty, the envisaged use of the ordinary legislative procedure and QMV amounts to an increase from 26 per cent to 34 per cent of all relevant rules (see Figure 5a). Yet, as regards procedural complexity, there will be only a modest reduction from 50 to 45 different types of procedures.

In view of the distribution of procedural profiles for single 'Categories of Competence' (Art. I-12), and despite the unified legal basis and legal instruments, it is already remarkable that the text of the TCE makes explicit mention of 'specific provisions relating to the common foreign and security policy' (Art. I-40), the 'common security and defence policy' (Art. I-41), as well as the 'area of freedom, security and justice' (Art. I-42). Also, in comparing the areas of each of the five categories, the procedural profiles show a high degree of variation between, and even within, categories of competence (see Table 2).

As a further way of testing our guiding thesis of a fusion ladder (see Figure 1, line d), the allocation of competences and decision-making procedures between the present EU Treaty (Nice version) and the Constitutional Treaty are compared (see Figure 5a–c). Figure 5a looks at the trends for both a vertical shift in the allocation of competences as well as horizontally, for the modes of decision-making in – and between – the Council and the EP in relative numbers of occurrence within the treaties as a whole.

As a first general conclusion, the evidence suggests that total EP participation has increased (see above); but even in those cases where the EP may not participate in the legislative process, QMV has nonetheless become a dominant, or at least equal mode of decision-making, and it has gained more importance – in relative and absolute terms – than any other mode across all areas (see especially Figure 5a). At the same time, the ordinary legislative procedure now applies to a good third of all provisions, showing a particularly significant rise for matters relating to the area of freedom, security and justice, as part of the shared competences.

A more detailed look at the absolute number of provisions in the Constitutional Treaty signals a further step in the escalator process. A clear horizontal shift towards the community method with the ordinary legislative procedure (formerly co-decision) and QMV is observed (see Figure 5b).

With regard to the areas of competence in the TCE, it is true that the relative distribution of provisions across the different categories may not show a general 'upward shift'. Yet, a look at the absolute numbers and the sheer quantity of new rules in all areas (see Figure 5c), especially the sharp increase in provisions for the area of freedom, security and justice, demonstrates a much greater extent and specification of treaty-based EU involvement than has previously been the case.

More specifically, several co-existing types of combination with respect to categories of competence and decision-making procedures are also noticed.

Table 2: Procedural Profiles in Categories of Competence

EP \ Council	Unanimity	QMV	Special QMV	Simple Majority	SUM EP Participation	%
(A) Exclusive competences (Art. I–13 TCE)						
No participation	5	8	5	–	18	64.29
Report	–	1	1	–	2	7.09
Consultation	–	7	–	–	7	25.00
Consent	–		–	–	–	
Ordinary legislation	–	1	–	–	1	3.57
SUM Council mode of decision	5 (17.86%)	17 (60.71%)	6 (21.43%)	0	28	100.00
(B) Shared competence (Art. I–14 TCE)						
No participation	2	6	–	–	8	7.08
Report	1	14	–	–	15	13.27
Consultation	18	11	1	1	31	27.43
Consent	5	1	1	–	7	6.19
Ordinary legislation	–	44	8	–	52	46.01
SUM Council mode of decision	26 (23.01%)	76 (67.25%)	10 (8.85%)	11 (0.88%)	13	100.00
(C) Supporting, co-ordinating or complementary action (Art. I–17 TCE)						
No participation	–	4	–	–	4	41.46
Report	–	–	–	–	–	
Consultation	–	–	–	–	–	
Consent	–	–	–	–	–	
Ordinary legislation	–	9	–	–	9	58.54
SUM Council mode of decision	0	13 (100%)	0	0	13	100.00
(D) Economic and employment policies (Art. I–15 TCE)						
No participation	–	1	5	–	6	25.00
Report	–	3	1	–	4	16.67
Consultation	2	6	1	1	10	41.67
Consent	–	–	–	–	–	
Ordinary legislation	–	4	–	–	4	16.67
SUM Council mode of decision	2 (8.33%)	14 (58.33%)	7 (29.17%)	1 (4.17%)	24	100.00
(E) CFSP and ESDP (Art. I–16 TCE)						
No participation	7	5	3	–	15	88.24
Report	–	–	–	–	–	
Consultation	2	–	–	–	2	11.76
Consent	–	–	–	–	–	
Ordinary legislation	–	–	–	–	–	
SUM Council mode of decision	9 (52.94%)	5 (29.41%)	3 (17.65%)	0	17	100.00
(F) Area of freedom, security and justice (Art. III-257 to 277 TCE) [a]						
No participation	–		–	–	–	
Report	–	1	–	–	1	2.80
Consultation	6	2	–	–	8	22.20
Consent	2	1	1	–	4	11.10
Ordinary legislation	–	15	8	–	23	63.90
SUM Council mode of decision	8	19 (22.22%)	9 (52.78%)	0 (25%)	36	100.00

Source: Treaty establishing a Constitution for Europe. CIG 87/1/04. 13 October 2004, compilation by Funda Tekin, Jean Monnet Chair, 2005.
Note: [a] These articles form part of the category of shared competences.

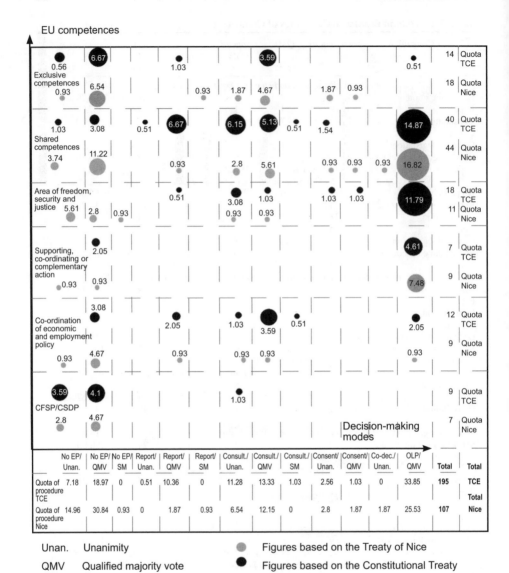

Figure 5a: Percentage Distribution of Provisions Based on the Treaty of Nice and the Treaty Establishing a Constitution for Europe (TCE), in Relative Numbers

Source: Treaty of Nice and Treaty establishing a Constitution for Europe (TCE), compilation by Funda Tekin, Jean Monnet Chair.

Notes: Only the TCE specifically defines the EU competences. For comparison, the articles of the Nice Treaty are not interpreted according to the pillar structure but in view of the TCE attribution. This method is based on Sénat (2004).

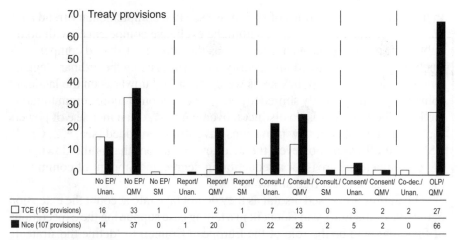

	No EP/ Unan.	No EP/ QMV	No EP/ SM	Report/ Unan.	Report/ QMV	Report/ SM	Consult./ Unan.	Consult./ QMV	Consult./ SM	Consent/ Unan.	Consent/ QMV	Co-dec./ Unan.	OLP/ QMV
☐ TCE (195 provisions)	16	33	1	0	2	1	7	13	0	3	2	2	27
■ Nice (107 provisions)	14	37	0	1	20	0	22	26	2	5	2	0	66

Figure 5b: Procedures as Specified in the Treaty of Nice and the Treaty Establishing a Constitution for Europe (TCE), in Absolute Numbers
Source: Treaty of Nice and Treaty establishing a Constitution for Europe (TCE), compilation and representation by Funda Tekin and Thomas Traguth, Jean Monnet Chair, 2005.

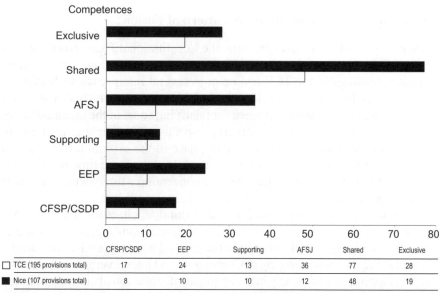

	CFSP/CSDP	EEP	Supporting	AFSJ	Shared	Exclusive
☐ TCE (195 provisions total)	17	24	13	36	77	28
■ Nice (107 provisions total)	8	10	10	12	48	19

Figure 5c: Competences as Specified in the Treaty of Nice and the Treaty Establishing a Constitution for Europe (TCE)[a] in Absolute Numbers
Source: Treaty of Nice and Treaty Establishing a Constitution for Europe (TCE), compilation and representation by Funda Tekin and Thomas Traguth, Jean Monnet Chair, 2005.
Note: [a] The method of comparison is based on 'Constitution Européenne. Comparaison avec les traités en vigueur' (Sénat, 2004); see also Figure 5a.

In line with the expectations of fusion, we see two complementary trends, i.e. that both the number of articles within the exclusive competences with no involvement of the EP has increased, as has the number of shared competences (including the area of freedom, security and justice) using the ordinary legislative procedure. Where policy areas were not shifted upwards on the ladder of competences, they mostly shifted towards the direction of more communitarian modes. Where there was no distinct movement towards an increase of powers for the EP, a number of new provisions have still been added (see, e.g., CFSP/CSDP). In all cases, however, the acid test of fusion, that is the downgrading of competence areas, or a reduction in degree and amount of community methods, has not occurred anywhere.

The figures are biased insofar as they do not take into account the extension of the role of the European Council; in a telling case supporting the expectations of fusion, it is to be the role of the European Council to 'define the strategic guidelines for legislative and operational planning within the area of freedom, security and justice' (see Art. III-258), whereas at the same time Community methods have gained in numerical importance (see Table 2F, Figures 5a and b above).

VI. Testing Trend Expectations: A Pattern of Fusion?

As in previous rounds of treaty reform, the Constitutional Treaty has not ended the ongoing debate on the Union's *finalité* and its institutional architecture. Repeated readings of the TCE can point to several interpretations leading in different directions. In line with the thesis of this article, several traces of fusion can be found, but also some evidence for falsifying some of the assumed logics of fusion. From a long-term historical perspective, the Constitutional Treaty might constitute and construct a further phase in the evolution of European states into a multi-level constitutionalism, while at the same time some provisions underline its restricted character as a conventional treaty with safeguards for national sovereignty.

As to the Union's institutional and procedural architecture, the provisions of the TCE have again strengthened existing medium-term trends towards shared, pooled responsibility between the EU and national levels. The parallel strengthening and close merging of Community and intergovernmental methods can be pinpointed most clearly in the aggregate distribution of competences and procedures, as well as in the office of the Union Minister for Foreign Affairs (see above). The ambiguous formulations of the text might lead, in the living constitution, to an even stronger institutional fusion with no clear delimitation of responsibilities. Discussing the effects on the integration ladder, the aggregate numerical picture indicates a major step towards a new level of integration.

Turning to the short-term view, crumbling EU legitimacy arising out of the ambiguities of the text of the new Treaty, combined with insufficient output from the Union, which could be notable, especially in the area of foreign and security policy, may fuel discussion over further-reaching constitutional steps. In the practical realms of the Union's living constitution, the grasping of new and revised opportunities will create pressures for further steps on the fusion ladder. These dynamics will also persist, should the Constitutional Treaty fail to be ratified by all Member States.

References

Ackermann, B. (2000) *We the People*. Vol. 2 (Cambridge: Transformations).

Ahern, B. (2004) 'Statement of the Taoiseach to the Dáil on the Outcome of the European Council and the Intergovernmental Conference held on 17–18 June, Brussels'. Available at «http://www.eu2004.ie».

Anderson, B. (1983) *Imagined Communities: Reflections on the Origin and Spread of Nationalism* (London: Verso).

Baldwin, R. and Widgrén, M. (2004) 'Council Voting in the Constitutional Treaty: Devil in the Details'. 23 June. Available at «http://www.cepr.org/pubs/dps/DP4450.asp».

Beck, U. and Grande, E. (2004) *Kosmopolitisches Europa* (Frankfurt: Suhrkamp).

Benz, A. (2001) *Der moderne Staat* (Munich/Vienna: Oldenbourg).

Blair, T. (2004) 'Statement to Parliament on the EU Constitutional Treaty, 21 June 2004'. Available at, e.g., «http://www.britischebotschaft.de/en/news/items/040621.htm»

Bogdanor, V. (2004) 'A Constitution for a House without Windows'. Federal Trust for Education and Research, *EU Constitution Project Newsletter* 7/2004. Available at «http://www.fedtrust.co.uk/uploads/constitution/News07_04.pdf».

Braudel, F. (1990) *L'identité de la France* (Paris: Flammarion).

Bulmer, S. and Burch, M. (1998) 'Organizing for Europe: Whitehall, the British State and European Union'. *Public Administration,* Vol. 76, pp. 601–28.

Bundesverfassungsgericht, Judgment of 12 October 1993, 2 BvR 2134/92 and 2 BvR 2159/92 (1994) 89 *Entscheidungen des Bundesverfassungsgerichts* 155–213; English translation in [1994] 1 *CMLR* 57.

Chirac, J. (2004)'Constitution pour l'Europe'. Paris, 19 June. Available at «http://diplomatie.gouv.fr/actu/article.asp?art=42838».

Churchill, W. (1946) Speech in Zurich, 19 September. Available at «http://www.churchill-society-london.org.uk/astonish.html».

Constantinecso, V. (2002) 'Europe Fédérale ou Fédération d'États-Nations'. In Dehousse, R. (ed.) *Une Constitution pour l'Europe?* (Paris: Presses de Sciences Po).

Council of the European Union (2005) Summary of Council Acts. Available at «http://ue.eu.int/cms3_applications/showPage.asp?id=551&lang=EN&mode=g.

Delors, J. (2004) *Mémoires* (Paris: Plon).

De Schoutheete, P. and Wallace, H. (2002) The European Council, 09/2002, Notre Europe. Available at «http://www.notre-europe.asso.fr/article.php3?id_article=186».

European Council (2001) 'Declaration of Laeken – The Future of the European Union'. Summit Conclusions of the Presidency, December, pp. 19–26. Available at «http://ue.eu.int/ueDocs/cms_Data/docs/pressdata/de/ec/68829.pdf».

European Parliament (2005) 'Resolution on the Treaty Establishing a Constitution for Europe'. 12 January (P6_TA-PROV(2005)0004).

Giscard d'Estaing, V. (2003) *La Constitution pour l'Europe* (Paris: Albin Michel).

Haas, E.B. (1958) *The Uniting of Europe 1950-1957* (Stanford: Stanford University Press).

Habermas, J. (1996) 'The European Nation State, its Achievements and its Limitations. On the Past and Future of Sovereignty and Citizenship'. 9 *Ratio Iuris* 125.

Hallstein, W. (1972) *Europe in the Making* (London: George Allen and Unwin).

Hesse, K. (1962) *Der unitarische Bundesstaat* (Karlsruhe: C.F. Müller).

Hix, S. (2001) 'Legislative Behaviour and Party Competition in the European Parliament. An Application'. *Journal of Common Market Studies,* Vol. 39, No. 4, pp. 663–88.

Hobe, S. (2003) 'Bedingungen, Verfahren und Chancen europäischer Verfassungsgebung: Zur Arbeit des Brüsseler Verfassungskonvents'. *Europarecht* 38, Bd. 1/2003, pp. 1–16.

Hughes, K. (2004) 'A New Division of Power in the EU'. Federal Trust: *EU Constitution Project Newsletter* 7/2004.

Inglehart, R. (1970) 'Public Opinion and Regional Integration'. *International Organisation,* Vol. 24, pp. 764–95.

Inglehart, R. (1977) *The Silent Revolution: Changing Values and Political Styles among Western Publics* (Oxford: Princeton University Press).

Kassim, H. and Menon, A. (2003) 'The Principal–Agent Approach and the Study of the European Union: Promise Unfulfilled?'. *Journal of European Public Policy,* Vol. 10, No. 1, pp. 121–39.

Kohl, H. (1994) Auswärtiges Amt (ed.) Gemeinsame Außen- und Sicherheitspolitik der Europäischen Union (GASP) – *Dokumentation,* 10. ed., Bonn, p. 511.

Lindberg, L. and Scheingold, S. (1970) *Europe's Would-Be Polity: Patterns of Change in the European Community* (Englewood Cliffs: Prentice-Hall).

Louis, J-V. and Ronse, T. (2005) *L'ordre juridique de l'Union européenne* (Basle: Helbing & Lichtenhahn).

Ludlow, P. (2004) 'The European Council and IGC of December, 2003. Why and How?'. *EuroComment Briefing Note,* No. 2.8, Brussels, pp. 329–39.

Magnette, P. and Nicolaïdis, K. (2004) 'The European Convention: Bargaining in the Shadow of Rhetoric'. *West European Politics,* Vol. 27, No. 3, pp. 381–404.

Majone G. (1994) 'The Rise of the Regulatory State in Europe'. *West European Politics,* Vol. 17, No. 3, pp. 77–101.

March, J.G. and Olsen, J.P. (2004) 'The Logic of Appropriateness'. Available at «http://www.arena.uio.no/publications/wp04_9.pdf».

Maurer, A. and Wessels, W. (2001) *National Parliaments on their Ways to Europe: Losers or Latecomers?* (Baden-Baden: Nomos).

Maurer, A. and Wessels, W. (2003a) *Das Europäische Parlament nach Amsterdam und Nizza: Akteur, Arena oder Alibi?* (Baden-Baden: Nomos).

Maurer, A. and Wessels, W. (2003b) 'The European Union Matters: Structuring Self-made Offers and Demands'. In Wessels, W. *et al.* (eds) *Fifteen into One? The European Union and its Member States* (Manchester: Manchester University Press).

Merton, R.K. (1968) *Social Theory and Social Structure*. 3rd edn (New York/London: Free Press).

Miles, L. (2003) 'The "Fusion" Perspective Revisited'. *Cooperation and Conflict*, Vol. 3, pp. 291–8.

Miles, L. (2005) *Fusing with Europe? Sweden in the European Union* (Aldershot: Ashgate).

Milward, A.S. (2000) *The European Rescue of the Nation-state*. 2nd edn (London: Routledge).

Monnet, J. (1975) *Mémoires* (Paris: Fayard).

Moravcsik, A. (1998) *A Choice for Europe* (Ithaca, NY: Cornell University Press).

Moravcsik, A. (2002) 'In Defence of the Democratic Deficit: Reassessing Legitimacy in the European Union'. *Journal of Common Market Studies*, Vol. 40, No. 4, pp. 603–24.

Moreau Defarges, P. (2004) *Comprendre la Constitution Européenne* (Paris: Editions d'Organisation).

Müller-Graff, P-C. (2003) 'Systemrationalität in Kontinuität und Änderung des Europäischen Verfassungsvertrags'. *Integration*, 4/2003, pp. 301–16.

Nicolaïdis, K. (2004) 'Making it our Own: A Proposal for the Democratic Interpretation of the EU Constitution'. Federal Trust: *EU Constitution Project Newsletter*, July 2004.

Olsen, J.P. (2000) 'Organising European Institutions of Governance. A Prelude to an Institutional Account of Political Integration'. Arena Working Papers WP 00/2, available at «http://www.arena.uio.no/publications/wp00_2.htm».

Pernice, I. (1999) 'Multilevel Constitutionalism and the Treaty of Amsterdam: European Constitution-Making Revisited?'. *Common Market Law Review*, 4/1999, pp. 703–50.

Pernice, I. (2000) 'Europäisches und nationales Verfassungsrecht'. *Veröffentlichung der Vereinigung der deutschen Staatslehrer*, 60, pp. 148–225.

Peterson, J. (1995) 'Decision-making in the European Union: Towards a Framework for Analysis'. *Journal of European Public Policy*, Vol. 2, No. 1, pp. 69–93.

Pinder, J. (2000) 'Steps Towards a Parliamentary Democracy for Europe: The Development of the European Parliament from the Seventies to the Nineties'. In Breuss, F., Fink, G. and Griller, S. (eds) *Vom Schuman-Plan zum Vertrag von Amsterdam, Entstehung und Zukunft der EU* (Vienna: Springer).

Pinder, J. (2004) 'The Constitutional Treaty: How Federal?'. Federal Trust: *EU Constitution Project Newsletter* 7/2004, available at «http://www.fedtrust.co.uk».

Pollack, M. (1997) 'Delegation, Agency, and Agenda Setting in the European Community'. *International Organization*, Vol. 51, pp. 99–134.

Quermonne, J-L. (1992) 'Trois Lectures du Traité de Maastricht. Essai d'Analyse Comparative'. *Revue Française de Science Politique*, Vol. 42, No. 5, pp. 802–18.

Risse, T. (2004) 'Social Constructivism and European Integation'. In Wiener, A. and Diez, T. (eds) *European Integration Theory* (Oxford: Oxford University Press).

Sénat (2004) 'Constitution Européenne. Comparaison avec les traités en vigueur'. Service des Affaires Européennes, Octobre, available at «www.senat.fr».

Tilly, C. (ed.) (1975) *The Formation of National States in Western Europe* (Princeton: Princeton University Press).

Tranholm-Mikkelsen, J. (1991) 'Neo-functionalism: Obstinate or Obsolete? A Reappraisal of the New Dynamism of the EC'. *Millenium: Journal of International Studies*, Vol. 20, No. 1, pp. 1–22.

Wallace, H. and Hayes-Renshaw, F. (2005) *The Council of Ministers*. 2nd edn (Basingstoke: Palgrave), forthcoming.

Weiler, J.H.H. (1997) 'Does Europe Need a Constitution? Reflections on Demos, Telos, Ethos and the Maastricht Decision'. In Gowan P. and Anderson P. (eds) *The Question of Europe* (London: Verso).

Weiler, J.H.H. (1999) *The Constitution of Europe. Do the New Clothes Have an Emperor?* (Cambridge: Cambridge University Press).

Wessels, W. (1997) 'An Ever Closer Fusion? A Dynamic Macropolitical View of the Integration Process'. *Journal of Common Market Studies*, Vol. 35, No. 2, pp. 267–99.

Wessels, W. (2004) 'A "Saut constitutionell" out of an Intergovernmental Trap? The Provisions of the Constitutional Treaty for the Common Foreign, Security and Defence Policy'. In Weiler, J.H.H. and Eisgruber, C.L. (eds) 'Altneuland: The EU Constitution in a Contextual Perspective'. Jean Monnet Working Paper 5/04, New York/Princeton.

Wessels, W., Maurer, A. and Mittag, J. (2003) *Fifteen into One? The European Union and its Member States* (Manchester: Manchester University Press).

JCMS 2005 Volume 43. Annual Review pp. 37–54

Governance and Institutions: A New Constitution and a New Commission

DESMOND DINAN
George Mason University

Introduction

Enlargement from 15 to 25 Member States and agreement on the Treaty establishing a Constitution for Europe were the two most remarkable developments in the EU in 2004. Whereas the accession of the new Member States was already well on track by the beginning of the year, the fate of the Constitutional Treaty was uncertain. Negotiations on the Treaty, which had ground to a halt in December 2003 at an acrimonious meeting of the European Council, resumed in the new year and ended successfully at the regular, end-of-Presidency meeting of the European Council in June. However, another important item of European Council business – nominating the next President of the European Commission – was every bit as acrimonious at the June summit as the treaty negotiations had been at the December summit. Only at a specially-convened summit at the end of June were national leaders able to announce their choice to head the new Commission: Portuguese Prime Minister José Manuel Barroso.

Five months later, at a splendid ceremony in Rome to sign the Constitutional Treaty, EU leaders faced the embarrassing fact that the outgoing Prodi Commission would have to stay in office for at least another few weeks beyond its planned departure date of 31 October. The reason for the change of plan was the European Parliament's refusal to accept one of the Commissioners-designate and its ability to force a reconfiguration of the proposed Commission. The struggle over the new Commission indicated the Parliament's continuing determination to assert itself politically by holding the Commission to account, regardless of the unexpectedly low turnout (45.5 per cent) in the recent direct elections.

Journal compilation © 2005 Blackwell Publishing Ltd, 9600 Garsington Road, Oxford OX4 2DQ, UK and 350 Main Street, Malden, MA 02148, USA

This article examines the conclusion of the Intergovernmental Conference (IGC); the nomination, parliamentary approval, and appointment of Barroso as Commission President; and the political manœuvring surrounding the Commission's investiture by the Parliament. Despite the achievement of the EU in concluding the Constitutional Treaty, holding direct elections, and putting a new Commission in place – not to mention taking in ten new Member States – the events of 2004 sent mixed signals about EU governance and inter-institutional relations. By the end of the year the primacy of the European Council was indisputable, yet its fractiousness was worrying. Although undoubtedly able to carry out its treaty-mandated tasks, the Commission remained politically weak. The Parliament's determination to use every opportunity to enhance its institutional authority was both obvious and exasperating. The challenges of managing all three institutions, which had increased in size and diversity as a result of enlargement, were daunting.

Implementation of the Constitutional Treaty would strengthen EU governance but would hardly bring harmony to the European Council or restore the inter-institutional balance, at least as the Commission sees it. Nor was the future of the Treaty assured. After all the heavy lifting of the Convention on the Future of Europe and the subsequent IGC, most politicians and officials involved in the two processes knew that the Treaty faced formidable hurdles on the road to ratification.

I. The Intergovernmental Conference

The year 2003 had ended on a glum note with the failure of the European Council to conclude the IGC, largely because of a disagreement between Poland and Spain, on the one hand, and France and Germany, on the other, over a new system for qualified majority voting in the Council. Poland and Spain wanted to maintain the current arrangement, so painfully agreed to in the Nice Treaty and so advantageous to them (they each had 27 votes compared to 29 votes each for the biggest Member States). France and Germany wanted the double majority system proposed by the Convention (50 per cent of the members of the Council representing at least 60 per cent of the population of the EU), an arrangement that would increase their relative voting weight. Most of the other Member States had little sympathy for any of the main protagonists, but acknowledged that the Nice arrangement was cumbersome and iniquitous and should probably be scrapped.

Media reports notwithstanding, the failure of the December 2003 summit was not tantamount to the failure of the IGC. Nor did it cause a crisis for the EU. Originally scheduled to start in 2004, the IGC would instead resume that year. The only question was when: during the Irish Presidency in the first semester or the Dutch Presidency in the second semester?

Even so, a successful outcome was by no means assured. The failure of the negotiations on institutional reform at the Amsterdam summit in June 1997, the unsatisfactory nature of the Nice arrangements, and the breakdown of the December 2003 summit weighed heavily on Member States' minds. The prospect of another failure or Nice-like debacle was repugnant to most participants and the Convention had generated considerable political momentum for success. But national leaders, with whom a final decision rested, had dug in their heels. Ill feeling over the war in Iraq and the disregard by France and Germany of the Stability and Growth Pact poisoned relations between EU leaders. As pointed out in last year's *Review*, the intimacy of the European Council was the institution's greatest strength but also, as events in December 2003 had shown, its greatest weakness.

A cooling off period seemed in order. Hence the talk in EU circles of waiting to resume the IGC under the Dutch Presidency. The Dutch themselves were ambivalent about the prospect. Nor, given the quirky nature of Dutch politics and changing attitudes in the Netherlands towards the EU, did the other Member States relish the idea of resuming the conference under Dutch chairmanship. Moreover, the changeover to a newly-elected European Parliament (after June 2004) and a newly-appointed European Commission (after November) meant that new representatives from the two institutions would have to be appointed to the conference. Although the Commission and the Parliament were marginal players in an avowedly intergovernmental process, it was better from their point of view, and in the opinion also of some Member States, to try to conclude an agreement with the existing cast of characters.

All of this played into the hands of Bertie Ahern, the fiercely ambitious but studiously understated Taoiseach. As soon as the December 2003 summit ended, Ahern was determined not only to resume the negotiations but also to bring them to a successful conclusion during Ireland's Presidency. A skilled negotiator used to tackling thorny issues (he had spent a decade dealing with Northern Ireland's notoriously obdurate politicians), Ahern relished the prospect of striking a bargain in Brussels. Without ever admitting what they were up to, Ahern, his Foreign Minister, and Irish officials quietly set the scene for a resumption of the IGC in early 2004.

Ahern's approach was in marked contrast to that of the excitable Commission President, Romano Prodi. At a press conference in Dublin in early January 2004, at the end of the six-monthly get-together between the Commission and the incoming Council Presidency, Prodi worried about a possible split in the EU, with France and Germany forming a 'pioneer' group of like-minded states. Ahern played down the idea, insisting that all Member States could and would move forward together. He then embarked on a series of bilateral meetings with his fellow national leaders, hoping to lay the groundwork for a decision at the next meeting of the European Council, in March 2004, to resume the IGC. Ahern's itinerary, like the conduct of other EU business, was complicated by the fact that there were now 25 players in the game, even though enlargement has not yet formally taken place.

Uncertainty about the state of the negotiations when they were broken off presented both a challenge and an opportunity to Ahern. Silvio Berlusconi, Italy's Prime Minister and Ahern's predecessor as Council President, had not kept notes of his bilateral 'confessionals' during the December summit or briefed his officials on the outcome. EU leaders therefore had different understandings of the state of play concerning the outstanding issues. That gave Ahern some wriggle room in his dealings with the main protagonists, but also made it more difficult for him to establish a common basis for a renewal of the negotiations. As Ahern conducted his diplomatic rounds, it became clear that renewed negotiations would have to be based on the Italian Presidency's 'global package' on the draft Constitutional Treaty, tabled following a conclave of foreign ministers in Naples at the end of November 2003 (the so-called post-Naples document).

The Irish Presidency identified 22 unresolved issues in the IGC. Apart from the system for qualified majority voting, the most contentious were:

- the size and composition of the Commission;
- the scope of qualified majority voting;
- the size of the European Parliament (the number of members and the size of national delegations);
- budgetary procedures (this was a highly sensitive issue for the European Parliament);
- whether to recognize Europe's 'religious' or 'Christian' heritage in the preamble of the Constitutional Treaty.

Without raising any of these issues, foreign ministers held their first talks on the draft Constitutional Treaty since the breakdown of the Brussels summit, at the end of January 2004. This amounted to an informal session of the IGC (the European Parliament's two representatives were present). A two-day hearing in mid-February on the state of the IGC, organized by the European Parliament's Constitutional Affairs Committee, brought together a number of the members of the Convention and added to the political pressure for a resumption of the negotiations. The Constitutional Affairs Committee held a similar hearing in mid-March, shortly before the meeting of the European Council at which EU leaders would decide on whether and when to resume the conference.

As he visited other national leaders before the summit, Ahern expressed pessimism about the likelihood of getting the negotiations going again. His doubt may have been tactical, intended to raise the stakes in the European Council and ensure a favourable result. Yet he seemed genuinely discouraged by the intransigence of the Spanish head of government, José Maria Aznar, and Polish Prime Minister Leszek Miller, both of whom had defended the Nice arrangement tenaciously at the December 2003 summit.

Ahern was well aware that the outcome of the Spanish general election, scheduled for mid-March (less than two weeks before the summit), could change the political landscape in Spain and the political dynamics in the European Council. Aznar had announced that he would be standing down in any case. Were his Conservative Party to win the election, as forecasters expected, then Spain would probably remain intransigent on the voting system. Were it to lose, however, the situation could change dramatically. Aznar would still remain in office for several weeks after the election, but he would be a lame duck. Moreover, the opposition Socialist Party had promised in its election programme to seek an agreement in the IGC on the basis of the draft Constitutional Treaty.

In the event, the socialists won, thanks in large part to public reaction against Aznar's initial response to the Madrid bombings, which took place on the eve of the election. The Spanish Foreign Minister-designate indicated at the meeting of the European Parliament's Constitutional Affairs Committee only days after the election that the new government would abandon the Nice formula. He did not say, however, that it would embrace the new system exactly as proposed in the draft Constitutional Treaty.

Apart from the outcome of the election, the shock of the Madrid bombings provided an impetus for the European Council to reach agreement on resuming the IGC, which would signal the EU's determination to strengthen its institutional and policy-making capacity especially in the areas of internal and external security. Ahern presented a paper outlining areas of possible agreement on some of the outstanding issues, while stressing that much work still needed to be done. Aznar, who attended the summit, was present at the working dinner where EU leaders discussed the IGC, but did not speak and left early. Polish Prime Minister Miller quietly abandoned his defence of the Nice formula (he was about to ousted as Prime Minister in any case).

EU leaders agreed without much difficulty that the IGC would resume at ministerial level in May following a series of meetings of the leaders' personal representatives (so-called focal points). They also pledged to reach agreement on the Constitutional Treaty no later than the next meeting of the European Council, in mid-June, a week after the European Parliament elections.

It was unclear if the IGC would have any impact on the elections. The failure of the December 2003 summit had not caused a political earthquake. On the contrary, Europeans seemed indifferent to it. Nevertheless, resuming the IGC in the run-up to the elections might help to raise the EU's profile among European voters. If so, poor progress in the IGC could negatively affect public perceptions of the EU and therefore contribute to lower voter turnout. Yet reaching an agreement before the elections risked turning them into a referendum on the Constitutional Treaty, which eurosceptics would easily exploit.

Foreign ministers again discussed the IGC at a meeting of the General Affairs Council on 26 April and agreed on a timetable for its resumption. A conference of the national focal points (senior government officials) in Dublin on 4 May helped to clarify the agenda. Meanwhile, Ahern had written to his fellow EU leaders, including the Presidents of the Commission and the Parliament, urging them to be flexible in the forthcoming negotiations. He also suggested that they try to resolve as many issues as possible before the June summit and not raise any new ones in the meantime. Ahern then set off on another, crucial round of visits to national capitals.

The conference officially resumed on 17 May, when foreign ministers met for a two-day session. The relatively late resumption of negotiations was due to the delay in putting a new Spanish government in place and to political changes in Poland. As a result, national governments had only three weeks in which to reach an agreement on the Constitutional Treaty, before concluding the conference at the next meeting of the European Council. Two other ministerial sessions took place before the summit, on 24 May and 14 June.

The Presidency sought to reduce the number of outstanding issues at each session (at ministerial or official level) of the IGC. Based on progress made at the previous session, the Presidency produced two papers for the next session: one was the latest version of the draft Treaty (including the most recently agreed provisions); the other was a progressively shorter list of outstanding issues. As in the closing stages of the Amsterdam and Nice negotiations, those issues included the system of qualified majority voting, the size and composition of the Commission, and the size and composition of the Parliament.

Much to the surprise of some other governments, the new Spanish government had not entirely abandoned its predecessor's reservations about the proposed new Council voting system. While accepting the principle of a double majority, the new government rejected the thresholds proposed in the draft Treaty (50 per cent of the Member States representing at least 60 per cent of the population of the EU). They also rejected the idea of simply deferring implementation of the proposed new system by accepting a lengthy transition period.

Instead, Spain proposed a qualified majority of 50 per cent of the Member States and 66 per cent of the population, a formula that would strengthen Spain's ability to form a blocking minority. Despite accepting the principle of a double majority, by proposing different thresholds the new government was trying to achieve what the old government had sought when it defended the Nice formula: maximum influence for Spain in Council decision-making. Clearly, interpretation of the national interest transcended party politics in Spain (and presumably in other EU countries as well). Indeed, the new Polish government was also obdurate on the question of Member State and demographic thresholds, in part because of deep-rooted Polish resistance to Franco-German ascendancy in the EU (the thresholds in the draft Constitutional Treaty were widely seen as a Franco-German demand).

Perhaps because the system for qualified majority voting risked once again becoming a deal breaker in the IGC, but also because Poland and Spain now accepted the principle of the double majority, France and Germany indicated their willingness to negotiate different thresholds. Most governments wanted to maintain the gap (10 per cent) between the Member State and demographic thresholds. In the run-up to the June summit, a consensus began to emerge on the formula of 55 per cent of the Member States representing 65 per cent of the population, with some qualifications. In particular, the small EU countries insisted that, given such a formula, the blocking minority should consist of at least four Member States, thereby preventing the three big Member States together from blocking legislation.

Although a resolution seemed possible, national leaders would have to thrash out the details at the June summit. The size and composition of the Commission would also be on the summit's agenda. The Convention had proposed a college of only 15 Commissioners, based on a system of equal rotation among the Member States with due regard to demographic and regional balance, with the remaining Member States allowed to have non-voting Commissioners. In the IGC, however, most of the small EU countries, especially those just coming into the Union, fiercely defended the principle of a unitary Commission with one Commissioner per Member State. They were motivated by calculations of national interest and prestige, and by concerns that the big Member States would dominate a restricted college. The question of the Commission's size seemed especially pertinent during the final stage of the IGC when, as a result of enlargement, the Commission had 30 members (a number that would fall to 25 in November, when the new Commission took office).

The size and composition of the European Parliament also remained a contested issue. The apportionment of seats to the acceding Member States and reapportionment among the existing Member States had been highly contentious in the IGC that resulted in the Nice Treaty. Given its large population and political influence, Germany had retained its representation of 99 parliamentarians, by far the largest national representation in the Parliament. Most other Member States, by contrast, saw their delegations shrink appreciably. At the conclusion of the accession negotiations in December 2002, by which time it was clear that Bulgaria and Romania would not join until 2007 at the earliest, the existing Member States and those just about to join decided to apportion among themselves, for the forthcoming direct elections (in June 2004), the seats already allocated to Bulgaria and Romania. That led to another round of intergovernmental bargaining, as a result of which many existing and soon-to-be Member States received additional seats, albeit temporarily (see Table 1).

If Bulgaria and Romania join before the next direct elections (in May or June 2009), the apportionment of seats agreed to at the Nice summit was to have applied to those elections, thereby adhering to the Nice Treaty's limit of 732 seats in the Parliament. During the period between their membership and the 2009 elections, however, Bulgaria's and Romania's delegations would push the total number of seats in the Parliament temporarily to 786, just as the arrival of 162 representatives from the countries that joined the EU in May 2004 pushed the total number of seats temporarily to 788 until the direct elections in June (the possible accession of Croatia was not factored into the equation).

The IGC on the Constitutional Treaty gave the smallest Member States an opportunity to reopen the question of apportionment. Whereas the draft Constitutional Treaty called for a minimum national representation of four seats, Cyprus, Malta, Estonia and Luxembourg pressed for a minimum of six seats. Those countries did not have much leverage by themselves, but they had the strong support of Britain and much sympathy from other Member States. By way of compromise, the Presidency proposed a minimum of five seats. The limit on the total number of seats in the Parliament would also have to be revised.

The scope of qualified majority voting was another issue that remained unresolved before the June summit. Contested areas included decision-making on judicial co-operation in criminal cases involving cross-border crime (whether Member States that were outvoted should have the right to refer the proposed legislation to the European Council, which would decide on the basis of unanimity), and the possible retention of the national veto in decision-making on taxation, social security and commercial policy. The British government, in particular, drew 'red lines' around some of these areas, meaning that it rejected outright the extension of qualified majority voting to them. Member States managed to resolve the dispute over the budget before the June summit, having secured agreement at the final ministerial session of the IGC whereby the Parliament would have the final say on the annual budget following a protracted co-decision procedure.

Table 1: Allocation of Seats in the European Parliament

Member State	Population (m)[a]	1999 Election	2004 Election
Germany	82.0	99	99
France	59.0	87	78
Britain	59.0	87	78
Italy	58.0	87	78
Spain	39.0	64	54
Netherlands	16.0	31	27
Belgium	10.0	25	24
Greece	11.0	25	24
Portugal	10.0	25	24
Sweden	9.0	22	19
Austria	8.0	21	18
Denmark	5.0	16	14
Finland	5.0	16	14
Ireland	4.0	15	13
Luxembourg	0.4	6	6
Poland	39.0	–	54
Czech Republic	10.0	–	24
Hungary	10.0	–	24
Slovakia	5.0	–	14
Lithuania	4.0	–	13
Latvia	2.0	–	9
Slovenia	2.0	–	7
Estonia	1.0	–	6
Cyprus	0.7	–	6
Malta	0.4	–	5
Romania	22.0	–	–
Bulgaria	8.0	–	–
Total	479.5	626	732[b]

Source: Data from «www.europa.eu.int».
Notes: [a] Population as of 2004. [b] According to the Constitutional Treaty the total number of seats in 2009 will be 750.

Whether to include a reference to Europe's Christian heritage in the preamble of the Constitutional Treaty became a vexed question in the final weeks of the conference. It first arose with a vengeance at the ministerial session of 17–18 May, when Poland's Foreign Minister pressed the case (he had strong support from the European People's Party in the European Parliament). On 20 May (Ascension Thursday), the leaders of six Member States (Poland, Italy, Slovakia, Czech Republic, Portugal and Malta), wrote to the Council Presidency urging the inclusion of the word 'Christian' in the preamble. France, Belgium, and Denmark were adamantly opposed; Germany and Hungary sympathetic; Sweden, Finland and Estonia disinclined. Under the new Socialist government, Spain abandoned its commitment to the cause. Ahern was grateful that, as Council President, he did not have to take a stand on the issue and risk alienating a sizeable segment of Irish opinion (either the religious conservatives or the secular avant-garde). Even before the European Council convened for the final negotiating session, it was clear that the preamble would not be revised to substitute 'Christian' for 'religious'.

The outcome of the conference was still unsure as EU leaders gathered for the summit on 17 June. Less than a week earlier, European voters had turned out in record low numbers in the European Parliament elections and, in most cases, had voted against the parties of incumbent governments. The IGC seemed to have had little impact (one way or the other) on the turnout or the results. However, the poor turnout possibly helped the conference by reminding national leaders, as they gathered for the decisive meeting of the European Council, of the symbolic importance of reaching agreement on the Constitutional Treaty. Another failure so soon after the disappointing European elections would have battered the EU's image even more.

Negotiations at the summit were difficult, although thanks to Aznar's absence the atmosphere at the meeting was less edgy than in December 2003. Yet British Prime Minister Tony Blair and French President Jacques Chirac grated on each other's nerves (as seen later in the chapter, they had a spectacular row over the selection of a new Commission President). Blair's announcement some weeks earlier that he would hold a referendum in Britain on the Constitutional Treaty angered Chirac and generally dismayed other national leaders. Yet it may have strengthened Blair's negotiating position by raising the domestic political importance of a favourable outcome for Britain in the negotiations. In the event, the outcome of the summit, and of the IGC as a whole, was highly satisfactory from Britain's point of view. Altogether, the IGC approved 80 amendments to the Convention's draft Treaty. Britain introduced nearly half of these and achieved all of its key demands. Even Chirac could not dispel the perception in France and elsewhere that the Constitutional Treaty bore a strong British stamp.

EU leaders and their assistants negotiated throughout the two-day summit, both together and in bilateral 'confessionals' with the Council President. As in previous sessions of the conference (at all levels), negotiations were based on two Presidency papers: a compilation of the agreements reached so far and an outline of the outstanding issues (mostly institutional affairs). Based on the deliberations during the first day, the Presidency submitted a new paper on the morning of the second day that included proposals for a final agreement. As expected at the beginning of the summit, the agreement eventually reached on the system for qualified majority voting was for a double majority of 55 per cent of the Member States and 65 per cent of the population of the EU. At the insistence of the small EU countries, the first threshold was expressed as a number as well as a percentage of Member States. Thus, the 55 per cent of Member States would have to include at least 15 EU countries (meaning that the threshold of Member States would in fact be higher than 55 per cent in the EU-25 and would approximate only 55 per cent in the EU-27).

As a concession to Poland, EU leaders agreed to include in the provisions for qualified majority voting a qualification that harks back to the Ioannina compromise, which Member States agreed to in 1994 in order to allay British and Spanish concerns in the run-up to enlargement (when Austria, Finland and Sweden would join) about the composition of a blocking minority. Thus, under the terms of the new Treaty, if a group of Member States somewhat less than a blocking minority opposed the adoption of a particular measure, the Council would do everything possible to reach a satisfactory compromise and allay the concerns of the group in the minority. This would be applicable until 2014, unless the Council agreed to extend it by a qualified majority vote.

The size and composition of the Commission remained a touchy issue until the end of the summit, when the small Member States finally agreed to a smaller Commission, but only in two Commissions' time. Thus, the Commission would retain one Commissioner per Member State until 2014, when the Commission would be limited to a number of Commissioners corresponding to two-thirds of the number of EU countries. Members of the smaller Commission would be chosen according to the principles agreed to in the Nice Treaty (strict and equal rotation among all Member States).

As for the European Parliament, EU leaders set a minimum threshold of six seats and an upper limit of 96 for Member States, thereby requiring Germany to trim the size of its delegation (this was a considerable concession on Chancellor Gerhard Schröder's part). Accordingly, they agreed to raise the number of seats to 750 (taking into account the expected accession of Bulgaria, Romania, and Croatia). The Constitutional Treaty does not provide for the allocation of these seats between national delegations but authorizes the European Council,

on a proposal from the Parliament (not the Commission) and with the assent
of Parliament, to allocate the seats before the 2009 direct elections.

National leaders settled the remaining issues, such as the extension (or
non-extension) of qualified majority voting to various policy areas, as well
as last-minute disputes about aspects of economic governance, in a flurry of
activity during the second evening of the summit. Poland's new Prime Minister
tried one last time to insert a reference to Europe's Christian heritage in the
preamble, but he was rebuffed. The European Council then wrapped up the IGC,
giving a delighted Ahern a standing ovation in recognition of the achievement
of his Presidency. Indeed, the conduct of the conference had demonstrated
the strength (in Ireland's case) and the weakness (in Italy's case) of the rotating Presidency, an institution destined to change radically under the terms of
the Constitutional Treaty – the European Council and the External Relations
Council would each have a permanent President; the Presidency of the other
Council formations would continue to rotate between EU countries for a six-
month period, according to a new rota based on groups of three Member States,
with each group containing a big and a small Member State and at least one
new Member State.

Overall, the version of the Treaty finally agreed to by the heads of state and
government bore a close resemblance to the Convention's draft, although many
of the last-minute deals on institutional provisions were retrograde steps. In
particular, the thresholds and provisos in the new system for qualified majority
voting were less elegant than the proposal in the draft Constitutional Treaty (and
also less congenial to the big Member States). Nevertheless, the conclusion
of the negotiations represented a major step forward politically for the EU. It
was the culmination of a process begun over three years previously when the
Convention first met in Brussels.

The Convention had done much of the preparatory work, but could not
substitute (either legally or politically) for the IGC, in which national governments had to take the political risks (and try to reap the political rewards) of
tough bargaining and deal-making. As in the two preceding IGCs (leading to
the Amsterdam and Nice Treaties), institutional issues proved the most challenging. Just as the failure of the Amsterdam negotiations to tackle thorny
institutional issues had prompted national leaders to try to do so in the Nice
negotiations, the inadequacy of the Nice Treaty had prompted them to try to
reach a more satisfactory institutional settlement in the Constitutional Treaty.
The new institutional bargain was far from ideal, but it was probably the best
that could have been hoped for in the circumstances.

Personal pique rather than entrenched political preferences had prevented an
agreement from being reached at the December 2003 summit (Chirac would not
countenance any concessions to Aznar). The same thing might have happened

had Aznar still been in office in June 2004, although the prospect of another failure might have impelled one or both leaders to seek a compromise. Even without Aznar, who would no longer have been head of the Spanish government by that time even if his party had won the general election, personal predilections inevitably played a part in the decisive summit, in particular because of strained relations between Blair and Chirac.

In whose interests were the leaders of Britain and France operating? Certainly in their own interests and those of their countries (at least as Blair and Chirac understood their countries' interests). What about the interest of the EU? That is very much a tertiary interest, although one that is bound up in the heads of state and governments' personal and national interests. The Commission President supposedly represents and promotes the European interest, as does the Council President. For Bertie Ahern, however, basking in the glow of the successful June 2004 summit, the European interest was relatively remote. As one of his aides observed, 'Getting agreement, that's what he really enjoys. It's the politics of it. It's the game' (*Financial Times*, 14 June 2004, p. 6).

II. The New Commission

Ahern had another difficult task in early 2004: shepherding the selection of a Commission President-designate through the European Council. When asked about it at the beginning of the Presidency, Ahern acknowledged that choosing Prodi's successor would not be easy. In his view the job did not have to go to a former or current prime minister, although most of the presumed contenders fitted that description. Early favourites included Jean-Luc Dehaene and Guy Verhofstadt of Belgium and Jean-Claude Juncker of Luxembourg.

According to the unofficial rota for the selection of the Commission President, it was the turn of a right-of-centre candidate from a small Member State to succeed Prodi, a left-of-centre politician from a big Member State. As Ireland's Presidency progressed, Ahern became well aware that many other factors would affect the selection process and that nominating the next Commission President was a political minefield. Despite the unusually tawdry nature of what happened before Barroso emerged, *deus ex machina*, to win the coveted nomination, the story of his selection serves as a useful guide to the abstruse and highly personal politics of choosing a Commission President.

Especially because Juncker seemed genuinely uninterested in the job, Verhofstadt was the odds-on favourite. Yet many of his fellow prime ministers resented Verhofstadt's close ties to Chirac and Schröder (Verhofstadt was generally seen as the candidate of France and Germany). By early June, in the run-up to the regularly scheduled summit at which national leaders should have made the nomination, opposition to Verhofstadt had gathered steam. Blair and

Berlusconi, with the support of the European People's Party, which emerged as the largest group in the European Parliament after the elections earlier in the month, led the charge against Verhofstadt (a member of the European Liberal Democrats) and campaigned instead for External Relations Commissioner Chris Patten. At a rancorous dinner on the first day of the summit, Chirac blocked Patten because the outgoing Commissioner's home country, Britain, was not in the euro area and because Patten spoke only passable French. Blair adamantly opposed Verhofstadt primarily because of the Belgian Prime Minister's strong opposition to the war in Iraq. Ahern tried to arbitrate, but even his skills were to no avail. The spat during dinner was especially embarrassing because Verhofstadt, who thought that the job was his, was present throughout.

A humiliated Verhofstadt withdrew from the race. That left Ahern searching for an acceptable candidate and fretting about having to pass a poisoned chalice to the Dutch Presidency. Barroso then emerged as an ideal alternative. His relative obscurity was an advantage, although his qualified support for the war in Iraq seemed likely to incur Chirac's wrath. By contrast, Barroso's reputation as an economic reformer appealed to Blair, who campaigned behind the scenes for his appointment. Perhaps because there were so few feasible candidates left, and because Barroso satisfied the key French criterion that the new President-designate come from a country within the euro area, Chirac relented (Barroso also speaks excellent French). Moreover, Chirac may have been mollified by the reappointment of Pierre de Boissieu as Deputy Secretary-General and *de facto* head of the Council Secretariat – an indicator of where France thinks that institutional power in the EU lies. Whatever the reasons, Chirac's acquiescence allowed Ahern to announce, after a special summit on 29 June 2004, that the heads of state and government were putting Barroso forward for the job.

Once nominated, Barroso had to be approved by the European Parliament. This was by no means a formality in a Parliament jealous of its prerogatives. The Parliament had shown ten years previously that it could not be taken for granted when it endorsed Jacques Santer by only a narrow margin. Although dissatisfied with the method of Barroso's selection, most Euro-parliamentarians, still settling in after the June elections, were not about to pick a fight with the national leaders (at least not yet).[1] It helped that Barroso belonged to the European People's Party, to which a majority of Euro-parliamentarians also belonged (see Table 2 for the composition of political groups in the Parliament

[1] Ironically, at the same time that it criticized the manner of Barroso's selection, the European Parliament chose its own President, Josep Borrell, on the basis of a deal between the two largest political groups that some members of the smaller groups claimed was unfair and undemocratic. Borrell, a member of the Party of European Socialists, will hold the Presidency for half of the Parliament's mandate; a member of the European People's Party (presumably Hans Gert Pöttering) will take over.

after the 2004 elections). In one of its first important votes, the newly-elected Parliament approved Barroso's nomination by a large margin (413 votes to 251) in July 2004.

Despite this endorsement, the nature of Barroso's nomination raised questions about his likely legitimacy and effectiveness as Commission President. In fact, the selection of the Commission President has usually been a messy affair. Jacques Delors, widely viewed as the most successful President in the Commission's history, was also a compromise candidate (coincidentally, Ireland was in the Council Presidency at the time of his selection). Regardless of how they select the nominee for Commission President, national leaders have the right to do so and insisted on retaining that right in the Constitutional Treaty.

Table 2: Political Groups in the European Parliament after the 2004 Elections

Group	Characteristics	Member States Represented	No. of Parliamentarians
Group of the European People's Party and European Democrats (EPP-ED)	Christian democrats and conservatives	25	268
Group of the Party of European Socialists (PES)	Social democrats	23	200
Alliance of Liberals and Democrats for Europe	Liberals and free marketers	19	88
Greens/European Free Alliance	Environmentalists and 'representatives of stateless nations' (e.g. Catalan, Scottish, Welsh nationalists)	13	42
Confederal Group of the European United Left/ Nordic Green Left	Far left-wing environmentalists, ex-communists and communists	14	41
Independence/Democracy Group	Disaffected eurosceptics	11	37
Union for Europe of the Nations Group	Heterogeneous group, mostly members of Italy's National Alliance and Ireland's Fianna Fáil	6	27
Unattached (independents)	Unaffiliated members	8	28

Source: Data from «www.europa.eu.int».

The legitimacy of the Commission President, however weak, derives from the strong legitimacy of the heads of state and government, from the approval of the Parliament, and from the effectiveness of the incumbent.

Barroso caused a stir in August when he allocated portfolios among the Member States' nominees to the Commission seemingly without regard to national preferences. His move was all the more surprising because of the presumption that, having won the grudging approval of the French and German leaders, Barroso would award important portfolios to the French and German nominees. Schröder, in particular, had pressed for the creation of a superportfolio for economic policy, to be given to Günter Verheugen, his Commission nominee (and a hold-over from the Prodi Commission). Instead, in a declaration of independence, Barroso did not combine the economic portfolios and allocated them to other nominees, mostly from small Member States, with track records as reformers. He relegated the French and German nominees to lesser (but not insignificant) portfolios, while taking the political precaution of appointing them Commission Vice-Presidents. Barroso's quick and audacious allocation of portfolios, announced when most national leaders were on their summer holidays, helped to establish his authority among the new Commissioners and with some of the national leaders.

Barroso may have acted too swiftly, however, in giving Rocco Buttiglione, Italy's commission nominee, the portfolio of justice, freedom and security. During the investiture procedure for the new Commission in September-October, the Parliament's Social Affairs Committee narrowly voted not to approve Buttiglione, a conservative Catholic with traditional views about women and gays.[2] This put Parliament as a whole and the Commission President-designate in a quandary. Should Barroso appease Parliament by sacrificing the Commissioner in question, or insist that Parliament vote on his entire college, as stipulated in the Treaty? Should Parliament confront Barroso and vote down his entire Commission for the sake of an unacceptable Commissioner-designate? Most national leaders had little sympathy for Buttiglione because of their general dislike for Berlusconi, Buttiglione's political patron. They were concerned, however, about the institutional implications of the looming political crisis.

At first Barroso held firm, buoyed by the support of Hans Gert Pöttering, leader of the Group of the European People's Party. When it became clear that a majority of parliamentarians would vote against the Commission despite Pöttering's assurances to the contrary, Barroso withdrew his support from the embattled Commissioner-designate, who fortunately withdrew from nomination. Barroso submitted a new Commission-designate to the Parliament (in an effort to save face and appease other criticism of his original

[2] This was the second set of hearings for new Commissioners in 2004; the first set, in May, was for the ten new members of the Prodi Commission from the acceding Member States.

list of Commissioners and their portfolios, it included one other new nominee and a reshuffle of two portfolios). Parliament held hearings for the two new Commissioners-designate on 15–16 November and, by 449 votes to 149, approved the new Commission on 18 November. The Barroso Commission finally took office on 22 November, three weeks later than expected.

The investiture crisis signalled Parliament's increasingly powerful oversight of Commission affairs and willingness to confront the European Council. Parliament won a commitment from Barroso to conclude a new framework agreement between the Parliament and the Commission President on parliamentary scrutiny of the Commission. Parliament's main demand was that, in the event that Parliament votes to withdraw confidence in an individual Commissioner, the President would either require that Commissioner to resign or justify a refusal to do so. According to Parliament's influential Committee on Constitutional Affairs, 'refusal to accept the Parliament's vote of no confidence ... will risk the survival of the President himself. [Members of the European Parliament] have found the escalator that will lead them, if necessary, to a position where they can use their 'nuclear option' – the power to sack the whole Commission' (European Parliament, 2005, p. 12).

The Committee justified what it described as this 'bloodthirsty' statement by pointing out that 'somebody somewhere [must be] responsible for running Europe' (presumably the Committee was referring to the Parliament in Strasbourg). Taking aim at the European Council rather than Barroso for the events of October-November 2004, the Committee concluded triumphantly that the outcome of the crisis was 'to have made the government of the Union a bit more parliamentary in character and a bit less presidential'. In another jab at the European Council, the Committee described as 'wholly formalistic' the process whereby the Council of Ministers, acting at the level of the heads of state and government, officially appoints the Commission. According to the Committee, national governments retained that process in the Constitutional Treaty 'solely in order to feed the pomposity of the Council' (European Parliament, 2005, pp. 10, 12). Such is the extent of parliamentary sniping at the Council of Ministers and the European Council in the EU today.

As for the Barroso Commission, the events surrounding its appointment suggested that it would have difficulty asserting itself. The new Commission contained a wealth of talent and a number of political heavyweights, including some former senior government ministers. There was no reason to believe that it would not carry out its responsibilities effectively. Nevertheless, Barroso's potential as Commission President, and therefore the Commission's potential as a political actor, seemed to be constrained. National leaders, including Barroso when he was Prime Minister of Portugal, were not looking for another Commission President like Delors. Though they paid lip service during the IGC to the importance of strong Commission leadership, they did not want a situation in which they could be overshadowed by the Commission President. Nor did they want the Commission to be in the driving seat of European integration.

While wishing Barroso well, national leaders knew that he could not over-reach himself. As the 'accidental President' who emerged after a host of other candidates had been rejected, as a politician from a small Member State, as a President lacking a compelling project for which the Commission could provide indispensable leadership (the Lisbon strategy does not have the political potential of the old single market programme) and, as the head of an unwieldy 25-strong executive body, Barroso has limited prospects. Compared to his immediate predecessors, he may shine, but compared to Delors during the golden years of the late 1980s, he is likely to disappoint.

Reference

European Parliament (2005) 'Draft Report on the Guidelines for the Approval of the European Commission'. Committee on Constitutional Affairs (2005/2024(INI)), 24 February.

The Irish Presidency: A Diplomatic Triumph

NICHOLAS REES
University of Limerick

Introduction

Ireland, which held the Presidency from January to June 2004, inherited a busy EU work programme from the Italians, and found itself in the driving seat at a key historical moment. It was likely to be a high-profile Presidency in the light of the Intergovernmental Conference (IGC), the impending enlargement, the appointment of the new Commission President and EP elections. The Taoiseach, Bertie Ahern was a skilled political operator, who clearly wanted a diplomatic triumph during the Irish Presidency. Other key players included Brian Cowen, the Minister for Foreign Affairs who, along with Mary Harney, the Tánaiste and Minister for Enterprise, Trade and Employment, was determined to improve transatlantic relations. Finally, other notable figures included Charlie McCreevy, Minister for Finance, and Dick Roche, Minister of State for European Affairs, as well as a number of high-profile Irish diplomats in the Department of Foreign Affairs and Permanent Representation.

The Irish Presidency's work programme, *Europeans – Working Together*, concentrated on four principal priorities: completing a successful enlargement, the Lisbon strategy, initiatives in the area of justice and home affairs, and global engagement, with a particular focus on working towards improved relations with the USA. However, given that the work programme of any individual Presidency now also forms part of both the annual operational programme, which in this case included the Dutch Presidency (July–December 2004), and the three-year multi-annual strategic programme, the scope for individual initiative is limited. Nevertheless, the Irish Presidency was particularly interested in moving forward the Lisbon agenda, reflecting Ireland's economic interest in competitiveness, economic growth and employment.

I. The Intergovernmental Conference

The December European Council charged the Irish Presidency with consulting its partners and determining whether progress could be achieved if the IGC were reconvened. The Taoiseach and Minister for Foreign Affairs deliberately adopted a low-key approach, seeking to minimize Member State expectations, while listening, assessing and ultimately reporting back to the March European Council. Thus, the Presidency's early weeks were dedicated to holding bilateral meetings with all Member States, identifying issues and building trust. By the time of the European Council on 24–25 March it had established that agreement might be possible and recommended that the IGC should be reconvened and concluded by June. The Irish strategy was to hold a sufficient number of meetings to resolve outstanding issues, but limit the number of issues being discussed and progressively close off items. An initial meeting of foreign ministers was held on 16–17 April in Ireland, at which a new timetable was agreed, while during early May, the Taoiseach engaged in a round of bilateral diplomacy, visiting all the EU capitals. In total, three meetings were held at foreign minister level on 17–18 and 24 May and on 14 June, with a further meeting at official level on 4 May in Dublin. The working method included circulation of both closed and open papers to Member States.

The IGC was formally reconvened on 17 June with a number of major open issues remaining for discussion, including the size of the Commission, voting thresholds in the Council, the number of EP seats, and some economic issues and matters relating to the Charter of Fundamental Rights. On 18 June, following a meeting of the European Council in the morning, the IGC was reconvened and the Taoiseach and Irish officials spent the remainder of the day meeting individual or groups of states. Final agreement was reached in the late evening, with the Taoiseach receiving a standing ovation from the Member States. All sides on the debate claimed the outcome as a victory and praised the Irish Presidency highly. The failure, however, to agree on a new Commission President left an unresolved issue, which was finally settled at the end of June when agreement was reached on the appointment of José Manuel Barroso, the Portuguese Prime Minister, as Commission President.

II. Internal Policies

The Irish Presidency placed considerable emphasis on making progress on the Lisbon agenda, with the stress on economic competitiveness, employment and social cohesion. However, the spring European Council meeting in March, which is usually devoted to discussing economic issues, was overshadowed by the Madrid bombings and the IGC. There was, however, agreement that Wim Kok, the former Dutch Prime Minister, would chair a high-level group charged with making recommendations on how further progress might be achieved. There was also agreement during the Presidency on a financial services action plan, the European health card, legislation concerning the mobility of citizens, businesses and services, a directive on intellectual property, consumer and environmental protection, and infrastructural development. Aside from the Lisbon agenda, the Irish Presidency made progress on early discussions on the financial perspective. Following publication of the Commission's 10 February communication on the policy challenges facing the Union between 2007 and 2013, it sought to consult Member States on their views and identified key issues. It presented its findings in an analytical report to the June European Council. The debate over the size of the budget was particularly poignant for Irish officials who, while recognizing what Ireland had received as a past beneficiary, were aware also that Ireland would soon be a net contributor.

There was also considerable progress in the area of justice, home affairs and internal security under the leadership of Minister for Justice, Equality and Law Reform, Michael McDowell, with agreement on a new directive on asylum qualification and political agreement on an asylum procedures direc-tive, both key elements of a common EU asylum system. Most of the attention was focused on terrorism in the light of the Madrid bombings on 11 March, with the European Council adopting a declaration on solidarity against ter-rorism, the appointment of the former Dutch minister, Gijs de Vries, as the EU's counter-terrorism co-ordinator, and the re-establishment of the counter-terrorism taskforce in Europol. The June European Council agreed that, every six months, Member States would review the EU's action plan/road map on terrorism to ensure future progress and give the process new impetus. Lastly, the European Council supported the High Representative's recommendation that intelligence capability be integrated into the Council Secretariat in order to gather information on terrorist threats. This was to be done by expanding the situation centre (SitCen), so as to enable it to assess both external and internal threats, rather than establishing an EU intelligence agency.

III. External Relations

The Irish Presidency also managed a complex international agenda, hosting a number of major summits (e.g. Russia, Canada, Switzerland, Japan, Latin America and the Caribbean), as well as making progress on international is-sues in the Mediterranean, Middle East and Africa. The historic enlargement of the Union on 1 May was a notable highlight. It was celebrated as a 'Day of Welcomes' in Dublin where European leaders, including the Presidents of the Commission and European Parliament, joined together in celebrating the enlargement. Meanwhile negotiations with Bulgaria and Romania continued, and further progress was made on opening accession negotiations with Croatia and Turkey. A particular priority was to improve and enhance relations with Canada and America. This culminated in a successful EU–US summit held in Dromoland Castle in June, at which President Bush declared his support for the EU and highlighted America's commitment to meeting its international obligations.

A further Irish Presidency priority was to highlight the plight of many African states and to make progress on EU–African relations, both through dialogue, support for the African Union, and effective leadership on HIV/Aids, all of which were aimed at ensuring that Africa was the focus of EU attention. The Presidency also continued work on developing the EU's approach to conflict prevention through early warning systems, working with civil society and NGOs, and building support with regional partners. Last, but by no means least, the Presidency was also charged with making progress on the European security strategy, an area that required sensitive handling, given Ireland's declared policy of military neutrality. The Presidency placed considerable emphasis on enhancing EU–UN co-operation, especially in crisis management, as well as working on the British and French proposals to develop the 'battle group' concept, and agreeing on new military capabilities (Headline Goal 2010). There was also agreement on launching the EU's first rule of law ESDP mission in Georgia, and military planning was undertaken in preparation for the launch of an ESDP operation in Bosnia-Herzegovina.

Conclusion

In conclusion, the Irish Presidency was highly successful, culminating in the agreement on the Constitutional Treaty, the appointment of the Commission President, and strengthened transatlantic ties. The Presidency achieved much of what it set out in its programme, and more given the challenges of the IGC, the Madrid bombings and other international events. It was a well-run Presidency, with the Taoiseach being praised by other European leaders for his negotiating skills. The Irish diplomatic corps also deserve particular praise, given the limited resources available to them. The limitations of a rotating Presidency – whether Irish or that of any other state – were clear, given the limited progress on the Lisbon agenda, perhaps reflecting the problem of relying on the open method of co-ordination (OMC), the practical problems of getting 15 (now 25) states to implement anti-terrorism measures, and the presence of ten new countries in the EU's institutions and at meetings.

JCMS 2005 Volume 43. Annual Review pp. 59–62

The Dutch Presidency: An Assessment

PETER VAN HAM
Netherlands Institute of International Affairs

Introduction

In his letter to the Dutch Parliament (28 May 2004), Minister of Foreign Affairs Ben Bot laid out a broad and ambitious agenda for the Netherlands Presidency in the latter half of that year. This probably being the last time that the Netherlands would be at the EU's helm, policy-makers in The Hague knew that, to be successful, it would take more than just minding the shop. What was required was both skill and ambition. Dutch ambitions ranged from developing the Union's capabilities in the area of justice and home affairs (JHA), making progress on the EU's economic Lisbon agenda, as well as in the areas of international terrorism, European defence, and relations with the United States.

The Dutch Presidency was the first to work (for the full six-month term) with no fewer than 25 Member States. New – and more – faces around the European Council table meant different working methods, especially since this coincided with a newly elected – and enlarged – European Parliament, as well as a newly appointed European Commission. The overall success of the Dutch Presidency showed that, even in an enlarged Union, decisions could still be made. Frequent *tours de tables* may no longer be practical during Council meetings, but this may well have added to the efficacy of EU decision-making.

I. 'Small Pearl' of the Presidency

The overall costs of the Dutch Presidency were around €100 million, of which €20 million were spent on security alone. Sixteen ministerial meetings were organized in South-Limburg, The Hague, Noordwijk, Amsterdam and Groningen. Two summits were held where all EU heads of state and government convened, on 4–5 November and 16–17 December (in Brussels). As European Council President, Dutch Prime Minister Jan Peter Balkenende received the leaders of Russia, China and India in The Hague. For a medium-sized country like the Netherlands, these high-level meetings offer the political advantages of organizing the six-month rotating Presidency at home. With all European Council meetings being held in Brussels in future, President Putin and Prime Minister Wen Jiaboa are likely to visit the Netherlands less often.

Although the EU still has to digest its enlargement to include ten new Member States in May 2004, it was decided that Croatia would be the next in line if Zagreb co-operated fully with the International Criminal Tribunal for the Former Yugoslavia (ICTY). Negotiations were also closed with Romania and Bulgaria, which meant that, in April 2005, accession treaties with both these countries could in principle be signed.

Balkenende labelled the start of accession negotiations with Turkey as the 'small pearl of our Presidency'. And indeed, like all pearls, the creation of this little miracle involved much friction and risked overall failure. Several EU Member States still had significant reservations about Turkey's possible entry into the Union, with Austria being the most wary for cultural reasons, and Cyprus for political reasons. Within the Netherlands, and even in Balkenende's own Christian Democratic Party, there was little love lost for Turkish EU membership, It required significant power-politics, with French President Jacques Chirac playing an important role, to convince his Cypriot counterpart, Tassos Papadopoulos, that the EU should open its doors to Turkey, before it was decided that Ankara and the EU would start accession talks on 3 October 2005. In the end, the compromise was historic, since Turkey now awaits a 15-year negotiation process where, as is formally stated in the final agreement, there is no assurance at all that full membership will be granted. The EU reserves the right to suspend negotiations in case of serious breaches of democratic and human rights.

III. Achievements

EU agreement on the so-called 'Hague Programme' on the exchange of information and the strengthening of judicial co-operation to fight international terrorism, can be considered a success of the Dutch Presidency. This five-year programme (which succeeds the Tampere programme) deals with the full spectrum of the Union's JHA policies, and the European Commission is now tasked to work out an action plan (in 2005). It was also agreed that work continue towards a common asylum policy in 2010, as well as an agreement to develop a new EU drugs strategy for 2005–12. The European Council also decided to establish a unit to develop *European* threat analyses on the basis of national intelligence.

The Dutch Presidency also put its weight behind the introduction of a multi-annual budgetary structure for the EU. As a net payer to the EU budget, the Dutch were keen to establish a clear link between budgetary options and political priorities. According to The Hague, the final agreement will now ensure more clarity and transparency, as well as a solid basis for future political agreement on the EU's new financial perspectives. The final decision should be made on this in 2005.

The Presidency took up the Lisbon strategy that focuses on the Union's economic competitiveness and reform agenda. It was a stated Dutch priority to work towards the streamlining and simplification of EU legislation. The agreement at the Ecofin Council on 7 December, where six Member States signed a renewed joint statement on regulatory reform (which includes a joint EU action plan for 2004–06 in order to reduce the burden of EU rules), was clearly a result of Dutch efforts.

During the Dutch Presidency, further steps were taken to make the European security and defence policy (ESDP) operational. On 2 December, the EU embarked on its first big military operation (named 'Althea', with around 7,000 troops) by taking over Nato's SFOR in Bosnia-Herzegovina. A few months earlier, an EU military capacities conference resulted in the establishment of 13 EU battle groups, offering the Union the military option to react effectively in conflict situations.

On foreign policy, the Dutch Presidency played a rather low-key role. The threat of a nuclear Iran was mainly dealt with by the EU's big three (the UK, France and Germany), whereas the so-called Orange Revolution in Ukraine was mainly the concern of the Union's foreign policy tzar, Javier Solana, and the Member State with the most expertise and the greatest strategic interests – Poland. Some irritation between the Netherlands and Russia occurred over the Union's response to the hostage drama in Beslan in September 2004, as well as with the United States over the EU's proposal to lift its arms embargo against China. The Dutch Presidency also annoyed French President Chirac when it decided to invite the interim Iraqi President Allawi to the European Council meeting of November.

Conclusion

What may have been the last Dutch EU Presidency can only be gauged a success. Living up to their existing record and their reputation as a competent and committed Member State, the Dutch have proved to be a safe pair of hands helping to steer the Union away from the edges of a number of political cliffs. Not only was the Constitutional Treaty signed in Rome in October 2004, but there were some major decisions in the areas of JHA, budgetary reform and further EU enlargement. In the end, The Hague managed to show off the 'small pearl' – the possible future EU membership of Turkey. It is one of the ironies of the dynamics of the EU Presidency that the Netherlands could well have been in the 'no' camp resisting full Turkish EU membership, were it not that its role as EU President during the crucial last phase of the negotiation process precluded it from taking sides. Instead, the Dutch Presidency had to use all its diplomatic skills and good offices to gain this outcome. Of all the achievements during the Netherlands' six-month stint as President, this is the one that will go into Europe's history books: the day that Turkey got a foot in the door of a still reluctant EU.

JCMS 2005 Volume 43. Annual Review pp. 63–84

Internal Policy Developments

DAVID HOWARTH
University of Edinburgh

Introduction

The most politically and economically significant development of the year – enlargement – brought about or encouraged several major alterations to Community policies. The Commission presented its proposal for the 2007–13 financial perspective that incorporated significant changes from the previous perspective, including major changes to the EU's cohesion policy. The Council began implementing the 2004–06 economic and social development programmes for the ten new EU countries and spending on the new Member States was incorporated into the 2005 budget. There were other significant developments in other areas. In competition policy, the modernized regulatory framework for antitrust and merger control came into force which included a new merger regulation designed to facilitate the referral of cases between the Commission and national authorities. In environmental policy, the Council agreed on a regulation bringing environmental liability to polluters throughout the EU. More negatively, with persistently high unemployment and sluggish economic growth in three of the four biggest EU national economies, 2004 saw the expression of growing doubt as to the ability of many EU countries to achieve the goals set out in the Lisbon process. The Kok report called for greater urgency in the Member States to be developed upon in the 2005 mid-term review of process. Bitter divisions between the Member States, the Commission and the European Central Bank (ECB) continued over the future of the Stability and Growth Pact.

I. Economic and Related Policies

The Lisbon Process: Competitiveness, Growth and Employment

In the lead up to the March 2005 mid-term review of the Lisbon strategy, the Commission set up a high-level group – presided over by the former Dutch Prime Minister, Wim Kok – to make proposals better designed to enable Member States to meet the strategy's goals. The Kok report, 'Facing the challenge – The Lisbon strategy for growth and employment' emphasized the need for greater urgency in implementing the strategy. In its 16 November conclusions, Ecofin called on the Commission to take into account certain elements of the report in the preparation of its proposals for the mid-term review. Ecofin stressed the need for stronger political commitment from governments, higher growth and employment, and notably in five key areas identified in the Kok report (knowledge society, internal market, entrepreneurship, labour market, environmental sustainability), the central role of the broad economic policy guidelines (BEPGs), multilateral surveillance, benchmarking of national performance and fiscal consolidation.

Employment and the European Employment Strategy (EES)

Addressing the problem of persistently high unemployment in several Member States of the EU remained firmly on the agenda. The Council adopted several measures to streamline further the European employment strategy started in 2003. The 4 March joint employment report presented three main objectives: full employment; work quality and productivity; enhanced social cohesion and inclusion. In an April communication, the Commission presented the case for reinforcing this strategy. On 23 September, the 'Employment in Europe 2004' report was published, providing an overview and analysis of recent labour market developments in the enlarged EU-25. The report explored the impact of labour market institutions on employment rates, the interrelationship of the different components of active employment policies, employment structures in the services sector and the impact of globalization on the labour market. On 14 October, the Council presented its recommendation on the implementation of Member States' employment policies based on the following approaches (as approved by the June European Council): 'increasing the adaptability of workers and enterprises; attracting more people to the labour market and making work a real option for all; investing more, and more efficiently, in human capital and lifelong learning; ensuring effective implementation of reforms through better governance' (Commission, 2005). The Commission presented several other employment related documents: (28 April) its final report on the activities pursued under the analysis, research and co-operation designed to monitor and contribute to the development of the employment strategy; (6 February) its mid-term assessment of the implementation of its action plan for skills and mobility; and (12 July) its report on the European employment services (EURES) network in 2002 and 2003, which was created to facilitate mobility in the European labour market.

Enterprise

The Lisbon strategy continued to direct EU enterprise policy in 2004 with the emphasis on enhancing competitiveness. At the March European Council four priorities in this area were highlighted: completion of the internal market; improving legislation; increased efforts in research; and strengthening the effectiveness of the institutional framework. The Commission also continued its work on defining an industrial policy to take advantage of the opportunities offered by enlargement, recommending action in three areas: better synergy between different Community policies, improving the regulatory environment for business (notably reducing the regulatory burden), and extending industrial policy to new sectors.

The Commission began work on relaunching and refocusing its innovation policy, emphasizing further European standardization to improve competitiveness. In its 11 February action plan to promote entrepreneurship, the Commission called for an improved administrative and regulatory framework for small and medium-sized businesses. The Commission proposed a series of actions to improve the visibility of the co-operative sector. Several directives and regulations were adopted in 2004 affecting various kinds of enterprises: modernization of the legislation on detergents to make it more ecological; harmonization of the control of certain drug precursors; updating of the legislation on pharmaceuticals, including the creation of a European Medicines Agency; codification of good laboratory practice; and extending the scope of the regulations on the construction of speed limitation devices to incorporate environmental and safety concerns. Taking additional steps to prepare European companies for the coming into effect of the multi-fibre agreement, the Commission proposed various actions to stimulate the competitiveness of the textiles and clothing sector. Work on laws on the registration, evaluation and authorization of chemicals (REACH) continued. The European Parliament and the Council set up the IDABC programme (2005–09) with the purpose of supporting the interoperable provision of pan-European e-government services to public departments, businesses and citizens.

'Information Society'

In 2004, one of the major themes of 'information society' policy was encouraging broadband access and use in under-equipped areas, including the ten new Member States and in disadvantaged communities. The European Network and Information Security Agency was officially established in 2004. In its mid-term review of the eEurope 2005 action plan, the Commission set out 15 actions designed to speed up the plan's implementation with regard to broadband, e-government (online public services) and e-business (electronic commerce). In a 30 June communication, the Commission spelled out the challenges to be addressed for the EU to exploit the social and economic benefits of mobile broadband services. On 19 November, the Commission launched a debate on the information society after 2005 in the context of the Lisbon strategy objectives and the wider deployment of information and communication technologies.

Throughout the year, the Commission presented several additional initiatives including proposals to: promote the existing programme on the safer use of the internet and online technologies (€50 million from 2005–08); establish an action plan for European e-health; reinforce the existing 2002 European directive on privacy and electronic communications to block spam more effectively; launch 'eContentplus' a 2005–08 multi-annual programme designed to continue and improve the eContent programme finishing in 2004. In a 2 December communication, the Commission judged as positive the implementation of the new regulatory framework for electronic communications in the Member States, as well as the state of the electronic communication services market. The Commission made preparations for the second phase of the United Nations world summit on the information society to be held in 2005.

Research

2004 saw several developments in the construction of a European research area (ERA). Launching the debate on the guidelines for future European research policy and activities, the Commission called for research funding to reach 3 per cent of GDP by 2010. Amongst other proposals, the Commission called for the development of research as a major strand of the future structural funds. In its 16 June communication, 'Science and technology, the key to Europe's future', the Commission set out six principal goals for future European research policy with the aim of contributing to growth, business competitiveness, employment and security: 'creating centres of excellence through inter-laboratory collaboration, launching major European technological initiatives, boosting basic research, making Europe more attractive to the best researchers, developing research infrastructure of European interest, and strengthening national research programmes' (Commission, 2005, ch. VIII, p. 3). The sixth framework programme resulted in over 100 calls for proposals for projects involving academics throughout the expanded Union and third countries and, in the first half of 2004, over 500 contracts were signed with some 4,400 participants.

The Commission sought to reinforce further the EU's independent capability in the field of satellite observation and remote sensing, with a plan for the second phase of global monitoring for environment and security (GMES) initiative (covering 2004–08). In the field of nuclear research, the Council allocated €30 million to a supplementary research programme for the operation of the European high flux reactor, with the joint research centre (JRC) given responsibility for implementing the programme. In a 12 May communication, the Commission pushed for the establishment of a European strategy for nanotechnology. International co-operation in research was enhanced through the renewal for a five-year period of the science and technology co-operation agreement with the United States and through bilateral co-operation agreements in the context of the sixth framework programme signed with Brazil, Egypt, Israel and Mexico.

Economic and Monetary Union (EMU)

Full macroeconomic policy co-ordination was extended to the ten new Member States, with the governments of all ten supporting euro area membership between 2007 and 2010. On 10 November, the Commission published its report on the practical preparedness of the new Member States for euro area membership, concluding that the introduction of the single currency would very likely take place more rapidly and smoothly than had been the case with the existing 12 Member States.

2004 was also noteworthy for tensions in macroeconomic policy co-ordination and in particular debates over the non-application of Stability and Growth Pact rules. France and Germany admitted to having exceeded the 3 per cent deficit threshold for the third year in a row and several other countries admitted to having done so in 2003. In January, the Commission referred to the European Court of Justice Ecofin's 25 November 2003 decision to suspend the application of the excessive deficit procedure (EDP) of the Stability Pact for Germany and France. In its 13 July decision, the ECJ revoked Ecofin's conclusions. Nonetheless, on 14 December, the Commission accepted the suspension of the EDP against these two Member States. On 3 September, the Commission presented a communication, 'Strengthening economic governance and clarifying the implementation of the Stability and Growth Pact', outlining four ways to refocus the Pact: to allow for more country-specific circumstances in defining the medium-term objectives of 'close to balance or in surplus'; to consider economic circumstances and developments in the implementation of the excessive deficit procedure; to place more emphasis on debt and the sustainability of public finances in the surveillance of budgetary positions; and to develop a more proactive surveillance of budgetary positions. The intense debate between the Member States on reforming the Pact continued into 2005 with the intention of reaching an agreement on reform prior to the March 2005 economic summit.

To reinforce the surveillance of macroeconomic policies, the Council adopted a 28 June regulation requiring Member States to produce data on their quarterly government debt. For its part, Ecofin made recommendations on necessary measures to be undertaken by the Member States in a situation of excessive deficit. However, it became unlikely that either France or Germany would respect their 2003 commitments to bring their deficit below 3 per cent by 2005. Ecofin presented opinions on the updated stability programmes and the convergence programmes of the 13 Member States not participating in the euro area. On 21 January, the Commission adopted a first report on the implementation of the 2003–05 BEPG that emphasized the deteriorating budgetary positions of several Member States and the need to step up the pace of structural reforms.

The Commission's analysis was supported by the Council, Parliament and European Council. On 5 July, the Council agreed to update the BEPG, confirming existing priorities (for example, increasing the flexibility of labour markets and ensuring the sustainability of public finances), and establishing the conditions for applying the guidelines to those Member States which were required to make adjustments to their fiscal policies (France, Germany, Greece, Italy, the Netherlands, Portugal and the United Kingdom) and to each of the ten new Member States. The Council expressed its concern (21 October, 16 November) about the failure of the Greek government to provide accurate data on debt and deficits for the 1997–2003 period, while the Commission initiated infringement proceedings against Greece at the ECJ. The Commission produced a report on 1 December proposing measures to improve 'statistical governance' in the Member States and strengthen monitoring mechanisms. The Council adopted its opinions on the euro area Member States' updated stability programmes; on the updated convergence programmes of the three 'old' euro-outsiders, Sweden, Denmark and the UK; and on the convergence programmes of the ten new Member States. On the basis of Commission reports and opinions, the Council adopted decisions (2 June, 5 July) noting excessive deficits in two of the current euro area Member States (Greece and the Netherlands) and six of the newest EU Member States (Czech Republic, Cyprus, Hungary, Malta, Poland and Slovakia) and recommending remedial action. Towards the end of the year, on 22 December, the Commission found that only one of the new Member States, Hungary, had failed to take effective action to meet the deficit target in 2005. In a 22 December recommendation, the Commission asked the

Council to find that the Greek government had taken no effective action since its notification of an excessive deficit on 5 July. On 11 May, the Council abrogated its 2002 decision on the existence of an excessive deficit in Portugal. On 5 July, the Council gave Italy an early warning on its deficit.

In July, the Commission published its report on macro-financial assistance to third countries in 2003. In 2004, new financing operations of the European Bank for Reconstruction and Development amounted to €3.8 billion, 88 per cent of which were loans and 12 per cent investments. Over 2004, the European Investment Bank granted loans amounting to €43.2 billion in support of European Union objectives (slightly up from €42.4 billion in 2003) of which €3.5 billion was spent in partner countries. On 26 May, the Commission presented its first annual report on the European Union solidarity fund.

Internal Market Developments

The Commission continued its efforts to improve the operation of the single market by encouraging Member States to deal with outstanding legislative issues such as the Community patent, and the incorrect or late transposition of Community directives into national law. On 13 January, the Commission proposed the 'Bolkestein directive' on establishing a legal framework for the elimination of obstacles to the free movement of services between Member States. Significant opposition from German and French governments and trade unions to this directive loomed.

The Commission took more modest steps in the area of financial services, presenting the final measures of its action plan, which included redesigning the directive on the capital adequacy of investment firms and credit institutions. On 21 April, a directive on markets in financial instruments was adopted to improve on existing provisions to allow financial services to operate throughout the EU on the basis of authorization in the home Member State. On 15 December, the Council and Parliament agreed a directive on 'transparency' designed to improve investor protection and the efficiency, openness and integrity of European capital markets. In the aftermath of several high-profile financial scandals involving EU companies (notably Parmalat), on 27 September the Commission presented a strategy on corporate malpractice. The Commission also sought to modernize directives governing the EU's statutory audit with the principal aim of ensuring greater transparency in accounting operations. The Commission requested Member States to strengthen the position of independent members on the supervisory or management boards of listed companies. The Council and EP agreed guidelines for the conduct of takeover bids. They also adopted a directive requiring Member States to take effective and preventive action against those involved in counterfeiting and piracy. On 19 February, the

Council adopted a regulation designed to enhance the Community trademark system set up in 1993. With the aim of avoiding distortion of competition, the Commission called for a regulation to harmonize the conditions for granting compulsory licences for the manufacture of pharmaceuticals. On 28 May, the Council signed an agreement with the United States permitting air carriers to transfer air passenger data to American customs authorities. The Council insists that the agreement upholds respect for EC law on personal data protection and non-discrimination against European passengers.

Two directives were adopted on 31 March on the co-ordination of contract award procedures for service and works in the field of public procurement in general, and for water, energy, transport and postal service sectors in particular. The principal aim of these directives was to clarify the criteria for the selection of tenders, increase transparency in the awarding of contracts, combat corruption and facilitate electronic procurement. The Commission published two major green papers (30 April and 23 September, respectively) with the aim of launching debate on desirable EU-level action on public–private partnerships, and Community law on public contracts and the adaptation of the European regulatory framework for defence equipment. On 21 April, the Council adopted a directive amending existing legislation on the mutual assistance between national authorities in the field of direct taxation, certain excise duties and taxation of insurance premia. The new directive contained provisions to speed up information flows between national tax authorities and to improve co-ordinated action against cross-border tax fraud. Amendments were made to the basic directive on VAT with the aim of simplifying and modernizing exemption procedures and to take into account issues arising from enlargement. The Commission made several proposals (notably reports of 2 April and 26 May) to clarify existing legislation on VAT and intra-Community movements of excisable products. Notably, the Commission proposed a directive to create a 'one-stop-shop' system allowing taxable persons to meet all their VAT obligations for activities throughout the EU in the Member States where they are established. The 2003 co-operation framework in the field of direct taxation was extended with agreements signed on tax on income from savings with Andorra, Liechtenstein, Monaco, San Marino and Switzerland. The various instruments of this framework were to enter into force on 1 July 2005. In its ongoing monitoring of the elimination of quantitative import and export restrictions between EU Member States, 60 new complaints were received in 2004, and four cases detected through the Commission's own investigations, with a total of 146 cases still under examination at the end of the year.

Competition and Industrial Policies

On 1 May, to coincide with enlargement, the modernized regulatory framework for antitrust and merger control came into force with wider decentralization to national competition authorities of the implementation of the competition rules based on Articles 81 and 82 of the EC Treaty. This new framework also involved the adoption of the new merger regulation designed to facilitate the referral of cases between the Commission and national authorities with the aim of optimizing case allocation before formal notification of a transaction and at the request of concerned firms. The reforms also sought to improve the role that complainants – including consumer associations – could play in enabling the Commission to undertake investigations. The reforms included a simplified procedure (regulation agreed on 20 January) for vetting certain mergers, and deadlines at different stages in the procedure for the submission of commitments by firms and the elimination of cumbersome notification procedures allowing the Commission to focus its efforts on major infringements of EC law. On 1 May, new rules also entered into force on technology transfer agreements (patents, knowhow and software copyright) to ensure policies more similar to those in the US. The Commission adopted a block exemption regulation on technology transfer agreements to clarify and simplify rules in this area. In its 20 April communication, entitled 'A proactive competition policy for a competitive Europe' the Commission clarified its own strategy. The Commission White Paper of 13 October explored the merits of maintaining or revising the existing exemption of maritime transport from competition rules.

On 7 July, the Commission established new guidelines on permissible state aid for rescuing and restructuring firms in difficulty, emphasizing that aid be kept to the minimum necessary to ensure the survival of the firm without distorting competition. In addition to social or regional policy considerations set out in the treaties, state aid could be allowed to help small and medium-sized enterprises (SMEs) and when the collapse of a company could lead to a monopoly situation. The Commission's monitoring of state aids was to focus on cases where there was likely to be a negative effect on competition. On 24 March, the Commission adopted an instrument to facilitate the preparation of state aid notifications by governments. On 18 February, the Commission proposed new rules to improve legal certainty for services of general economic interest. On 30 March, the Commission adopted a set of instruments supplementing an existing regulation to modernize the procedures for managing restrictive agreements and abuses of dominant positions.

The Commission issued several decisions prohibiting illegal cartels. It also reinforced its efforts against companies abusing their dominant market position. In one noteworthy decision on 24 March, the Commission found that

Microsoft abused its dominant market position in the group server operating systems and media player markets, imposed a fine of €497 million (one of the largest fines ever imposed by the Commission) and required Microsoft to take corrective measures. The Commission examined numerous merger cases, blocking (on 9 December) one transaction between Portuguese electricity and gas operators. On state aids, the Commission adopted numerous decisions, although it allowed 95 per cent of cases of aid it examined. The Commission continued its efforts to require the repayment of illegal aid.

On 20 April and 16 November, the Commission published updated versions of its state aid scoreboard, noting that 'the majority of Member States appear[ed] to be responding positively to the call for "less but better targeted State aid"' (Commission, 2004b). The Commission found that levels of state aid in the EU continued to fall, albeit less sharply than in the late 1990s and that aid is being redirected to so-called horizontal objectives (including research and development, SMEs, environment and regional economic developments). In 2002, as in 2001, Germany, France and Italy (in that order) provided the most state aid (calculations excluding support for railways). As a percentage of GDP, Finland provided the most at 1.28 per cent, followed by Portugal, Spain and Germany, with the UK providing the least at 0.25 per cent, with state aid throughout the EU reaching 0.56 per cent of GDP. However, if aid to agriculture and fisheries is eliminated from calculations, Finland has one of the lowest levels of state aid in the EU, with 0.17 per cent of GDP, with Denmark having the highest at 0.72 per cent, Germany, Spain and Portugal at around 0.55 per cent and an EU average of 0.39 per cent. The Commission continued to co-operate with the US on cartels and worldwide mergers, and strengthened its links with other trading partners through the establishment of competition policy dialogue with China, in May, and South Korea in October.

Structural Funds and Regional Policy

2004 can be seen as a turning point for the EU's cohesion policy. First, the Council adopted and began implementing the 2004–06 economic and social development programmes for the ten new Member States, with the financing of around 30 projects in 2004. Second, on 14 July, the Commission outlined the structure for post-enlargement cohesion policy and submitted proposals for the 2007–13 financial perspective. The Commission recommended more targeted assistance, devoting most available resources to the least-developed Member States and regions. It also recommended several reforms to improve the implementation of policy, including increased decentralization of responsibilities and stronger partnership. The Commission proposed a series of regulations to provide a framework for cohesion policy from 2007 with a view to improving consistency, complementarity and efficiency. The Commission also made specific proposals with regard to reforming existing funds – the European social fund, the European regional development fund and the cohesion fund – and proposed the establishment of a new instrument, the European grouping of cross-border co-operation (EGCC). On 26 May, the Commission proposed the main elements of a stronger partnership for the Union's outermost regions. The Commission's 15th annual report on the implementation of the structural funds (28 October) noted that payments reaching €26.2 billion in 2003 were at their highest level ever and there was important progress in budgetary implementation of the funds. The Commission and the Member States carried out a mid-term review of the programmes financed under the structural measures, making some adjustments to allocations. It was decided that Ireland was no longer eligible for support under the cohesion fund.

In commitments made during 2004 – as in the previous year – Spain, Greece, Italy, Portugal and Germany were the major recipients of objective 1 funding (regions where per capita income is below 75 per cent of the EU average), although Germany surpassed Portugal in total commitments. Poland, with €1.9 billion of commitments under objective 1, took sixth place. These six Member States received approximately 90 per cent of total objective 1 funding. The major beneficiaries of objective 2 funding (regions undergoing structural change) were – in the same order as 2003 – France, UK, Germany, Italy and Spain; and the major beneficiaries of objective 3 funding (modernization of education, training and employment systems) were – in the same order as 2003 – Germany, UK, France, Italy and Spain. Over half the commitments under the cohesion fund (totalling €5,620,718,220) went to Spain and Poland (respectively 30 and 25 per cent).

II. Social Policies

2004 saw the completion of several social policy projects that were begun or revived in 2003. Regulations were adopted on the co-ordination of national social security systems (29 April) and the simplification of procedures for patients in need of healthcare in a Member State other than their own (23 December). Starting on 1 June 2004, the European health insurance card – created to simplify the procedure for receiving medical treatment during a temporary stay in a Member State – began to be introduced by certain Member States. This card will replace existing forms (E111 and E110). On 29 April, the Council adopted a directive on the right of EU citizens and members of their family to move and reside within the territory of the Union. In a 20 April communication, the Commission proposed to apply the open method of co-ordination to an examination of different social protection systems and the difficulties arising from an ageing population. In the field of health and safety at work, several directives were adopted, including one on the protection of workers from the risks related to exposure to carcinogens or mutagens at work (29 April) and on exposure to electromagnetic fields (29 April).

On 8 October, the social partners reached collective agreement on work-related stress and initial moves were taken to consult the social partners on three issues: workplace violence, carcinogens and musculo-skeletal disorders. A tripartite social summit was held in Brussels on 25 March to exchange views on the new partnerships for change and a special summit was organized on 4 November focusing on the Kok report on the Lisbon strategy. In a 12 August communication, the Commission set out its views on the functioning, results and future of the European social dialogue.

The Commission made several proposals to combat forms of social exclusion. On 28 May, it presented a green paper on progress in the elimination of practices contributing to discrimination on the grounds of sex, race, religion, age, disability and sexual orientation. In December, on the basis of the new Member States' national action plans for social inclusion, the Commission published a report on combating poverty and social exclusion, and promoting greater social cohesion in these Member States. On 22 September, the Commission made recommendations on the modification of existing arrangements for the organization of working time to reconcile various concerns, including worker health and safety, and the flexibility to be allowed Member States and companies in the management of working time. On 14 July, the Commission proposed creating a new instrument for the 2007–13 financial perspective in the form of an integrated programme for employment and social solidarity (progress). On 19 February, the Commission published its report on the progress and challenges in the pursuit of gender equality in 2004. On 29 April, the Council and Parliament adopted an action programme to support organizations promoting equal opportunities for women and men, and on 13 December, the Council adopted a directive on equal treatment in the supply of and access to goods and services. The June European Council expressed its support for the creation of a European Gender Institute and called on the Commission to draw up a proposal.

III. Finances

2004 was an important year for EU finances principally because, on 10 February, the Commission outlined the new financial framework in a communication entitled 'Building our common future – Policy challenges and budgetary means of the enlarged Union 2007–13'. It was recommended that EU policy objectives be supported on a multi-annual basis and be targeted at the aims of the Lisbon strategy and additional specific priorities, including the promotion of sustainable development, the development of European citizenship and the strengthening of the EU as a global partner. The Commission considerably restructured headings (broad categories of expenditure) for the new financial framework. In July, the Commission proposed the simplification of certain mechanisms for the management of the financial framework, while keeping the same basic principles of budgetary discipline (see Table 1 for a summary of the full financial framework proposed). The annual average ceiling on payment appropriations for the period 2007–13 was set at 1.14 per cent of the EU-25 gross national income (GNI), providing a significant margin under the own resources ceiling of 1.24 per cent GNI, varying, depending on the year, between 0.09 per cent and 0.16 per cent of GNI.

On 14 July, the Commission presented a communication outlining the progress achieved since February on assessing the value-added of EC action, examining the resources needed to achieve the proposed project and simplifying and rationalizing the instruments delivering the project. The Commission flanked this communication with several proposals on its budgetary plans: the renewal of the 1999 inter-institutional agreement on budgetary discipline and improvement of the budgetary procedure; the creation of a mechanism for the correction of budgetary imbalances; and changes to the own resources system (the replacement of the British budget rebate mechanism with a 'generalized correction mechanism' and the introduction of a genuine fiscal own resource based on the taxation of energy consumption, value added tax or corporate income tax from 2014 to replace the current VAT resource and part of the GNI resource).

On 10 February, the Commission issued recommendations on clarifying the rules on the stages of investigation by the European Anti-Fraud Office (OLAF) and the sharing of information between OLAF and other EC institutions and bodies. On 9 August, the Commission adopted a new action programme for 2004–05 continuing the protection of financial interests and the fight against fraud and strengthening the regulatory framework for the operation of OLAF. On 21 September, the Commission adopted a standard financial regulation for the implementation of the operating budget of each of the executive agencies carrying out Community programmes. On 29 September, the Commission expanded the package of proposals in various areas of activity. For example, in its communication 'Instruments for external assistance', the Commission proposed replacing existing financial instruments with a simpler, more efficient framework.

On 16 December, the European Parliament adopted the 2005 budget – the first to cover expenditure for 25 Member States over the whole year – with appropriations for commitments reaching €116.5 billion and appropriations for payments at €106.3 billion. This increase was accepted as necessary due

Table 1: Financial Framework 2007–13 (€million, 2004 prices)

Appropriations for Commitment	2006 [a]	2007	2008	2009	2010	2011	2012	2013	
1. Sustainable growth	46 621	58 735	61 875	64 895	67 350	70 660	72 865	75 950	
1a. Competitiveness for growth and employment	8 791	12 105	14 390	16 680	18 965	21 250	23 540	25 825	
1b. Cohesion for growth and employment [b]	37 830	46 630	47 485	48 215	48 385	49 410	49 325	50 125	
2. Preservation and management of natural resources of which:	56 015	57 180	57 900	58 115	57 980	57 850	57 825	57 805	
Agriculture – market related expenditure and direct payments	43 735	43 500	43 673	43 354	43 034	42 714	42 506	42 293	
3. Citizenship, freedom, security and justice	2 342	2 570	2 935	3 235	3 530	2 970	4 145	4 455	
4. The EU as a global partner [c]	11 232	11 280	12 115	12 885	13 720	14 495	15 115	15 740	
5. Administration [d]	3 436	3 675	3 815	3 950	4 090	4 225	4 365	4 500	
Budgetary compensations [e]	1 041	120	60	60					
Total appropriations for commitment	120 688	133 560	138 700	143 140	146 670	150 200	154 315	158 450	
Total appropriations for payment [b, c]	114 740	124 600	136 500	127 700	126 000	132 400	138 400	143 100	Average
Appropriations for payment as % of GNI (%)	1.09	1.15	1.23	1.12	1.08	1.11	1.14	1.15	1.14
Margin available (%)	0.15	0.09	0.01	0.12	0.16	0.13	0.10	0.09	0.10
Own resources ceiling as % of GNI (%)	1.24	1.24	1.24	1.24	1.24	1.24	1.24	1.24	1.24

Source: Commission of the European Communities (2005) *General Report on the Activities of the European Union* (Luxembourg: OOPEC), Chapter XXII: 'Financing of Community activities, resource management, protection of the Communities' financial interests/Financial perspective: preparation of the 2007–13 financial framework', pp. 3–4.

Notes: [a] 2006 expenditure under the current financial perspective has been broken down according to the proposed new nomenclature for reference purposes and to facilitate comparisons. Expenditure under headings 3 and 4 includes amounts corresponding to the solidarity fund (€961 million at 2004 prices) and the EDF (estimated at €3 billion).

[b] Includes expenditure for the solidarity fund (€961 million at 2004 prices) as from 2006. However, corresponding payments are calculated only as from 2007.

[c] The integration of the EDF is assumed to take effect in 2008. Commitments for 2006 and 2007 are included only for comparison purposes. Payments on commitments before 2008 are not taken into account in the payment figures.

[d] Includes administrative expenditure for institutions other than the Commission, pensions and the European schools.

[e] Amounts in the European Union common position for the Accession Conference with Bulgaria.

principally to enlargement, the reform of the CAP and the increased use of the structural funds by the Member States. The appropriations for commitments rose by 5.2 per cent over the 2004 budget, while the appropriations for payments rose 5.4 per cent. This should be compared to the drop in commitment appropriations from 2002–03 (by 0.3 per cent) and increase in payment appropriation by 2.3 per cent. Payments as a percentage of EU gross national income (GNI) reached 1.04 per cent, up from 0.98 per cent in 2003 which was the smallest initial budget since 1990. However, the 2005 payment commitments were much lower than the ceiling agreed for 2005 (at 1.08 per cent of GNI).

The final budget was somewhat below the Commission's preliminary draft budget of 28 April calling for appropriations for commitments of €117.2 billion and appropriations for payments of €109.5 billion (1.03 per cent of the EU 25 GNI) – an increase of €9.7 billion over 2003 payments. However, these Commission proposed appropriations were also much lower – by €4.7 billion – than the ceiling agreed for 2005. The final budget was only slightly above the Council draft budget of 16 July calling for €115.977 billion in appropriations for commitments and €105.221 billion in appropriations for payments (0.99 per cent of EU-25 GNI). The Parliament accepted final payment appropriations well below the €111.5 billion in the budget it adopted following the first reading. The implementation of appropriations for commitment from 31 December for the EU-25 is shown in Table 2 while, on the revenue side, the own resources are shown in Table 3. On 21 April, following a Council recommendation, the Parliament granted the Commission a discharge in respect of implementation of the 2002 budget.

On other politically significant financial matters, on 25 November, the Parliament and Council agreed in a conciliation meeting to accept the use of the flexibility instrument to provide €185 million to the rehabilitation and reconstruction of Iraq. This amount – considerably above the €115 million proposed by the Commission in June – was symbolic of the easing of intergovernmental tensions on the Iraq war. In effect rewarding the Turkish Cypriot community for having supported Cypriot reunification and accession to the EU, on 25 November the Council also agreed to provide €120 million as part of the multi-annual pledge to Turkish north of Cyprus of €259 million proposed by the Commission on 7 July. The Council also agreed to the provision of €105 million to finance the pre-accession strategy for Croatia.

Table 2: 2005 Budget (Appropriations for Commitments)

Heading	2005 Budget	2004 Budget	Financial Perspective 2005	% Diff. 2005 over 2004
1. Agriculture	49 676 450 000	45 081 285 000	51 439 000 000	10.2
Margin	*1 762 550 000*	*4 223 715 000*		
Agricultural exp.	42 835 450 000	38 545 285 000	44 598 000 000	11.1
Agriculture and rural devt	42 514 275 000	38 248 310 000		11.2
Fisheries	33 200 000	33 075 000		0.4
Health and consumer protection	287 975 000	263 900 000		9.1
Rural devt and accompanying measures	6 841 000 000	6 536 000 000	6 841 000 000	4.7
Agriculture and rural development	6 841 000 000	6 536 000 000		4.7
2. Structural operations	42 423 497 444	41 030 673 000	42 441 000 000	3.4
Margin	*17 502 556*	*4 327 000*		
Structural funds	37 291 564 455	35 348 673 000	37 247 000 000	5.5
Objective 1	27 283 055 007	25 468 722 770		7.1
Objective 2	3 544 290 085	3 619 049 248		2.1
Objective 3	3 911 064 342	3 834 809 871		2.0
Other structural operations (except Objective 1)	180 026 162	174 900 000		2.9
Community initiatives	2 258 572 465	2 138 663 280		5.6
Innovative measures and technical assistance	114 556 394	112 527 831		1.8
Cohesion fund	5 131 932 989	5 682 000 000	5 194 000 000	9.7
3. Internal policies	9 052 000 000	8 704 761 754	9 012 000 000	4.0
Margin	*40 000 000*	*17 238 246*		
Economic and financial affairs	83 294 577	99 840 000		16.6
Enterprises	234 998 000	210 000 000		11.9
Competition	800 000	800 000		0.0
Employment and social affairs	178 237 000	172 128 000		3.5
Agriculture and rural development	41 110 000	51 735 000		20.5
Energy and transport	1 298 440 000	1 246 833 000		4.1
Environment	235 537 000	250 200 000		5.9
Research	3 307 900 000	3 172 000 000		4.3

Table 2: 2005 Budget (Contd)

Heading	2005 Budget	2004 Budget	Financial Perspective 2005	% Diff. 2005 over 2004
Information society	1 222 292 000	1 141 480 000		7.1
Direct research	365 800 000	304 900 000		20.0
Fisheries	106 164 543	93 635 979		13.4
Internal market	12 100 000	11 400 000		6.1
Regional policy	15 000 000	35 955 775		58.3
Taxation and customs union	58 210 000	50 050 000		16.3
Education and culture	896 586 880	847 600 000		5.8
Press and communication	67 715 000	65 500 000		3.4
Health and consumer protection	120 553 000	107 930 000		11.7
Area of freedom, security and justice	540 234 000	492 276 000		9.7
External relations	11 000 000	11 000 000		0.0
Trade	1 400 000	1 400 000		0.0
Enlargement	146 000 000	240 000 000		39.2
Measures to combat fraud	11 700 000	12 050 000		2.9
Commission's policy co-ordination and legal advice	9 000 000	4 500 000		100.0
Administration	34 000 000	28 605 000		18.9
Statistics	53 928 000	52 943 000		1.9
Total research framework programme	5 047 000 000	4 815 000 000		4.8
4. External actions	5 219 000 000	5 176 551 000	5 119 000 000	0.8
Margin	*100 000 000*	*94 551 000*		
Economic and financial affairs	82 200 000	90 200 000		8.9
Agriculture and rural devt	5 920 000	5 795 000		2.2
Energy and transport	5 000 000	5 000 000		0.0
Environment	16 000 000	17 000 000		5.9
Fisheries	196 000 000	194 000 000		1.0
Taxation and customs union	1 700 000	1 550 000		9.7
Education and culture	19 000 000	18 000 000		5.6
Health and consumer protection				
External relations, of which:	3 369 780 000	3 359 331 000		0.3
Multilateral relations and general external relations matters	97 550 000	81 660 000		19.5
Common foreign and security policy	62 200 000	62 237 898		0.1

Table 2: 2005 Budget (Contd)

Heading	2005 Budget	2004 Budget	Financial Perspective 2005	% Diff. 2005 over 2004
European Initiative for Democracy and Human Rights (EIDHR)	111 630 000	118 625 000		5.9
Relations with non-EU OECD countries	16 000 000	16 890 000		5.3
Relations with eastern Europe, the Caucasus and the central Asian republics	483 580 000	483 925 000		0.1
Relations with the western Balkans	466 500 000	592 501 000		21.3
Relations with the Middle East and the southern Mediterranean	1 047 673 000	986 800 000		6.2
Relations with Latin America	310 625 000	293 575 000		5.8
Relations with Asia	634 000 000	591 125 000		7.3
Policy strategy and co-ordination of policy area external relations	20 605 000	17 900 000		15.1
Trade	10 700 000	10 050 000		6.5
Development and relations with African, Caribbean and Pacific States (ACP), of which:	1 017 200 000	985 625 000		3.2
Development co-operation policy and sectoral strategies	794 086 000	772 522 660		2.8
Relations with sub-Saharan Africa, the Caribbean, Pacific and Indian Ocean and overseas countries and territories	166 000 000	171 500 000		3.2
Policy strategy and co-ordination of policy area Development	16 200 000	11 800 000		37.3
Enlargement Humanitarian aid	495 500 000	490 000 000		1.1
5. Administration	6 351 199 258	6 121 983 823	6 360 000 000	3.7
Margin	*8 800 742*	*35 016 177*		
Commission (excluding pensions)	3 129 731 309	3 032 176 924		3.2

Table 2: 2005 Budget (Contd)

Heading	2005 Budget	2004 Budget	Financial Perspective 2005	% Diff. 2005 over 2004
Other institutions (excluding pensions)	2 355 540 949	2 274 730 699		3.6
Pensions (all institutions)	865 927 000	815 076 200		6.2
6. Reserves	446 000 000	442 000 000	446 000 000	0.9
Margin	*0*	*0*		
Economic and financial affairs	223 000 000	221 000 000		0.9
Reserves	223 000 000	221 000 000		0.9
7. Pre-accession strategy	2 081 000 000	1 733 261 220	3 472 000 000	20.1
Margin	*1 511 000 000*	*1 721 738 780*		
Agriculture and rural development	250 300 000	226 700 000		10.4
Regional policy	525 700 000	454 261 220		15.7
Education and culture	2 500 000	2 500 000		0.0
Enlargement	1 302 500 000	1 049 800 000		24.1
Phare pre-accession instrument	896 300 000	807 200 000		11.0
Turkey	286 200 000	242 600 000		18.0
8. Compensation	1 304 988 996	1 409 545 056	1 305 000 000	7.4
Margin	*11 004*	*454 944*		
Total commitment appropriations	116 554 135 698	109 700 060 853	119 594 000 000	6.2
Margin	*3 039 864 302*	*5 907 939 147*		
Compulsory expenditure	45 743 787 944	41 490 416 176		10.3
Non-compulsory expenditure	70 810 347 754	68 209 644 677		3.8
Payment appropriations				
Total payment appropriations	106 300 000 000	101 806 602 380	114 235 000 000	4.4
Margin	*7 935 000 000*	*9 747 397 620*		
Compulsory expenditure	45 784 806 944	41 544 750 814		10.2
Non-compulsory expenditure	60 515 193 056	60 261 851 566		0.4
Payment appropriations as % of GNP	1.00	1.01		

Source: Commission (2004).

Table 3: Budget Revenue (€m)

Field	2004	2005
Agricultural duties	1 313.40	819.40
Levies and other duties in the sugar sector	401.60	793.60
Customs duties	10 580.40	10 750.00
VAT own resources	13 679.30	15 313.50
GNI-based own resources	69 061.60	77 583.00
Balance and adjustments to balances of	232.80	
VAT own resources from previous years	−232.20	
Balance and adjustments to balances of		
GNP/GNI own resources from previous years	5 693.00	
Surplus available from previous year	2 623.60	1 040.50
Other revenue		
Total	103 353.50	106 300.00
	% of GNI	
Maximum own resources which may be assigned to the budget	1.24	1.24
Own resources actually assigned to the budget	0.95	0.99

Source: Commission (2005) Chapter XXII: 'Financing of Community activities, resource management, protection of the Communities' financial interests/Budgets' (pp. 11–19).

IV. Agriculture

In 2004, the Commission adopted several regulations to implement the fundamental reform of the CAP agreed in 2003. On 29 April, the Council also widened the scope of the reform by agreeing to extend it to the new Member States through modifications to the Accession Treaty and by extending the principle of decoupling aid from production to additional products (cotton, hops, olive oil and tobacco). The Commission also made reform proposals (14 July) to the sugar sector to make it conform to broader reform objectives. The Commission proposed several initiatives and specific actions to address product quality concerns (for example, in a 5 April report it recommended changes to improve the process of information and promotion of agricultural products). On 10 June, responding to the rapid rise in the number of organic farms in the EU, the Commission presented an action plan for organic food and farming, with 21 practical measures. On 24 February, the Council adopted a regulation reinforcing EC-level legal protection for organic farming methods and, on 24 April, agreed a regulation to set up a programme for the conservation, collection and utilization of genetic resources in agriculture. The Commission proposed reforms to reinforce Community policy on rural development and simplify its implementation, with three central objectives:

strengthening the competitiveness of the agricultural and forestry sector; protecting the environment and countryside; and improving the quality of life in rural areas.

In its proposals for the 2007–13 financial perspective, presented on 14 July, the Commission proposed a new basic regulation on the financing of the CAP and the establishment of two new funds corresponding to the two pillars of the CAP: a European agricultural guarantee fund (EAGF) and – a single instrument for financing and programming rural development policy – a European agricultural fund for rural development (EAFRD). The Commission recommended that the latter be implemented under a more bottom-up approach allowing Member States, regions and action groups to have a greater say in the design of rural development programmes to meet local needs. A breakdown of EAGF spending (from 16 October 2003 to 15 October 2004) showed that Poland received the highest payments, followed by France and Germany. At international level, the EU requested the opening of tariff negotiations on banana imports in the World Trade Organization.

V. Environmental Policy

The most significant development in environmental law in 2004 was the 21 April adoption by the Council and Parliament of the directive on environmental liability that put into the practice the 'polluter pays' principle in the EU. On 11 February, the Council and Parliament agreed to a directive setting a more ambitious recovery and recycling targets for waste packaging, and the Commission made progress on designing recycling strategies for other products. Legislative work continued on the Reach programme involving the registration, evaluation, authorization and restriction of chemicals. On 9 June, the Commission submitted a multi-annual (2004–10) action plan as part of its ongoing efforts to design a European environment and health strategy. On 28 January, the Commission presented its action plan to encourage the development of environmental technologies to protect the environment and boost the competitiveness of companies. As part of its broader efforts to promote sustainable development, on 11 February the Commission also set down the foundations for a thematic strategy for the urban environment. On 1 June, the Commission published its first review of the Cardiff process aimed at integrating environmental considerations into the EU's sectoral policies with an examination of developments in nine sectors and recommendations on ways to revitalize the process. The Commission also proposed the integration of Natura 2000 network funding into Community policies through existing funds rather than establishing a specific fund for this network. In the context of the financial perspective 2007–13 package, on 29 September, the Commission proposed Life+ to become the EU's sole financial instrument targeting only the environment. The aim is to use Life+ finance to adopt programmes in priority areas such as protecting biodiversity, combating climate change and adverse environmental impacts on human health.

In 2004, the EU focused special attention on the implementation of its international environmental commitments and in particular the UN framework convention on climate change and the Kyoto protocol. On 11 February, the Parliament and the Council adopted a decision to establish a mechanism for monitoring greenhouse gas emissions. On 11 February, these two institutions adopted a directive concerning the measurement of CO_2 emissions and fuel consumption of light commercial vehicles, while on 13 September, they adopted a directive designed to include other flexible mechanisms provided for under the Kyoto protocol in the pre-existing directive establishing a Community scheme for greenhouse gas emission allowance trading. The Commission gave its approval to over 5,000 industrial plants to enter, from January 2005, the CO_2 emissions market set up to help EU Member States meet their emissions targets under the Kyoto protocol. The Commission proposed several legal amendments and proposals concerning the application of international agreements on persistent organic pollutants and the Aarhus convention on access to information, public participation in decision-making and access to justice in environmental matters. The EC acceded to the Stockholm convention concerning the regime applicable to certain polluting substances and to the protocol to the Barcelona convention for the protection of the Mediterranean sea against pollution.

References

Commission of the European Communities (2004a) *Bulletin of the European Union*, various months (Luxembourg: OOPEC).

Commission of the European Communities (2004b) *Report: State Aid Scoreboard*, Brussels, 20 April/19 November.

Commission of the European Communities (2005) *General Report on the Activities of the European Union* (Luxembourg: OOPEC).

EU Observer (2004) (various).

The European Central Bank in 2004

DAVID G. MAYES
University of Stirling

I. Monetary Policy

In prospect the ECB must have thought that 2004 was at last going to be the year when inflation fell back below 2 per cent despite the historically low level of interest rates. But no, there were just enough unexpected shocks particularly from rapidly rising oil prices in the second half of the year to keep it up above that figure (see Figure 1).[1] This has meant that the ECB has been pushing the bounds of credibility by continuing to forecast that the fall in inflation is only a few months into the future. This can be seen from the measure of inflation expectations in Figure 1.[2] Nevertheless that is exactly what other forecasters have been saying as well, so this is not merely an example of central bank 'cheap talk'. An examination of the Eurosystem's forecasting record shows that they have on average been optimistic about the prospects for both real economic growth and inflation. However, given that the period since these forecasts began to be published has been characterized by below average growth and above target inflation, it is not a surprising outcome. If it were maintained through a complete cycle then it might be an indication of bias. What is more likely is that ECB projections tend to revert towards the mean of past experience the further ahead they look. However, projecting on the unrealistic basis of constant interests rates does not help (Kontulainen *et al.*, 2004).

---

[1] I am grateful to Kristina Gustafsson for compiling Figure 1.
[2] This measure of expectations is drawn from the prices of 2012 inflation-indexed French government bonds. It does not allow for variations in risk premia. Surveys of knowledgeable sources by the ECB suggest inflation expectations around 1.9 per cent.

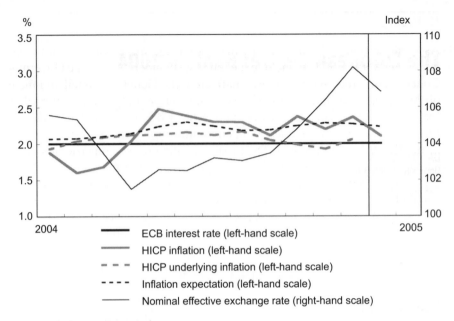

Figure 1: Inflation Expectations
Sources: ECB, Eurostat and Reuters.

The Governing Council did not change the setting of monetary policy during the year, in the sense of altering their interest rate settings, but a glance at the exchange rate movement during the year shows that the effective rate tightened by about 6 percentage points. While opinions vary about the equivalence of the impact of the exchange rate and the ECB interest rate on future inflation and output, this is equivalent to a tightening of at least 50 basis points.

If we exclude the energy and raw food elements of the harmonized index of consumer prices (HICP), we can see that over the year underlying inflation remained at around 2 per cent. Thus external factors were largely responsible for the unwanted inflation. Nevertheless, while unseasonable climatic variations may be unpredictable, the extent of world-wide demand pressure and the lack of opportunities for substantial increases in supply made oil price rises seem a plausible prospect. However, since oil prices are denominated in US$ and the dollar itself fell against the euro, the impact on the euro area was muted and, in real terms, oil prices did not reach their previous highs. The unwelcome surprise for the ECB was thus the poor recovery of the euro economy given the degree of world demand, the fiscal pressure with the effective easing of the Stability and Growth Pact, and the historically low interest rates.

II. Enlargement

As with the other EU institutions, the big change in 2004 has been the enlargement of the ESCB to include the ten new members. While the Governing Council and Executive Board are unaffected, the General Council and many of the Committees have changed their composition and to some extent their focus. Committees such as the Monetary Policy Committee meet in two forms, Eurosystem composition and extended composition, where all the members of the ESCB are represented. Thus issues relating to econometric modelling and public finance are dealt with in extended composition and only the clearly Eurosystem issues, such as agreeing material to go in the *Monthly Bulletin* are handled by the smaller group. There was no dramatic change on 1 May as the new members had already been participating as observers. The agenda had also already changed its orientation with concerns about possible new membership of the euro area gaining more prominence.

Estonia, Lithuania and Slovenia joined ERM2 at the earliest opportunity (28 June) and are hoping to be admitted to membership of the Eurosystem in mid-2006 when the next convergence report is due, with a view to adopting the euro as early as 2007. Since these are all small countries, the logistical problems of handling the issue of new currency is quite small. Problems in the countries themselves may be harder but since the two Baltic States have already been operating with a fixed parity to the euro, acceptance should be relatively easy. With currencies biased towards notes rather than coins, the physical costs of the changeover may be more limited and the problems with the changeover of accounting systems in the bank and non-bank sectors are well known from the experience of existing members. Hence, from the point of view of technical implementation, a tight timetable may be possible. Similarly, meeting the convergence criteria may be possible in short order, although the requirement to have inflation within 1.5 per cent of the lowest three *EU* not *euro area* members may be harsh unless reasonable treatment of 'outliers' can be agreed, as there can be many reasons why an individual country can have a recorded HICP considerably lower than its underlying inflationary pressure would imply in any particular year.

III. Transparency and Independence

Under its new President, the Governing Council has continued to work on making its communication of monetary policy decisions clear, consistent and rapid. The press statement after the Governing Council meetings and the subsequent open session for questions are very much filling the role of minutes and, combined with the *Monthly Bulletin*, the role of inflation reports. The ECB has continued to expand its conferences with academics and has published the results of a review of its research. The Eurosystem has continued to define its independence, with an attempt by the government of Finland to acquire some of its central bank's reserves being deemed inconsistent with the Treaty and attempts by Germany to persuade the Bundesbank to sell some of its gold to help reduce the embarrassing excess fiscal deficit being rebuffed.

IV. Other Issues

There have been two changes in the Governing Council during the year. Domingo Solans's period of appointment to the Executive Board ended in June and he was replaced without debate by José Manuel González Páramo, Economics Professor and Member of the Board of the Bank of Spain, perpetuating the idea that the four large countries have some sort of entitlement to a seat. Matti Vanhala resigned through ill health in March (and sadly died in September) and was replaced by Finland's Commissioner in Brussels and former Finance Minister Erkki Liikanen. Domingo Solans died in November. New Directors-General of Economics (Wolfgang Schill from inside the ECB), and Research (Lucrezia Reichlin from the Free University of Brussels), were appointed at the end of year.

In December, the ECB published its first *Financial Stability Review*, reinforcing its increasing oversight of the European financial system. It has already been producing regular reports on the stability of the banking system. It is sustaining pressure to see an efficient cross-border payment and settlement system and is continuing the development of an enhanced version of Target (imaginatively labelled Target2), its own real time gross settlement system. When the annual report for 2004 comes out, it will no doubt reveal substantial losses as the rise in the value of the euro will have lowered the value of the ECB's foreign exchange reserves. There would be a clear policy contradiction if a central bank tried to protect its balance sheet against changes in its own exchange rate.

Reference

Kontulainen, J., Mayes, D. and Tarkka, J. (2004) 'Monetary Policy Assumptions in Central Bank Forecasts'. *Bank of Finland Bulletin*, 4/2004, pp. 28–35.

JCMS 2005 Volume 43. Annual Review pp. 89–107

Legal Developments

MICHAEL DOUGAN
Liverpool Law School, University of Liverpool

Introduction

The outstanding legal development of 2004 was, of course, the signature of the final Treaty establishing a Constitution for Europe.[1] If and when ratified by all Member States, this Treaty will usher in major reforms to areas such as the Union's constitutional architecture and institutional framework; the principles underpinning Union and Member State competences (especially in the fields of foreign and security policy, and the area of freedom, security and justice); the protection of human rights and fundamental freedoms; the Union's legal instruments; and the jurisdiction of the Union courts. In addition, 2004 saw its fair share of new Community legislation across diverse fields of policy activity: for example, equal treatment between men and women in access to and the supply of goods and services;[2] environmental liability with regard to the prevention and remedying of environmental damage;[3] co-operation between national authorities responsible for the enforcement of consumer protection laws;[4] quality and safety standards for the procurement, testing, processing, storage and distribution of human tissues and cells;[5] takeover bids for the securities of companies governed by Member State laws;[6] and the creation of a 'single European sky' as part of the common transport policy,

---

[1] Published in the Official Journal at OJ 2004 C 310.
[2] Directive 2004/113, OJ 2004 L 373, p. 37.
[3] Directive 2004/35, OJ 2004 L 143, p. 56.
[4] Regulation 2006/2004, OJ 2004 L 364, p. 1.
[5] Directive 2004/23, OJ 2004 L 102, p. 48.
[6] Directive 2004/25, OJ 2004 L 142, p. 12.

with a view to enhancing safety and efficiency for general air traffic within Europe.[7] The free movement of persons was particularly blessed, with the adoption of a new umbrella directive on the free movement of Union citizens and their family members,[8] and the long-awaited revision of the system for co-ordinating national social security systems.[9] The flood of Union legislation dealing with justice and home affairs also continued unabated, with measures on the admission of third country nationals for the purposes of study and voluntary service,[10] minimum standards for the qualification and protection of third country nationals and stateless persons as refugees or persons otherwise in need of international protection,[11] and compensation to victims of crime.[12] Furthermore, there were major overhauls of the existing legislative regimes in fields such as public procurement,[13] and mergers between undertakings.[14] As usual, however, this review will focus on highlighting a handful of the most important judgments delivered by the Community courts.

I. Free Movement and Equal Treatment of Union Citizens

In landmark judgments such as *Grzelczyk*, *Baumbast* and *D'Hoop*, the Court established that Article 18(1) EC confers directly upon every Union citizen the right to move and reside freely across the Member States. Exercise of that right is subject to the limitations and conditions laid down under Community law – which, as regards economically inactive citizens, refer especially to the requirements of 'sufficient resources' and 'sickness insurance in respect of all risks' contained in the three residency directives adopted between 1990 and 1993.[15] However, these limitations and conditions must themselves be applied by the Member States in accordance with the general principles of Community law – including the principle of proportionality. Moreover, provided they are lawfully resident within the national territory, economically inactive migrant Union citizens are entitled to equal treatment with own nationals in accordance with Article 12 EC – though the Member State may be entitled to restrict access to social benefits to those with a 'real link' with the host society.[16] These broad

---

[7] Regulation 549/2004, OJ 2004 L 96, p. 1. Also, e.g., Regulation 550/2004, OJ 2004 L 96, p. 10; Regulation 551/2004, OJ 2004 L 96, p. 20; Regulation 552/2004, OJ 2004 L 96, p. 26.
[8] Directive 2004/38, OJ 2004 L 158, p. 77.
[9] Regulation 883/2004, OJ 2004 L 166, p. 1.
[10] Directive 2004/114, OJ 2004 L 375, p. 12.
[11] Directive 2004/83, OJ 2004 L 304, p. 12.
[12] Directive 2004/80, OJ 2004 L 261, p. 15.
[13] Directive 2004/17, OJ 2004 L 134, p. 1 and Directive 2004/18, OJ 2004 L 134, p. 114.
[14] Regulation 139/2004, OJ 2004 L 24, p. 1.
[15] Directive 90/364, OJ 1990 L 180, p. 26, Directive 90/365, OJ 1990 L 180, p. 28, and Directive 93/96, OJ 1993 L 317, p. 59. Now repealed and replaced by Directive 2004/38, OJ 2004 L 158, p. 77 (referred to above).
[16] Case C-184/99 *Grzelczyk* [2001] ECR I-6193; Case C-413/99 *Baumbast* [2002] ECR I-7091; Case C-224/98 *D'Hoop* [2002] ECR I-6191.

principles urgently demanded further clarification, and 2004 saw the Court deliver several judgments that usefully elaborate upon its earlier case-law.

For example, *Trojani* concerned a French national residing in a Salvation Army hostel in Brussels as part of a socio-occupational reintegration programme. The question arose as to whether he was entitled to a right of residence directly under Article 18(1) EC; and whether he could claim award of the Belgian minimex (minimum subsistence allowance) on the basis of Community law. The Court confirmed that it would not be disproportionate for Belgium to refuse any right of residence to a Union citizen who patently lacked 'sufficient resources' to provide for his own subsistence. However, insofar as it appeared that Belgium had in fact already granted Trojani a residence permit, he was to be considered lawfully resident within the host territory – and thus entitled to equal treatment as regards social benefits such as the minimex – unless and until the national authorities took steps to rescind that residence permit and remove Trojani from Belgium.[17] The lesson for Member States? Control over economically inactive foreigners seeking membership of the national welfare society is located most effectively within the field of domestic immigration law – because once the Member State chooses to admit Union citizens to the territory, and to ratify their residency there, they become entitled to the full range of social benefits on equal terms with own nationals.

The Court further explored the inter-relationship between residency, equal treatment and social benefits in its judgment in *Collins*, which concerned an Irish national who arrived in the United Kingdom in search of employment (workseekers being treated as quasi-economically active persons under Community law with a secure right to residency so long as they are actually looking for work and have genuine chances of becoming engaged). Collins' application for jobseeker's allowance (a non-contributory subsistence benefit) faced two hurdles. First, it was apparently settled case-law that workseekers are not entitled to claim equal treatment under the economic free movement provisions as regards social benefits. However, the Court held that such case-law had to be reconsidered in the light of more recent developments under Articles 18 and 12 EC. Migrant workseekers are still Union citizens, and provided they are lawfully resident in the host territory by virtue of their active search for employment, they are also entitled to claim full equal treatment with own nationals – including financial benefits intended to facilitate access to the host state's employment market. Moreover, since their right to residence is secure under Community law, it would appear that Member States cannot simply use their immigration powers to exclude such workseekers from public support within the host territory. The second hurdle was that jobseeker's allowance was limited to those who were 'habitually resident' within the United Kingdom – a

---

[17] Case C-456/02 *Trojani* (Judgment of 7 September 2004).

requirement which discriminated only indirectly against foreign nationals and hence could be objectively justified by the Member State. For these purposes, the Court accepted that it was legitimate for the United Kingdom to insist on the existence of a genuine link between claimants of welfare benefits and the national employment market. Nevertheless, the requirement of 'habitual residence' – while admittedly an appropriate means of establishing the existence of the necessary link – had to be applied in accordance with the principle of proportionality (for example, involving clear criteria known in advance and capable of being judicially reviewed).[18] The lesson for Member States? Restrictions on Union citizens seeking membership of the national welfare society may also be imposed within the field of social policy itself – but direct discrimination which blatantly targets foreigners will be much more difficult to justify than indirect discrimination which seeks ultimately to safeguard the moral and financial integrity of the domestic welfare system.

Another interesting development emerged in *Zhu and Chen*, which concerned a Chinese national who went to Belfast to give birth to her second child. Thanks to the peculiarities of the relevant domestic laws, baby Catherine was not entitled to British or Chinese nationality, but was automatically able to obtain Irish citizenship. As such, she simultaneously found herself *both* a Union citizen *and* a cross-border migrant. The family were completely independent of public funds in the United Kingdom, and were covered by a private sickness insurance scheme. The Court held that Catherine clearly fulfilled the conditions, laid down in the applicable residency directive, required to exercise her right to residence under Article 18(1) EC. For these purposes, it was irrelevant that the necessary resources were provided by a third person rather than belonging to Catherine personally. The Court then found that for the United Kingdom to refuse residence also to the mother – a third country national with no apparent entitlement to protection under any express provision of Community law – would render the exercise of Catherine's right to free movement totally ineffective, i.e. by separating the child from her primary carer. The Court explicitly rejected the contention that the Treaty was being abused for improper ends, it having been admitted that the sole purpose of the Belfast birth was to enable Catherine to acquire Irish nationality and thereby secure a long-term right of residence under Community law for her third country national mother.[19]

The *Zhu and Chen* dispute played a (not entirely savoury) role in the public debate surrounding Ireland's referendum on reform of its nationality rules.[20] However, the case is primarily of interest because of its 'effectiveness' approach

---

[18] Case C-138/02 *Collins* (Judgment of 23 March 2004).

[19] Case C-200/02 *Zhu and Chen* (Judgment of 19 October 2004).

[20] Cf. *The Citizenship Referendum: Implications for the Constitution and Human Rights* (School of Law, Trinity College Dublin, 2004).

to the free movement rights of Union citizens: even *non-discriminatory* restrictions imposed by the host state which would undermine the exercise of individual freedoms may well be caught by the Treaty and require objective justification. The question which future cases will surely explore is just how 'effective' free movement rights must be: for example, would a Member State's refusal to grant entry to the third country national unmarried (heterosexual or homosexual) partner of a migrant Union citizen create an unlawful barrier to enjoyment of the latter's own residency rights under Article 18(1) EC?

II. Legal Aspects of Economic and Monetary Union

Perhaps the most high-profile dispute to be addressed by the Court during 2004 concerned the political imbroglio surrounding France and Germany's difficulties in meeting the standards of budgetary discipline underpinning economic and monetary union.

Article 104 EC establishes the excessive deficit procedure, which seeks to encourage and, if necessary, compel Member States to observe budgetary discipline. The multi-stage procedure consistently divides institutional responsibility between the Commission (which makes appropriate recommendations for action) and the Council (which then adopts decisions and recommendations addressed to the relevant Member States). In particular, Article 104(6) EC provides that the Council shall (acting on a Commission recommendation) decide whether an excessive deficit exists. If so, Article 104(7) EC states that the Council shall (also acting on a Commission recommendation) make recommendations to the relevant Member State with a view to bringing the excessive deficit to an end within a given period. If that Member State persists in failing to put into practice the Council's recommendations, Article 104(9) EC provides that the Council may (again acting on a Commission recommendation) decide to give notice to the Member State to take the necessary measures to reduce its deficit within a specified time limit. So long as a Member State fails to comply with a decision adopted under Article 104(7) EC, the Council may decide to apply or intensify certain measures (including the imposition of fines) as detailed in Article 104(11) EC. These primary treaty rules are supplemented by the European Council's Resolution on the Stability and Growth Pact [SGP] 1997,[21] and Regulation 1467/97 on speeding up and clarifying the implementation of the excessive deficit procedure.[22] The latter, *inter alia*, establishes a framework of deadlines for institutional action, and defines the conditions for holding the procedure in abeyance.

---

[21] Resolution on the Stability and Growth Pact, OJ 1997 C 236, p. 1.
[22] Regulation 1467/97, OJ 1997 L 209, p. 6.

The Council decided in 2003 that excessive deficits existed in France and Germany, and adopted recommendations setting those Member States a deadline for taking corrective measures, in accordance with Articles 104(6) and (7) EC. After expiry of that deadline, the Commission recommended that the Council adopt decisions, finding that France and Germany had failed to respond adequately to the Council's earlier recommendations, and giving those Member States notice to take the necessary measures to reduce their deficits under Article 104(9) EC. However, when the Council voted on the Commission's recommendations, at its meeting on 25 November 2003, it failed to obtain the necessary majority. Instead, the Council decided to go off on a frolic of its own – adopting conclusions stating that the excessive deficit procedures should be held in abeyance with regard to France and Germany, and addressing fresh recommendations for correcting their deficits, having regard to certain commitments proffered by those Member States. A furious Commission – feeling that its own institutional prerogatives under the excessive deficit procedure, the credibility of the SGP within and outside the euro area, and indeed the reputation of the Union as an organization governed by the rule of law, had all been undermined – brought an action for annulment of these Council conclusions.

The Court in *Commission* v. *Council* accepted that the Council has a margin of discretion when implementing the excessive deficit procedure: for example, the Council may modify recommendations made by the Commission as regards the assessment of economic data and the appropriate measures to be taken by the relevant Member State. However, the Council cannot depart from the rules set down in the Treaty itself or contained in Regulation 1467/97. In that regard, the disputed Council conclusions were indeed legally flawed. First, Regulation 1467/97 defines exhaustively the situations in which the excessive deficit procedure may *de jure* be held in abeyance. It is true that the procedure may also *de facto* be held in abeyance if a Commission recommendation is not adopted by the Council because the latter cannot achieve the required majority. However, the disputed conclusions went further than this: insofar as the excessive deficit procedure would be held in abeyance for as long as France and Germany complied with their own unilateral commitments, the Council had purported to restrict its power to give notice to those Member States under Article 104(9) EC on the basis of the Commission's recommendations (and using the previous Council recommendations adopted under Article 104(7) EC as the appropriate frame of reference). Secondly, it was clear from Article 104 EC that, where the Council has adopted recommendations for correction of an excessive deficit, it cannot subsequently modify them without being prompted to do so by a fresh Commission recommendation. The disputed Council conclusions infringed the Commission's right of initiative under Article 104 EC, since they were not preceded by a Commission recommendation seeking the adoption of new Council recommendations for correcting France and Germany's excessive deficits, different from those the Council had adopted previously.[23]

To this extent, the judgment is a victory for the Commission: the Court emphasized that the excessive deficit procedure, for all its political importance, also has an enforceable legal dimension focused on the inter-institutional balance; in particular, whatever horse-trading between Member States might occur within the Council, the Commission retains an important role as agenda-setter, particularly when it comes to revisiting recommendations already adopted by the Council under Article 104(7) EC. And in keeping with the Commission's underlying role as impartial guardian of the treaties, for large and small countries alike, this should help ensure that the rules on which EMU is based will be applied consistently to all Member States. However, the Court was also prudent not to go further than necessary in addressing the legal parameters of the excessive deficit procedure: even though it was accepted that the procedure may *de facto* be held in abeyance simply because the Council fails to muster enough votes to adopt a decision recommended by the Commission, the Court deliberately refrained from expressing any view as to whether, pursuant to Article 104(9) EC, the Council is under a legal obligation to adopt a decision where the relevant Member State persists in failing to put into practice adequate measures to reduce its deficit as previously recommended by the Council under Article 104(7) EC.[24]

The Commission eventually decided (in December 2004) that no further steps were necessary against France or Germany, which were judged to have made sufficient efforts to reduce their budget deficits below the crucial benchmark of 3 per cent of GDP, taking into account the reasonable expectations of those Member States under the annulled Council conclusions.[25] Nevertheless, one of the important side effects of the Court's judgment has been to increase the already significant momentum for reform of the SGP. In particular, the Commission (in September 2004) proposed enhancing the flexibility available to Member States over the whole of the economic cycle, and taking greater account of the heterogeneous state of the various national economies across the Union; together with increased emphasis on *ex ante* prevention, rather than *ex post* sanctions, through the system of multilateral surveillance established under Article 99 EC.[26]

---

[23] Case C-27/04 *Commission* v. *Council* (Judgment of 13 July 2004).

[24] See also paras 25–36 of the judgment on the procedural inadmissibility of the Commission's claim for annulment of the Council's failure to adopt formal instruments under Articles 104(8) and (9) EC pursuant to the Commission's recommendations.

[25] See Commission Press Release IP/04/1471.

[26] See, in particular, the Commission's views as contained in COM(2004) 581 final.

2004 gave the ECJ the opportunity to deal with another touchy aspect of EMU: price rises connected with the introduction of the euro. Article 3 of Regulation 1103/97 contains the principle that (subject to any contrary agreement between the parties) the introduction of the euro shall not affect the continuity of contracts. Article 4 provides that conversion rates (adopted as one euro expressed in terms of each participating national currency) shall be adopted with six significant figures and cannot be rounded or truncated when making conversions. However, according to Article 5, 'monetary amounts to be paid or accounted for', when a rounding takes place after a conversion into the euro unit pursuant to Article 4, are to be rounded up or down to the nearest cent.[27] O_2, which operates a mobile telephone network in Germany, converted its price-per-minute tariffs from German marks into euros and rounded them to the nearest cent. Consumer association Verbraucher-Zentrale objected to this rounding practice, which it claimed resulted in an increase in O2's prices. The national court hearing the dispute sought guidance from the ECJ about which rounding rules apply under Community law to tariffs for goods and services.

The first question in *Verbraucher-Zentrale* v. O_2 *(Germany)* was whether tariffs should be considered 'monetary amounts to be paid or accounted for' and therefore subject to the compulsory rounding rule contained in Article 5. For these purposes, the Court observed that the provisions of Regulation 1103/97 are intended to ensure that the transition to the euro should be neutral, i.e. without affecting obligations already entered into by citizens and firms. Such neutrality requires that a high degree of accuracy in conversion operations should be achieved. For purely practical reasons, Article 5 imposed upon certain situations a (potentially) relatively inaccurate rounding rule that contradicted the underlying principle of neutrality. It was therefore inappropriate to adopt a broad construction of the 'monetary amounts to be paid or accounted for' which are subject to the compulsory provisions of Article 5: while this concept should embrace monetary amounts which can indeed be expressed only to the nearest cent (such as cash prices and invoices), in the case of tariffs such as O_2's per-minute prices, there was no such pressing reason to require the amount to be rounded in every case to two decimal places. Such amounts are not actually invoiced to and paid by consumers, and are not entered as such in any accounting document or statement of account.

The second issue was whether, even if Regulation 1103/97 did not *require* tariffs such as O_2's per-minute prices to be governed by the rounding rule in Article 5, Community law nevertheless *permitted* economic operators to follow the same rounding rule in situations other than those referred to in Article 5. In this regard, the Court observed that the regulation did not on its face lay down any rounding rules in respect of monetary amounts other than those referred

[27] Regulation 1103/97, OJ 1997 L 162, p. 1.

to in Article 5, such as per-unit tariffs for goods and services or intermediate amounts used for calculating monetary amounts to be paid or accounted for. But this does not mean that such operations are exempt from the general principle of continuity of contracts, or can disregard the underlying objective of neutrality in the transition to the euro. So, even if Regulation 1103/97 does not generally preclude monetary amounts other than those referred to in Article 5 being rounded to the nearest cent, that rounding method must not in any case affect existing contractual obligations or have a real impact on the price actually to be paid. It was for the German courts to ascertain whether O_2's decision to round all of its per-minute tariffs to the nearest cent overstepped those parameters.[28]

III. Scope of Community Competition Law

The Court continues to be confronted with disputes about the impact of Community economic law on the structure and substance of welfare provision within the Member States, posing difficult choices about how far national social policies should be exposed to the rigours of the internal market.

AOK Bundesverband concerned the German statutory health insurance scheme, which requires almost all employees to be affiliated to one of the national sickness funds (independently managed public law bodies). Insured persons are free to choose between sickness funds, which compete with each other as regards the contribution rates for employees and employers, though the obligatory benefits in kind provided to insured persons are essentially identical. Moreover, sickness funds operate within a solidarity mechanism whereby funds insuring the least costly risks contribute to the financing of funds insuring more onerous risks. Sickness funds pay pharmacies for their medicinal products, up to the fixed maximum amount determined in accordance with the law. If the price of the medicinal product exceeds this fixed maximum amount, the insured person must pay the difference. Fixed maximum amounts are determined according to a two-stage procedure: representatives of doctors and sickness funds identify the groups of medicinal products for which ceilings are to be laid down; sickness fund associations then jointly determine the maximum amounts applicable to the selected medicinal products. Several pharmaceutical companies (disgruntled at changes to the ceilings applicable to their medicinal products) challenged the compatibility of this system with Community competition law, in particular, Article 81 EC prohibiting anti-competitive agreements, decisions and practices between undertakings or associations of undertakings.

---

[28] Case C-19/03 *Verbraucher-Zentrale* v. *O2 (Germany)* (Judgment of 14 September 2004).

However, the Court of Justice found that sickness funds in the German statutory health insurance scheme were involved in the management of the social security system, fulfilling an exclusively social function founded on the principle of national solidarity and which was entirely non-profit-making. This finding could not be called into question by the fact that sickness funds enjoyed some latitude in setting contribution rates, and thus engaged in a limited form of competition with each other to attract members. The German legislature introduced this element of competition in order to encourage sickness funds to operate in accordance with principles of sound management, i.e. in the most effective and least costly manner possible, in the interests of the proper functioning of the German social security system. Since the activities of bodies such as the sickness funds are not economic in nature, those bodies do not constitute undertakings for the purposes of Article 81 EC. It is indeed possible, admitted the Court, that sickness funds could (besides their exclusively social functions) engage in certain operations which have a primarily economic purpose. However, that could not be said of the sickness funds' involvement in the procedure for determining fixed maximum amounts for purchasing medicinal products – by which the funds merely perform an obligation imposed on them under German law and integrally connected with their social activities within the framework of the statutory health insurance scheme. It was therefore unnecessary for the Court to investigate any further whether the sickness funds had engaged in anti-competitive conduct prohibited under Article 81 EC.[29]

By acknowledging that some degree of competition, designed to increase efficiency, does not fundamentally alter the social character of public health systems, the Court in *AOK Bundesverband* effectively enlarged the safe space within which Member States may modernize their embattled welfare regimes without being equated to economic market actors. Moreover, although direct comparisons are difficult, the judgment in *AOK Bundesverband* suggests that the Court is adopting a more protective approach towards the welfare state under the competition rules than that embodied in its recent case-law on the free movement of health services under Article 49 EC (which has significantly liberalized the conditions under which individuals may seek extra-mural and, to a lesser extent, intra-mural treatment abroad at the expense of their domestic sickness funds).[30]

Another interesting judgment from 2004 addressed the outer boundaries of Articles 81 and 82 EC. In *Meca-Medina and Majcen*, the Court of First Instance

---

[29] Joined Cases C-264/01, C-306/01, C-354/01 & C-355/01 *AOK Bundesverband* (Judgment of 16 March 2004).
[30] E.g. Case C-158/96 *Kohll* [1998] ECR I-1931; Case C-368/98 *Vanbraekel* [2001] ECR I-5363; Case C-157/99 *Peerbooms* [2001] ECR I-5473; Case C-385/99 *Müller-Fauré* [2003] ECR I-4509.

(CFI) was called upon to determine whether the anti-doping rules adopted by the International Olympic Committee (IOC) (including penalties such as suspension for doping offences, imposed by the various international sporting federations, subject to an appeal to the Court of Arbitration for Sport, and in turn to the Swiss Federal Court) were subject to scrutiny under Community competition law. The CFI recalled that sport is subject to free movement law insofar as it constitutes an economic activity: for example, paid employment under Article 39 EC or the provision of a remunerated service under Article 49 EC. However, it is also established case-law that, for the purposes of the free movement provisions, disputes will fall outside the scope of the Treaty if they concern rules which are of purely sporting interest, have nothing to do with an economic activity, and are inherent in the organization and proper conduct of sporting competition. The same basic approach could equally be extended as regards the application of Community competition law to sporting regulations. Consequently, only rules which are not purely sporting, but concern the economic activity which sport may represent, are capable of being the subject of proceedings under Articles 81 and 82 EC. Against that background, the CFI held that a campaign against doping – even within the context of professional sport – does not pursue any economic objective. It is intended to advance the purely social objective of preserving the spirit of fair play, and also to safeguard the health of athletes against the potential negative effects of doping products. The same approach applied to the specific anti-doping legislation at issue in this dispute. The IOC's regime was accepted as being entirely non-discriminatory. Even if the anti-doping rules were to be considered harsh or excessive, particularly as regards their economic repercussions for affected athletes, that could not in itself affect their purely social character and bring them within the scope of the Treaty's competition rules. In conclusion, the CFI found that the applicants should properly have pursued their grievances against the application of the IOC's anti-doping rules before the Swiss Federal Court.[31]

IV. Equal Treatment on Grounds of Sex

Does the ECJ have a soft spot for transsexuals? *K.B.* is the latest judgment to suggest the answer is 'yes'. The case concerned English rules preventing transsexuals from marrying in their acquired sex: marriages are void when not contracted between a male and a female partner; a person's sex is deemed to be that appearing on his/her birth certificate; and the record of original sex on a birth certificate cannot subsequently be amended. One important side-effect

[31] Case T-313/02 *Meca-Medina & Majcen* (Judgment of 30 September 2004).

of this regime is that partners in a relationship which includes a transsexual are not entitled to benefits (*in casu*, a survivor's pension under the NHS Pension Scheme Regulations) which are dependent on a relationship of marriage. The question arose whether this state of affairs involved unlawful discrimination contrary to the principle of equal pay between men and women contained in Article 141 EC.

The ECJ found that, while a survivor's pension granted under a scheme which essentially relates to the spouse's employment relationship constitutes 'pay' for the purposes of Article 141 EC, the decision to restrict certain benefits to married couples while excluding all persons who live together without being married is for the Member State to determine, and individuals cannot on that basis claim to have suffered unlawful discrimination on the grounds of sex. Nevertheless, the Court went on to observe that, even though the inequality of treatment suffered by transsexuals does not directly undermine enjoyment of a right protected by Community law, it does affect one of the conditions for the grant of that right. In other words, the inequality of treatment at is-sue relates not to the award of a survivor's pension but rather to a necessary precondition for the grant of such a pension: the capacity to marry. In this regard, the European Court of Human Rights had already held that to deny transsexuals the right to marry someone of their original sex, on the grounds that for the purposes of civil registration the couple would belong to the same sex, constitutes a breach of their fundamental rights. According to the ECJ, legislation which, in breach of the ECHR, prevents a couple from fulfilling the marriage requirement which must be met for one of them to benefit from a survivor's pension must be regarded as being, in principle, incompatible with Article 141 EC. However, since it is for the Member State to determine the conditions under which legal recognition is given to a change of gender, it fell to the English court to determine whether the claimants could actually rely on Article 141 EC to gain recognition of the right to nominate a transsexual partner as the beneficiary of a survivor's pension.[32]

K.B. is an impressive demonstration of the ECJ's strong desire to ensure justice for vulnerable citizens. But that desire can sometimes leave the Court stuck between a rock and a hard place. On the one hand, *K.B.* is not the first judgment which advances individual rights by perhaps over-stretching the natural scope of application of Community law – bringing within the purview of the Treaty disputes which might seem better left to domestic and (where appropriate) ECHR law alone.[33] After all, it is far from obvious why Article 141 EC should not only prohibit discrimination between men and women in the field of remuneration, but also obstacles to one's capacity to earn a wage

---

[32] Case C-117/01 *K.B.* (Judgment of 7 January 2004).
[33] Consider, in particular, Case C-60/00 *Carpenter* [2002] ECR I-6279.

in the first place, which are not themselves tainted by discrimination on the grounds of sex, but rather by the Member State's failure to respect certain of its obligations under an international agreement (to which the Community itself is not even party). On the other hand, the reasoning in *K.B.* demonstrates that the Court's determination to see justice done has its limits. In effect, *K.B.* is an affirmation of the transsexual's right to pursue a traditional heterosexual lifestyle. There is little in the judgment to suggest that the Court would adopt a similarly generous approach towards homosexual couples who, in many Member States, are deprived of the right to marry, and thus of financial benefits related to employment such as a survivor's pension. It might well be that such an interpretation of Article 141 EC would indeed constitute one legal step too far, but that hardly tallies with the reasonable expectation that Community law address arbitrary inequalities of treatment – an expectation generated (at least in part) by the Court's own expansive conception of the proper scope of the Treaty in cases such as *K.B.*[34]

On a different track, *Österreichischer Gewerkschaftsbund* concerned Austrian legislation under which, for the purposes of calculating termination payments, employers were obliged to take into account as length of service the duration of military or equivalent civilian service (performed mostly by men) but were not required to take into account for the same purpose the duration of parental leave (taken mostly by women). The question arose whether this discrepancy constituted unequal treatment on grounds of sex prohibited under Article 141 EC. The ECJ recalled that the principle of non-discrimination always assumes that the male and female workers to whom it applies are in comparable situations – and this could not be said of the two types of leave at issue. On the one hand, parental leave is taken voluntarily by a worker in order to bring up a child (and is distinct from maternity leave as regards its purpose, its legislative framework and the periods when it may be taken). On the other hand, the performance of national service corresponds to a civic obligation laid down by law in the public interest, to be performed at a time the individual worker does not choose (and imposes constraints regardless of the size of the undertaking or the employee's length of service). Even though national service may be voluntarily extended, such extensions are still governed by the public interest, insofar as they remain subject to military requirements. Given that the reasons for suspension of the contract of employment are different, workers who benefit from parental leave and those who perform national service are not in comparable situations – and so any difference in treatment between the two groups, when it comes to calculating continuity of employment for the

---

[34] Cf. the contrast between Case C-13/94 *P* v. *S and Cornwall County Council* [1996] ECR I-2143 and Case C-249/96 *Grant* v. *South West Trains* [1998] ECR I-621.

purposes of awarding termination payments, cannot be treated as discrimination under Article 141 EC.[35]

V. Implications of the Principle of Supremacy

It is well established in the Court's case-law that an unimplemented directive cannot of itself impose obligations on individuals and therefore cannot be relied upon as such in litigation between two private parties (so-called horizontal direct effect).[36] However, several perplexing judgments which appeared to contradict this proposition led many academic commentators to speculate about whether the Court's jurisprudence might be evolving towards a more nuanced understanding of the potential direct effect of unimplemented directives.[37] One increasingly popular theory involved drawing a distinction between cases of 'substitution' (involving the direct and immediate application of Community law) and cases of 'exclusion' (involving the mere setting aside of incompatible national rules). In the former situation, the principle of direct effect sets out certain threshold criteria for the justiciability of treaty norms, including the prohibition on horizontal direct effect for unimplemented directives. In the latter situation, the principle of supremacy alone provides a sufficient legal mechanism for determining the status of domestic law *vis-à-vis* treaty norms, without any need to examine the threshold requirements inherent in the concept of direct effect, and may thus result in the imposition of fresh legal obligations on private parties.[38]

This theory in fact highlighted an important division in academic understandings not only of the horizontal direct effect problem, but more fundamentally of the entire relationship between the principles of direct effect and supremacy. Advocates of the substitution-exclusion theory – whether consciously or not – seemed to postulate what might be termed a 'civil law' view of supremacy: the latter is a *constitutional fundamental* describing the relationship between treaty norms and the national legal systems; that principle is not dependent for its operation on the relevant Community rules being cognizable in the sense of having direct effect, but may be triggered in any case where there is a conflict between Community and domestic provisions. However, many other EU lawyers subscribe to what might be termed a 'common law' view of supremacy: the latter is merely a *practical remedy* to be applied in individual cases where

---

[35] Case C-220/02 *Österreichischer Gewerkschaftsbund* (Judgment of 8 June 2004).

[36] In particular: Case 152/84 *Marshall* [1986] ECR 723; Case C-91/92 *Faccini Dori* [1994] ECR I-3325.

[37] E.g. Case C-441/93 *Pafitis* [1996] ECR I-1347; Case C-129/94 *Ruiz Bernáldez* [1996] ECR I-1829; Case C-194/94 *CIA Security International* [1996] ECR I-2201; Case C-443/98 *Unilever Italia* [2000] ECR I-7535.

[38] E.g. Lenz, M., Sif Tynes, D. and Young, L. (2000) 'Horizontal What? Back to Basics'. 25 *ELRev* 509; Tridimas, T. (2002) 'Black, White and Shades of Grey: Horizontality of Directives Revisited'. 21 *YEL* 327.

effect. Viewed from this perspective, the distinction between 'substitution' and 'exclusion' not only appears rather formalistic (surely every exclusion implies some form of substitution, and *vice versa*, since there can be no such thing as a legal vacuum); but also seems to short-circuit the entire theoretical framework for understanding how Community law produces independent effects within the domestic legal orders (whereby supremacy is meant to be a consequence of direct effect and as such indivisible from it).[39]

The Court seems to have treated the dispute in *Pfeiffer* as an opportunity to settle this long-running and crucially important disagreement. The case involved German legislation that, by and large, correctly implemented the working time directive rules concerning the maximum 48-hour working week.[40] However, the national legislation also contained a derogation permitting collective agreements to prescribe longer working hours in the case of contracts involving significant periods of 'duty time' (*in casu*, emergency workers required to make themselves available to their employer at the place of employment and able to act as and when the need arose). Having established that this derogation was incompatible with the requirements imposed under the working time directive, the next question concerned the potential legal effects of the misimplemented directive for the purposes of a horizontal dispute involving two private parties. In fact, the Court of Justice (which was sitting as a Grand Chamber) reopened oral proceedings and sought further observations in response to a structured series of questions on precisely this issue. Advocates of our 'civil law' conception of supremacy would surely have reasoned as follows: it is perfectly possible to invoke the working time directive so as to set aside the conflicting rule of German law creating an exception in favour of certain collective agreements; that does not involve horizontal direct effect for the directive, since the employees are not seeking to substitute any new rule derived from the directive which does not already exist under German law; it is merely an example of the exclusionary effects *vis-à-vis* incompatible domestic norms which flow inexorably from the overarching supremacy of Community law.

But the Court in the end seemed to prefer the 'common law' interpretation of the relationship between direct effect and supremacy: affirming that the relevant provisions of the working time directive were sufficiently clear, precise and unconditional to enjoy direct effect in principle, it remained a consistent tenet of Community law that directives cannot of themselves impose obligations on individuals and cannot therefore be relied on as such against individuals; even a clear, precise and unconditional provision of a directive seeking to confer rights or impose obligations on individuals cannot of itself apply in proceedings exclusively between private parties. The most the ECJ would do was offer

[39] See further, e.g., Dougan, M. (2001) Commentary on *Unilever Italia*. 38 *CMLRev* 1503.
[40] Directive 93/104, OJ 1993 L 307, p. 18.

(admittedly rather extensive) guidance to the national court now charged with interpreting existing German law as far as possible to achieve an outcome consistent with the objectives pursued by the working time directive.[41] *Pfeiffer* might therefore look like the *coup de grâce* for the substitution-exclusion theory. But that still leaves our several perplexing judgments to hobble on with no satisfactory conceptual model to explain their apparent defiance of the 'no horizontal direct effect' rule.

The full legal implications of the principle of supremacy were further explored by the Court in *Kühne & Heitz*, which concerned a Dutch authority's decision that certain poultry meats had been wrongly classified under the customs tariff nomenclature and demanding partial repayment of the relevant export refunds. Kühne & Heitz's appeal to the competent Dutch courts failed, though the latter did not seek any guidance from the ECJ using the preliminary reference procedure under Article 234 EC. Three years later, the ECJ in another dispute delivered a judgment which supported the interpretation originally advocated by Kühne & Heitz – who then requested the Dutch authority to revisit is earlier decision. That request was refused on the grounds that, through the judgment of the Dutch courts, the administrative decision had acquired definitive legal effect. The question arose under which circumstances the principle of supremacy of Community law might require national authorities to reopen decisions which have become final, where it becomes apparent from a subsequent judgment from the ECJ that those decisions were based on a misinterpretation of Community law.

The Court's response was relatively cautious. On the one hand, an interpretation provided by the Court under Article 234 EC clarifies the meaning of the relevant Community provisions as from their coming into force. On the other hand, legal certainty is one of the general principles of Community law, and implies that administrative bodies should not be required, in principle, to reopen a decision which has become final upon the expiry of reasonable limitation periods or the exhaustion of available legal remedies. However, under Dutch law, administrative bodies always have the power (and sometimes an obligation) to reopen a final decision. The Court held that, against that background, Community law could also, in the present circumstances, require the national authorities to revisit their apparently final decision. In particular, the decision's finality derived from a judgment of the national court against which there was no further appeal; that judgment was based on a misinterpretation of Community law which was not referred to the ECJ for guidance; and Kühne & Heitz had complained to the Dutch authority immediately after becoming aware of the ECJ's subsequent favourable judgment. However, in accordance

---

[41] Joined Cases C-397/01 to C-403/01 *Pfeiffer* (Judgment of 5 October 2004).

with Dutch law, reopening the disputed decision should not have the effect of adversely affecting the interests of third parties.[42] This judgment is so carefully tied to the particular facts of the dispute in *Kühne & Heitz* that it is difficult to extract any firm principles to determine the relationship between the principle of supremacy and respect for legal certainty, save for a general feeling that the Court is prepared to interfere with legitimate domestic concerns for administrative finality only in fairly compelling circumstances.

VI. Non-Contractual Liability of Member States and the Community

In *Peter Paul*, the Court delivered an important judgment on the relationship between regulation in the public interest and the possibility of compensation for private losses under Community law. Directive 94/19 requires each Member State to ensure that officially recognized deposit guarantee schemes exist within its territory, and that all credit institutions are affiliated to such a scheme. The national authorities must exercise supervisory functions in respect of credit institutions' compliance with their obligations as members of deposit guarantee schemes. The directive further provides that, in the event of deposits being unavailable, a depositor's aggregate deposits are to be covered by the guarantee scheme up to ECU 20,000.[43] When Germany failed to implement the directive within its time limit, it was accepted that the state could be held liable to depositors for losses incurred up to ECU 20,000. But the question arose whether depositors could seek compensation for losses in excess of that sum, on the grounds that the competent German authorities had failed properly to comply with their banking supervisory obligations under Directive 94/19 or any other Community directives on banking law. The main hurdle for the claimants was that, under German law, the functions of the national authority responsible for supervising credit institutions are to be fulfilled only in the public interest – thus precluding individuals from seeking compensation for private losses resulting from defective supervision by that national authority.

The Court in *Peter Paul* was therefore called upon to determine whether such German legislation was compatible with Community law. It held that, provided compensation up to ECU 20,000 is provided in accordance with Directive 94/19, the latter does not grant to depositors any right to have the competent authorities adopt supervisory measures in their interest. It was therefore legitimate for German law to prevent individuals from seeking compensation for damage resulting from defective supervision by the relevant national authority. Furthermore, an examination of other Community legislation in the field of banking law, although imposing on national authorities certain supervisory

---

[42] Case C-453/00 *Kühne & Heitz* (Judgment of 13 January 2004).

[43] Directive 94/19, OJ 1994 L 135, p. 5.

obligations *vis-à-vis* credit institutions, did not suggest that those directives were intended to confer rights on depositors in the event of their deposits being unavailable as a result of defective regulatory supervision. Moreover, insofar as the claimants might seek compensation not only under German law but as a matter of Community law itself, in accordance with the principles of Member State liability developed under the *Francovich* case-law,[44] their action was bound to fail for the same reasons: the relevant Community legislation was not intended to confer rights on individuals, over and above the compensation expressly provided for under Directive 94/19.[45]

Peter Paul is one of the only cases in which the Court has denied Member State liability under *Francovich* on the grounds that there was no 'intention to confer rights' on the part of the Community legislature. But the judgment highlights a difficult task which must now be addressed by the Court: how to develop a coherent theoretical approach to the circumstances in which private individuals may be called upon to assist in the enforcement of legislation intended primarily to protect the general interest, including the possibility of seeking compensation for any personal losses they may have suffered. This task seems all the more thorny given that existing case-law in analogous contexts, involving 'public interest' legislation on environmental protection and agricultural quality, clearly contemplates a greater role for 'private enforcement' than that recognized by the Court in *Peter Paul*.[46]

2004 also saw several significant judgments dealing with the non-contractual liability of the Community itself. From these one might highlight the dispute in *Lamberts*, which concerned an action for compensation brought under Articles 235 and 288 EC against the European Ombudsman based on the latter's alleged failure adequately to investigate a complaint of maladministration against the Commission. The CFI held that the action was admissible but unfounded, since the claimant had not demonstrated any breach by the Ombudsman of his official duties. The Ombudsman appealed against this judgment, arguing that the CFI should have dismissed the action as inadmissible without even entering upon its merits. For example, it was argued that judicial scrutiny of the Ombudsman's activities is precluded by the supervisory powers exercised over him/her by the European Parliament. However, the ECJ rejected this submission: neither the Ombudsman's obligation to report to the European Parliament, nor the possibility of dismissal based on an overall appraisal of the Ombudsman's performance, amount to review by Parliament of the proper performance of the Ombudsman's duties when dealing with a citizen's complaint. It was

---

[44] Cases C-6 & 9/90 *Francovich* [1991] ECR I-5357.
[45] Case C-222/02 *Peter Paul* (Judgment of 12 October 2004).
[46] Consider, e.g. Case C-201/02 *Wells* (Judgment of 7 January 2004); Case C-253/00 *Muñoz* [2002] ECR I-7289.

also argued that judicial review of the Ombudsman's activities would call into question his/her independence. Again, however, the ECJ rejected this contention: a finding of liability based on the Ombudsman's activities does not concern him/her personally, but rather the Community as a whole; and such liability will in turn be assessed, within the framework of legal principles for engaging the Community's non-contractual liability, having regard to the specific nature of the Ombudsman's obligation merely to use best endeavours, and to his/her wide margin of discretion. Nevertheless, even if judicial review must be limited, it remains possible that 'in very exceptional circumstances', a citizen may be able to demonstrate that the Ombudsman has committed a sufficiently serious breach of Community law in the performance of his/her administrative duties. Consequently, the CFI did not err in law when it declared the claimant's action admissible.[47]

---

[47] Case C-234/02P *European Ombudsman* v. *Lamberts* (Judgment of 23 March 2004).

External Policy Developments

DAVID ALLEN AND MICHAEL SMITH
Loughborough University

I. General Themes

The EU's successful enlargement to ten new Member States in May 2004 was widely described as its most successful external policy. In addition, the Member States signed the Constitutional Treaty, which contains some radical proposals for the formulation and implementation of EU external policy. These include: the creation of the post of an elected President of the European Council; a European Foreign Minister (EFM) by 'dual-hatting' the current responsibilities of the CFSP High Representative and that of the Relex Commissioner; a European external action service (EEAS); and a European defence agency (EDA). Whilst many of the innovations will be translated into policy only if and when the Treaty is ratified by all the Member States, some have already been implemented and some, like the EEAS, are under active consideration. After much drama in the autumn, a new Commission was eventually sworn in at the end of 2004. Benita Ferrero-Waldner has the Relex portfolio which now includes the new European neighbourhood policy (ENP), but she will have to relinquish this post to Javier Solana (who was appointed to be the first European Foreign Minister) if the Treaty is ratified. Louis Michel is the development Commissioner, Peter Mandelson has the trade portfolio and Olli Rehn is responsible for enlargement and relations with the candidate countries. Significantly, Commission President José Barroso announced that he will chair the meetings of Commissioners with external relations responsibilities presumably until Solana becomes a Commissioner.

The Commission, as part of its proposals for the new financial perspective has called for a 36 per cent increase on the €5bn currently spent on external policies to meet the objectives of the EU security strategy.

Notwithstanding the preparations for the European external action service (see below), the Commission has continued with its programme of reform of its external services, including budgetary devolution to the delegations. A new delegation was opened in Saudi Arabia, new regional delegations were opened in New Zealand and Yemen, and a number of representations, and regional and local offices were converted into delegations and regional delegations. At the end of 2004 the Commission had 123 delegations and offices and it was represented by 99 heads of delegation.

During 2004 the EU developed its plans for a European neighbourhood policy, designed to provide an overall framework for its dealings with those of its neighbours for whom EU membership is not a current (or likely?) consideration. The states to be covered by this policy come from both the former Soviet Union (Russia, Ukraine, Moldova, Armenia, Azerbaijan and Georgia and, eventually, Belarus) and the Mediterranean and the Middle East (all those engaged in the Barcelona process and eventually Libya). Ironically the EU's intention seems to be to conduct the ENP on a bilateral basis, albeit within a multilateral framework, and thus there seem to be few incentives in the ENP for the EU's immediate neighbours to develop or improve regional links between themselves despite the supposed attraction of the EU model.

Thus it is envisaged that an initial series of individual action plans (Israel, Jordan, Morocco, Moldova, the Palestinian Authority, Tunisia and Ukraine) would eventually be extended to all ENP participants with a view to then transforming them into European Neighbourhood Agreements, which would presumably replace both the partnership and co-operation agreements already in place with the former Soviet states and the association agreements still being negotiated with Mediterranean and Middle East states within the Barcelona process. Similarly the Commission is seeking, within the framework of the next financial perspective, to replace financial assistance currently given under the Meda and Tacis programmes with a new 'European neighbourhood and partnership instrument' (ENPI).

Common Foreign and Security Policy

The European security strategy, agreed at the end of 2003, and the Constitutional Treaty provided the framework for CFSP/ESDP planning and activities in 2004. Javier Solana was reappointed as the High Representative for the CFSP until the Constitutional Treaty is ratified, at which point he will assume the responsibilities of the EU's first Foreign Minister. Solana began work in consultation with the President of the Commission and the Member States on outline proposals for the planned European external action service (EEAS). By the end of 2004 it was clear that the size, role, mix (meaning the numbers of staff to be drawn from the Commission, the Council and the diplomatic services of the Member States), and the institutional home of the EEAS, were already the source of much contention, in particular between the European Commission and the Council of Ministers. To date most of the preparatory work has concentrated on the 'headquarters' role of the EEAS in Brussels, with Solana expressing a clear preference for an institution which would look like a European Foreign Ministry designed to support his role as Foreign Minister, and which would be based slightly apart from both the Commission and the Council. Solana and Barroso were due to present their further proposals to the European Council in June 2005, and only then will their recommendations for both the Brussels HQ and the EU's external delegations become clear.

Other aspects of the Constitutional Treaty also made progress in 2004. The European Council adopted a declaration on terrorism and a declaration of mutual solidarity in the face of terrorist attack 'in the spirit' of what was then (March) the draft Constitutional Treaty. Within the framework of ESDP the European defence agency (EDA) proposed in the Treaty was established in July under the interim direction of Nick Whitney, with an initial budget of €2 million. The EDA will report to Javier Solana, all the Member States except Denmark are participating in it, and it is envisaged that in 2005 its staff will grow to around 80. Their job will be: to develop defence capabilities for crisis management; to encourage arms co-operation; to strengthen the EU defence industrial base; and to create a competitive equipment market. The EDA is seen as a facilitator; it will have no significant budget beyond its own staff costs, and there remain significant differences between the Member States as to its ideal role.

As described below in the regional sections, ESDP operations continued to expand in 2004, with Operations Althea (Bosnia), Eujust– Themis (Georgia), Eupol-Kinshasa (Democratic Republic of Congo: DRC) being added to the EUPM (Bosnia) and Proxima (Macedonia). In anticipation of future operations to support the UN – possibly in the Sudan, Iraq, Cyprus, Haiti, Burundi, and the Ivory Coast – the EU Member States accepted a proposal from the UK, France and Germany that it should create 1,500-strong battle groups based loosely on the model used in Operation Artemis in the DRC. By November sufficient troops had been committed to contemplate the eventual (by 2010) creation of 13 such battle groups, each deployable within two weeks; some would be based on forces from single Member States, but most would draw their forces from several Member States.

During 2004, the EU adopted seven new joint actions and defined 20 common positions. The mandate of the special representatives for Afghanistan (Francesc Vendrell), the EUMM in the western Balkans (Maryese Daviet), the southern Caucasus (Heikke Talvitie), Macedonia (see below), the Great Lakes region (Aldo Ajello), Bosnia and Herzogovina (Lord Ashdown) and for the Middle East Peace Process (Marc Otte) were all extended. Soren Jessen-Petersen was appointed to replace Alexis Brouhns as EU special representative to Macedonia, and he was in turn replaced by Michael Sahlin, whilst Kevin Carty was appointed as Head of Mission/Police Commissioner of the EU Police Mission (EUPM) in Bosnia and Herzegovina. The EU and the Presidency issued 123 declarations, which are listed in the European Commission's 2004 *General Report on the Activities of the European Union* (point 540, Table 12).

External Trade and the Common Commercial Policy

As a result of the accession of ten new Member States in May, a wide range of existing EU undertakings in trade and commercial policy needed to be reviewed and in many cases substantially amended. Thus, in the World Trade Organization (WTO) context, the Commission had to renegotiate such framework agreements as that on public procurement, whilst in specific trade sectors there was a variety of agreements that needed to be revised (for example those concerning steel with Russia, the Ukraine and Kazakhstan). In other areas, the reality of enlargement changed the context within which the EU's commercial policies were already under review (for example, in the banana trade, where the move from the EU's existing 'illegal' quota-based regime to a tariff-based regime had to take account of the demands of new members). Another knock-on effect of enlargement was felt in the EU's visa arrangements with the USA – an area with strong commercial policy implications. Here, the visa waiver arrangements made by Washington with the existing Member States did not automatically extend to the ten new members, and for a while there was the possibility of the EU imposing reciprocal demands for visas on Americans in order to reflect the interests of the accession countries.

At the same time as the effects of enlargement were being felt, the Union (and more specifically the Commission acting on behalf of the Community) had to deal with the 'hangover' from the failure of the WTO's Doha development agenda (DDA) in 2003 (see *Annual Review 2003*). In January 2004, Robert Zoellick, the US Trade Representative, made overtures to all WTO members, and this was followed up with action by Pascal Lamy, the Commissioner for Trade, during the spring. A meeting in London at the beginning of May, between Zoellick, Lamy and other key players from countries such as Brazil, India and South Africa, led to a new momentum and, in early May, Lamy made a crucial move by offering to negotiate the disappearance of all EU agricultural export subsidies. There was disagreement over how valuable this offer was, and it was conditional on all others making the same kind of move, but it certainly created a new atmosphere. The offer was coupled with new flexibility on the part of the EU towards negotiations on the so-called 'Singapore issues' (investment, trade facilitation and other areas), which contributed significantly towards the final setting of a negotiating framework at the end of July 2004. Negotiations in the DDA are scheduled to last at least until the end of 2005, and are a major item on the agenda of Peter Mandelson, the new Trade Commissioner. At the same time his predecessor, Pascal Lamy, threw his hat into the ring as a candidate for the Director-Generalship of the WTO.

During the year, the Union was involved in 27 WTO disputes, 15 of them as the plaintiff and 12 as the target. Although nine trade partners were involved in the range of disputes, 15 of them involved the EU and the USA; in ten of these the EU was the plaintiff. Notable among the disputes was one involving the legality of the EU's sugar trade regime, which led in the autumn to a finding against the Union; this in turn fed into the 'internal' re-consideration of the EU's policy in the sector. Alongside this activity of dispute management, the EU was also actively involved in matters of WTO membership, pursuing negotiations with a number of potential accession states. The most important of these were with Russia, and in May the EU concluded a market access agreement with Moscow. Observers noted that it was immediately after this agreement that the Russians seemed to become markedly more willing to ratify the Kyoto protocol on climate change; the subsequent ratification in the autumn meant that the USA was largely isolated in its refusal to ratify the protocol.

As usual, the work on 'framework issues' and global problems in trade was accompanied by a host of more specific negotiations and measures. The EU undertook a review of its generalized system of preferences (GSP), a set of arrangements applying particularly to less developed countries, and in July 2004 it proposed new guidelines for the period 2006–15 with a strong emphasis on sustainable development and the needs of the poorest countries. In October, a new regulation was adopted as the basis for conduct of the GSP during 2006–08. Customs co-operation was another significant area of activity: a new agreement was signed with the United States (although the year also saw some friction over variations in customs practices between EU Member States, which the US saw as a potential barrier to trade). An agreement between the EU and China was also initialled, whilst one with India was proposed. The Chinese factor also entered strongly into the EU's approach to a major change in world trade: the elimination of quotas on the trade in textiles, which arose from the Uruguay round in the mid-1990s and was due to take place in January 2005. Given the potential consequences of liberalized trade not only for EU producers, but also for producers in EU partner countries such as Bangladesh, the Commission was anxious to monitor events closely and retain the option of some kind of safeguard measures. On another front, the external ramifications of the EU's policy on the control of chemicals (the Reach proposals) became a commercial policy issue, with the Americans and others concerned at the complexity and administrative demands it would impose.

During 2004, the EU continued to be active in the use of 'trade defence' instruments such as anti-dumping and anti-subsidy measures. Whilst the use of these measures is declining at the global level, the Commission was nonetheless engaged in ten anti-dumping cases where definitive duties were applied; it confirmed or amended duties in 31 procedures and terminated a further ten without renewing the measures. There were 29 notices of initiation of new anti-dumping actions, 41 notices of initiation of reviews, and in five cases provisional anti-dumping duties were imposed. On the anti-subsidy front, the EU imposed definitive duties in two new cases, confirmed or amended duties in five cases, and adopted new provisional measures in one case.

Development Co-operation Policy and Humanitarian Aid

Possibly as part of a strategy aimed at the forthcoming negotiations for the next financial perspective, the UK launched a major critique of the EU's development policy during 2004, arguing for the repatriation of expenditure on development aid from the EU to the national level. The UK government was critical of the Commission's record of implementing spending decisions despite the fact that the UK House of Lords found, in its own investigations, that EU implementation had been greatly improved following the reforms developed through EuropeAid (including country strategy papers, financial devolution and deconcentration of tasks to Commission delegations). The Lords report did argue that the Commission now needed to turn its attention to improving the co-ordination of multilateral EU aid with bilateral Member State aid, and it highlighted poor internal co-ordination on aid matters within the Commission – in particular between the Development and Agriculture DGs.

The UK and others also drew attention to the fact that the EU, despite committing itself publicly to aiding the very poorest states in the international system, nevertheless increasingly privileges its immediate neighbours rather than the very poor states, so that their share of EU aid dropped from 70 per cent to under 50 per cent in the last decade. Citizens in Mediterranean states receive $100 per annum from the EU, whereas citizens in Asia receive just $1 per annum. For its part, the EU Commission stated its opposition to British proposals for using international loan facilities, underpinned by Member State guarantees, to write off third world debt.

Despite being the world's largest aid donor, the EU and its Member States collectively have, to date, managed only 0.39 per cent of EU GNP towards the UN target of 0.7 per cent of GNP for development aid. The European Commission has now been given responsibility for monitoring progress towards this 0.7 per cent target.

In 2004 the European Community humanitarian office (Echo) allocated €570 million in humanitarian aid. The bulk of this aid (€300 million) went to the African, Caribbean and Pacific (ACP) countries, including €91 million for the Darfur region of the Sudan. The Commission provided €419 million in food aid and food security programmes.

II. Regional Themes

The European Economic Area and EFTA

June 2004 saw the tenth anniversary of the European Economic Area (EEA) agreement; it was not without irony that almost simultaneously the agreement was being revised to reflect the accession of ten new Member States to the EU. As a result, the ten new members acceded to the EEA agreement at the same time as they entered the Union. The wheels of this process were oiled by a contribution of €100m over five years from the non-EU members of the EEA, designed to enhance the social and economic cohesion of the enlarged EEA. The enlargement might have been expected to make some of the non-EU members think about the implications of their continued exclusion from EU decision-making processes. Although there was some discussion of the position of Norway, nothing solid in the way of renewed interest in EU membership had emerged by the end of 2004. Whilst Iceland began negotiations with the Union on liberalization of agricultural trade, this was again not in the context of any broader intensification of interest in membership.

2004 was a year of active negotiation and agreement with Switzerland, which is not a member of the EEA, but is a member of the European Free Trade Association (EFTA). During 2003, there had been efforts on the part of the Union to get the Swiss to agree on the treatment of savings, in particular the imposition of a withholding tax. This had been complicated by issues surrounding the Swiss banking system, in particular its secrecy, but it was clear that if the EU legislation was going to work it had to have Swiss agreement and subsequent action, as well as that of other financial centres in Andorra, Monaco and San Marino. Finally, in October 2004, a set of nine agreements was signed with the Swiss, including the vital savings agreement. Given the delay, it was still uncertain whether the savings arrangements could be implemented on 1 January 2005 as planned, and it was also unclear whether the implementation of the withholding tax would bring significant returns; but at least it was an agreement. The other agreements in the set of nine also covered some major areas of concern: double taxation, media, statistics, free movement, treatment of asylum applications, and trade in some processed food products.

Western Balkans

In the Western Balkans 2004 was a difficult year, with the EU concerned about riots in Albania, violence in Kosovo, the failure of the Croatian and Serbian governments to deliver notorious war criminals to the International Criminal Tribunal for the former Yugoslavia (ICTY) and the growing reliance of the Serbian government of Vojislv Kostunica on the support of Slobodon Milosovic's Socialist Party. Within the framework of the Stability Pact for South Eastern Europe (which celebrated its fifth anniversary) the EU continued to develop the stabilization and association process: Croatia was recognized as an EU candidate country although accession negotiations in 2005 will begin only if co-operation with the ICTY improves. Macedonia's application for membership was submitted in March (Macedonia hopes to join the EU by 2009) and its stabilization and association agreement (SAA) entered into force in April, whilst European partnerships (designed to focus preparations for further integration into the EU) were agreed with Albania, Bosnia and Herzegovina, Macedonia and Serbia and Montenegro. Although it has stated the ambition of joining the EU by 2012, Serbia and Montenegro remains the only former Yugoslav state yet to make any significant progress towards a SAA and, unlike Bosnia, it has not yet reached even the feasibility stage. Questions remain both about the continuation of the federal arrangements binding Serbia and Montenegro together and, more seriously, those involving the future status of Kosovo.

Under the ESDP, the EU decided to continue (at least until December 2005) with its police mission (Eupol Proxima) in Macedonia, although it capped the budget allocation for this mission at €6.5million. In Bosnia and Herzegovina the mandate of the EU police mission (EUPM) was extended for another year and €17million allocated to it. More significantly, in July the Council approved the principle of another ESDP mission (Althea) whereby the EU from early December would continue with SFOR's task of providing a secure environment for the implementation of the Dayton peace accords. Althea will involve the deployment of around 7,000 troops under the local command of a British General, David Leakey. Althea forces will enjoy the use of Nato assets and capabilities under the 'Berlin plus' arrangements agreed between the EU and Nato. The operational commander for Althea will be another British General, John Reith, who is also Nato's Deputy Supreme Commander for Europe (D-SACEUR).

Russia and the Soviet Successor States

2004 saw the EU harden its stance towards Russia in the second of the two annual summits and then directly oppose Russia in respect of the result of the Ukrainian presidential election. At the start of the year the forthcoming enlargement of the EU caused some tensions, as Russia prevaricated about the extension of the partnership and co-operation agreement to the ten incoming EU Member States. However, these issues were resolved by the time of the first EU–Russia summit in May at which the EU pledged its support for Russian entry into the World Trade Organization (WTO) and Russia agreed to ratify the Kyoto protocol.

By the time of the second summit in November, relations had worsened, partly as a result of economic difficulties (for instance Russia was accused of using discriminatory freight railway rates against ports like Riga and Tallinn in the Baltic States in favour of St Petersburg and Kaliningrad), and partly as a result of Russia's heavy-handed resolution of the Beslan school hostage incident in which over 350 people, many of them children, were killed. Before the summit the EU, aware of Russia's ability to undermine its common positions by dealing unilaterally with its larger Member States (especially France and Germany), decided to take a firm line on Russia's perceived 'cherry-picking' of the four agreed 'spaces' (economic; freedom, security and justice; external security; research and education) common to the EU and Russia which provide the framework for ongoing negotiations. Russia is seen to be unresponsive on issues that concern the EU like visa-free travel, human rights in Chechnya and South Ossetia, judicial reform and the withdrawal of Russian troops from Moldova and Georgia. When problems arose in Ukraine in December, the atmosphere worsened as Russia accused the EU of 'destructive external interference'.

Relations with Ukraine in the early part of the year centred around the development of the ENP, with Ukraine unhappy that this policy framework was seen to fall short of offering the prospect of eventual EU membership. When the EU (along with Nato and the OSCE) supported the growing wave of protest inside Ukraine and rejected the electoral process that saw Viktor Yanukovich elected as President, a key role in subsequent developments was played by Javier Solana. The EU High Representative, assisted by the Presidents of Poland and Lithuania, played a major interventionist role as events unfolded in Kiev. The result was a new round of elections which saw Viktor Yushchenko eventually triumph in a Ukraine which nevertheless remained divided between those who sought closer links with the EU and those who preferred a closer relationship with Russia. Finally, Ukraine suggested a temporary solution to the EU's deficiency in 'heavy lift' aircraft for its ESDP missions by offering the same Antonov aircraft that the EU had 'borrowed' for Operation Artemis in the DRC.

In Moldova, despite the declared interest and offers of assistance (via the ENP) from the EU, negotiations over the disputed Transdniestra region, in which the rule of law is increasingly subverted by the actions of the mafia (much as is the case in Kaliningrad), were conducted between Russia and the US without reference to the EU.

In the Caucasus region, the prospect of an ENP caused difficulties for Azerbaijan to the extent that it might require closer relations with Armenia, whilst the Ngorno-Karabkh dispute, involving the occupation of part of Azerbaijan by Armenian troops, remains unresolved. In Georgia, following the peaceful revolution that had taken place in 2003, the EU decided in 2004 to launch an ESDP 'rule of law' mission entitled Eujust Themis. This involves 12 EU civilian legal experts, based in government departments, assisting in the reform of the criminal code and other aspects of the justice system. In addition the EU Commission promised some €125 million to assist the reform process in Georgia.

Finally, in central Asia, the EU opposed Kazakhstan's candidacy for the OSCE Presidency because of its dubious election held in September. In March, Commissioner Patten met with representatives from Uzbekistan, Kazakhstan, Tajikistan and Kyrgyzstan to discuss a proposal from Uzbekistan that a new centre against drug trafficking and terrorism be established in Tashkent. In October the EU signed with Tajikistan its first ever partnership and co-operation agreement to include clauses dealing with the fight against terrorism and weapons of mass destruction.

The Mediterranean and the Middle East

The EU's strategy towards this part of the world has for a long time been developed within the framework of the multilateral Barcelona process. The development of the European Neighbourhood Policy would seem to be moving the EU towards a greater focus on bilateral relations. The most obvious beneficiary of this move would appear to be Israel, for whom progress within the confines of the Barcelona process has always proved difficult because of its differences with most other Mediterranean and Middle Eastern states over the Arab–Israeli conflict.

During 2004, the EU made significant progress towards normalizing its relations with Libya after the Ghaddafi regime accepted responsibility for the Lockerbie bombings (including payment of compensation), and agreed to allow weapons inspectors to operate within Libya. In October, after Ghaddafi had visited Brussels the EU, following the US, agreed to lift its sanctions against Libya. Libya, for its part, co-operated with the EU, and in particular with Malta and Italy, in a bid to prevent illegal migrants from Sudan, Chad and Niger entering the EU by boat from Libya.

The EU's relations with Israel were not helped by the Sharon government's continued construction of a security wall around the territory controlled by the Palestinian Authority. The death of Yasser Arafat towards the end of the year was, however, seen by the EU as an opportunity for it to extend its role in the search for peace in the Middle East, through both its own bilateral action and its participation in the Quartet (EU, UN, US and Russia). The objective remains the implementation of the 'road map' and its two-state solution – both given an apparent new impetus by the death of Arafat and the re-election of US President Bush. During the year, fears were expressed within the EU (but not in Israel) that the EU's enlargement would lead to a divided EU position because of the pro-US, and therefore pro-Israeli, sentiments of many of the new Member States. So far this has not happened, and the distinct EU position supporting the existence of both Israel and Palestine but giving considerable economic assistance to the Palestinian Authority has been maintained. Thus Israel seeks to accuse the EU of losing its 'honest broker' status, and therefore deserving to be excluded from the peace process, whilst Javier Solana is heard to comment that 'we will be involved whether you like it or not'. During 2004 the EU anti-fraud office (OLAF) reported that it could find no evidence to support Israeli charges that EU aid to the Palestinian Authority had been diverted to support terrorist activities against Israel.

Towards the end of the year the conclusion of an ENP action plan for Israel, despite Israeli objections to references to weapons of mass destruction, seemed to give Israel the opportunity for participation in the EU single market without any of the political conditionality associated with the Barcelona process. There thus seems to be a degree of contradiction between the permissive features of the ENP action plan for Israel and the human rights conditions that are a part of the EU–Israel association agreement and the Quartet's road map.

The death of Arafat did make the EU, led by Javier Solana, step up its diplomacy, promising to assist the Palestinian Authority with its presidential and other elections and with the further training of a police force in anticipation of an Israeli withdrawal from Gaza and the West Bank.

On Iraq, the EU has overcome most of the internal divisions caused by the prosecution of the war and appears to be united in its determination to play a part in Iraq's reconstruction. Whether agreement about what might be thought of as civilian assistance (financial assistance, possibly a police mission and a contribution to the restoration of the rule of law) can eventually be extended to the notion of military assistance, remains to be seen. The EU allocated €160 million to Iraq in 2004 and agreed to a further €200 million for 2005.

Britain, France and Germany invited Javier Solana to join them in their joint diplomatic bid to persuade the Iranians to comply with international (primarily US) concerns about its nuclear policy. The EU's bargaining counter is the promise of trade concessions within the framework of a trade and co-operation agreement but, by the end of the year, the chances of reaching an acceptable agreement seemed to have lessened and the EU position put forward by the 3+1 had hardened, becoming closer to that of the US than when the talks began in 2003.

2004 proved to be a potential turning point in the gradual evolution of EU–Turkey relations. In October, despite the public dissent of several Commissioners, the Commission voted to recommend that accession negotiations be opened with Turkey and this was accepted by the European Council in December – even though several Member States expressed considerable reservations about and resistance to eventual Turkish membership of the EU.

Africa

The EU's involvement in African affairs is steadily increasing. The Union is the largest donor of aid to Africa (more than 50 per cent) and has the largest share of African trade (45 per cent, which is three times larger than intra-African trade). In 2004 the EU, within the overall framework of the European security strategy, agreed a peace and security action plan for Africa designed to enhance capacity-building and thus the means (via ESDP) to support the disarmament, demobilization and reintegration of combatants. Building on the success in 2003 of the limited ESDP operation (Artemis) in the Democratic Republic of the Congo, it was agreed in 2004 to support the establishment of an integrated police unit in the DRC to be assisted in 2005 by a EU police mission (Eupol Kinshasa). In the Dafur region of the Sudan the EU has committed significant funds (from the European development fund (€100 million), from the peace facility for Africa (€80 million) and bilaterally from EU Member States (€200 million)), as well as civilian and military personnel to support both a negotiated ceasefire and the conflict prevention and resolution activities of the African Union.

The EU also used the human rights 'conditionality' provision (Article 96) of the Cotonou agreement to renew the suspension of development assistance to Zimbabwe, the Ivory Coast and to Liberia (but not as yet to Uganda despite the fact that several Member States have done so and despite warnings about the need for conflict prevention measures in that country) whilst lifting similar restrictions previously imposed on Guinea-Bissau. Under the Cotonou agreement, the enlarged EU of 25 held it first ministerial Council with the ACP states, at which significant progress was made towards the conclusion of economic partnership agreements with the African regions. These agreements are designed to replace the Cotonou trade provisions after 2008 and in 2004 the EU extended the negotiations that had been started with central and west African regional bodies to the eastern and southern region and to the Southern African Development Community (SADC). In 2004 the European Commission held its first ever meeting with the Commission of the newly established African Union, at which the two main topics were the fight against terrorism and development aid. In 2004 African countries received a total of €1849 million directly from the European development fund plus a share of €534 million EDF money allocated to non-geographic programmes.

Asia

The biennial Asia–Europe Meeting (ASEM) met for the fourth time in 2004, from 7–9 October in Hanoi, the capital of Vietnam. Until the very last minute, it was not certain that this meeting would take place: the perennial problem of Burma/Myanmar, which is subject to EU sanctions on human rights grounds but is a member of the Association of Southeast Asian Nations (ASEAN) and thus formally entitled to participate in the ASEM, continued to bedevil the arrangements. Two ASEM ministerial meetings were cancelled as a result in the early part of 2004, and it fell to the Dutch Presidency to try to find a compromise as the basis for the full ASEM going ahead. Eventually they did so: Burma/Myanmar could participate but would be represented at ministerial (not head of state/government) level and, in the aftermath of the ASEM, the EU would look at intensification of their existing sanctions because of the continuing failure of the Burmese to release opposition leader Aung San Suu Kyi. Such intensification was discussed, and new measures devised, but these explicitly excluded existing investments in Burma/Myanmar, such as those of the French oil company Total.

The ASEM focused especially on economic co-operation issues, and included a call for a free trade area by 2025 as well as greater use of the euro for transactions between ASEM members. Alongside ASEM, the EU's new strategy for relations with ASEAN (introduced in *Annual Review 2003/04*) relies on bilateral discussions within a multilateral framework with the aim eventually of producing an ASEAN–EU free trade area. The strategic priorities for this initiative were agreed by the EU in early 2004 and by the end of the year bilateral negotiations had been authorized with a number of ASEAN Member States, focusing especially on regulatory issues.

In a host of interconnected areas, the EU is concerned with what happens in China. During 2004, for example, the reluctance of the Chinese to revalue their currency continued to mean that the terms of trade between the EU and

China were to the latter's advantage; the fact that the Chinese yuan is pegged to the (rapidly declining) US dollar means that this situation is exacerbated as the dollar falls. The development and dynamism of the Chinese economy also means that domestic demands there will affect the availability of resources at the global level and to the EU: an obvious example is oil, where Chinese demand is a key factor producing record high prices, but another less publicized example causing concern in 2004 was coal, where the Chinese have been major suppliers to the EU but now restrict the export of such specialist items as coke because they need it at home. As noted earlier, the textiles issue promises to be a key element shaping EU trade concerns in the near future. Finally, in bilateral EU–China trade relations, the EU is faced with the question of whether to declare China a 'market economy': a designation which has ramifications for the EU's capacity to act against Beijing for example through anti-dumping procedures. In July, the EU decided not to certify the Chinese in this way, much to Beijing's frustration, but the question has certainly not gone away.

China, however, is not only an economic issue. During 2004, this was brought home to the EU on a number of fronts. Perhaps most sharply, it was focused by the French-led push to lift the arms embargo on Beijing, and to rely instead on the EU's non-binding code of practice for arms sales. Not only did some EU Member States consider this inappropriate, it was also strongly opposed by the USA, with threats of (unspecified) measures to be taken against EU interests if the embargo were to be lifted. This was in turn linked with the question of Taiwan, where the push in some quarters for a referendum on independence from China led again to divisions in the EU and cautionary words from Washington.

Other bilateral relationships between the EU and Asia, as usual, showed a picture of diversity. Significantly, the Union declared during 2004 that it wished to pursue a 'strategic partnership' with India: the only other declared partnerships of this kind so far are with the USA and China. The 'strategic partnership' was launched at the EU–India summit held in November, and aims to enhance relations in trade, innovation and technology, the economy, and the fight against terrorism. Relations between the EU and Pakistan centred on the possibility of concluding the third generation partnership and co-operation agreement – a process which was resisted by the European Parliament, but which was approved by the Council in April 2004. The EU continued to play an active role in the reconstruction of Afghanistan and its transition to democracy, and welcomed the decision to hold presidential elections in October; but the delivery of EU aid was put at risk on occasion by the ways in which civilian assistance efforts had become intermingled with military operations. Development Commissioner Poul Nielsen had occasion in May 2004 to complain vehemently about this trend. Meanwhile the mandate of Francesc Vendrell, the EU Special Representative in Afghanistan, was extended to 28 February 2005.

During 2004, the Union committed €274m to financial and technical co-operation with Asian countries. Afghanistan received €185m in support of rehabilitation and reconstruction; there was €25m for operations to support uprooted peoples; €3.4m for rehabilitation projects; and an additional €107.2m for political, economic and cultural co-operation. Right at the end of 2004, the EU dedicated an initial €23m in emergency humanitarian aid to countries affected by the tsunami which caused widespread devastation and loss of life across the Indian Ocean.

Latin America

During 2004, the key event in EU–Latin American relations was the third EU–Latin America/Caribbean summit in Guadalajara, Mexico, on 28 May. This was also the occasion for a number of 'sub-regional' meetings between the EU and such groupings as the Andean countries. The focus of the Guadalajara meeting was particularly on growth and multilateralism – and implicitly also on the extent to which the EU could provide a rival focus to the USA for Latin American or Caribbean countries. A total of 58 countries attended: the 25 EU Member States, 17 Latin American countries and 16 Caribbean countries. From the point of view of some Latin American or Caribbean participants, the meeting was disappointing in that it led to no major progress in the establishment of free trade arrangements, but it did promise a new focus on 'bi-regional' and other forms of co-operation. A programme to enhance regional economic and social cohesion ('Eurosocial') was agreed with an initial €30m budget, and arrangements for political dialogue and scientific co-operation were made with a number of Latin American countries.

The most ambitious EU–Latin America negotiations, those between the EU and the Mercosur grouping, made little progress in 2004. For the past few years the aim has been to establish a free trade area between the two regional economic groupings but, in 2004 as before, the question of agriculture proved a key stumbling block. The EU's reluctance to concede on this, along with other issues concerning public contracts, meant that an October deadline for the completion of negotiations was missed, and prospects for future progress lay with the new Commission.

In bilateral relations, the predominantly economic agreements with Mexico and Chile, established in the past few years, were amended during 2004 to take account of the enlargement of the EU. At the same time, a long-standing problem reared its head in the form of the EU's arrangements for banana imports. Proposals made by Pascal Lamy towards the end of the year for a major increase in import tariffs on Latin American bananas, evoked complaints from Ecuador and others, and raised the prospect of a new dispute – ironically precipitated in part by efforts to implement a solution to the dispute of the late 1990s. Relations with Cuba, frosty since EU protests about the imprisonment of dissidents in 2002–03, improved marginally towards the end of the year as there was evidence of some relaxation and release of some of those imprisoned; such a thaw was vigorously pursued by the new Spanish Prime Minister, José Luis Zapatero.

The United States, Japan and Other Industrial Countries

The EU's relations with the United States had been not only complex and messy during 2002 and 2003, but also acrimonious (see previous *Annual Reviews*). On this basis, and on the grounds that 2004 was a US presidential election year, it might have been expected that the tensions would continue. It might also have been expected that a key factor in the development of relations would be US domestic politics, in which the EU did not loom large: a Gallup Europe poll conducted in the summer of 2004 revealed that 77 per cent of Americans knew little or nothing about the EU. Nonetheless – and despite the fact that the annual EU–US summit held in Ireland during June lasted only a total of three hours including lunch – there were some signs of reconstruction, as well as continuing signs of potential trouble as the year developed. By the latter part of the year a number of groups had put forward proposals for the revitalization of the transatlantic relationship, including the creation of a free trade area by the year 2010. There was also general agreement that despite quite widespread support in the EU for John Kerry as a potential president, the actual impact of a Kerry Presidency on EU–US relations would be minimal. As it turned out, of course, such speculation was just that and the EU was confronted with 'Bush II'.

At the political and institutional level, the echoes of Iraq continued to be heard, with frictions between Brussels and Washington over proposals for relief of Iraqi debts and Iraqi observer status in the WTO. The antipathy to US policies in Iraq was extended in the Union by the Madrid bombing of March 2004, which led to the almost immediate installation of the Zapatero government; this change in the internal balance of feeling was significant in the evolution of EU policies and alignments during the rest of the year. But whilst Iraq (along with US views on the 'greater Middle East' and the Israel–Palestine conflict) continued to be a focus of resentment, there were other more hopeful signs. The EU – and specifically the 'EU-3' (Britain, France and Germany) continued to play a leading role in dealing with the issue of Iran's nuclear programme, pursuing a diplomatic rather than a confrontational line. Whilst the Iranians played hard to get for much of the year, the EU-3 were able to extract concessions; during the autumn, they hardened their line by letting it be known that they would have to go along with the US request for a UN Security Council referral if the Iranians did not budge, and the eventual result was an agreement by Tehran to cease all uranium enrichment activities. Another key focus of EU–US diplomatic interaction was China. The discussions within the EU on whether to lift the arms embargo during the latter part of 2004 were closely watched by Washington (see above) and any signs of wavering in Brussels met with concern and the exercise of diplomatic pressure.

On a more positive note, during 2004, the EU and the US reached agreement on the Galileo satellite system, which allows the Europeans to develop it fully and established a mechanism for ensuring compatibility between Galileo and the US-controlled GPS system. This agreement was noted as the first in which the US had agreed to release classified intelligence to the EU. Another EU–US agreement on information-sharing was rather more controversial: the Commission, the Council and the US administration came to an agreement about the release of data on air passengers heading towards the USA, but this was opposed by the European Parliament on the grounds of data protection, and referred by the EP to the European Court of Justice on an advisory vote. Despite this resistance, the agreement went ahead.

The decline of the US dollar, highlighted earlier as a factor in EU–China relations, was also a key concern in transatlantic dealings, with its implications for trade and investment (both predominantly negative) much debated. As noted earlier, the linkage of EU and US activities in the revitalization of the Doha development agenda of the WTO gave rise to hope that there would be a more active and constructive concertation of policies in world trade. At the same time, the ratification of the Kyoto protocol by Russia meant that the US refusal to ratify stood out all the more, and there were those in the EU who were prepared to argue that the US would sign up eventually in the face of isolation. The transatlantic business dialogue (TABD) was relaunched in 2004, and found itself immediately embroiled in the debates about global trade negotiations; it also emphasized the growing linkage between the kinds of deregulation and enhanced competitiveness at the heart of the Lisbon strategy and the future balance of transatlantic relations.

2004 saw the implementation of the trade sanctions authorized by the WTO in the dispute over US foreign sales corporations; these were applied in a progressive way, as the revised US legislation inched its way through Congress. The WTO also authorized the EU (along with others) to apply countermeasures in two other cases: those of the so-called Byrd amendment, which allows US firms to reap the benefits of anti-dumping cases in cash, and the 1916 trade legislation that allows the US to apply triple duties to products found to be dumped. European companies continued to experience the burden of the Sarbanes-Oxley legislation, passed in the aftermath of the Enron affair and other corporate scandals, which gives no concessions to companies registered in both the US and the EU; only the threat that many EU companies might de-list from the New York Stock Exchange seemed to bring any movement.

Negotiations on a so-called 'open skies' deal between the EU and the US faltered during 2004, largely due to perceptions in the EU that the Americans were unwilling to offer any realistic access to their domestic airline market; this led to a breakdown of negotiations in the summer, to legal action by the Commission against those EU Member States that had concluded 'illegal' bilateral deals with the USA, and to the prospect of increased tensions in 2005. Increased tensions were also caused by the perennial dispute over subsidies for large civil aircraft (i.e. the Airbus–Boeing dispute). During the summer, there was increased pressure from the Americans aimed at getting the Europeans to reduce their launch aid for key Airbus projects. This turned into the first big test for the new European Trade Commissioner, Peter Mandelson, and led to friction with outgoing US Trade Representative Robert Zoellick.

Japan, for so many years a source of concern to the EU, hardly merited a mention in 2004, although the annual summit in June did produce agreement on investment promotion. The Union and Japan did find themselves embroiled in a contest over the siting of a major new nuclear fusion project (the €10bn Iter facility) in which the Union was supported by China and Russia and Japan by the USA. South Korea, and particularly its shipbuilding industry, remained a focus of interest especially when, late in the year, the WTO ruled only partly in favour of the measures the EU had taken to support its industry. With Canada, there were negotiations on a new 'partnership agenda', focused especially on bilateral trade and investment enhancement. Finally, Australia and New Zealand received scant attention, except that Australia was involved as leader of the Cairns group of agricultural exporters in the machinations around the resumption of WTO negotiations, and New Zealand was favoured with the establishment of a dedicated Commission delegation in Wellington (whereas previously they had been covered by the Canberra delegation).

JCMS 2005 Volume 43. Annual Review pp. 127–30

Enlarging the European Union

JULIE SMITH
University of Cambridge

2004 was a momentous year in the EU enlargement process as ten new Member States from central, eastern and southern Europe finally acceded on 1 May. This 'big bang' enlargement could easily have served to impede any further expansion of the Union as existing Members struggled to come to terms with the first wave of newcomers. However, it was clear from an early stage that the accession of the ten would not be the end of the process. Bulgaria and Romania began 2004 with the desire of joining their neighbours by 2007; Croatia and Macedonia sought acceptance as candidates by the Union; and Turkey was hoping to be given a date to start accession negotiations.

Bulgaria and Romania were recognized as candidate states in 1997 and began to negotiate membership when the Union decided to adopt a 'regatta approach' to enlargement, designed to ensure that states could negotiate and accede according to their individual progress. Neither state was able to catch up with the other central and east European applicants, but each hoped to join by 2007 and the Union offered them a clear strategy for completing the accession process in the form of road maps and revised accession partnerships.

The Commission's Regular Reports on Bulgaria and Romania presented in October 2004 (Commission, 2004c, d) argued that both countries had made good progress towards meeting the Copenhagen criteria, political and economic. Much work was still to be done in terms of administrative capacity and judicial reform, but the Commission was satisfied that, if the two states continued along the same reform trajectory, they would be ready to join in 2007. The Commission indicated that the pre-accession strategy would remain until accession, and made it clear that Bulgaria and Romania would have to continue 'reinforcing administrative and judicial capacity' once they were members (Commission, 2004b, p. 4). The Commission pledged to continue to monitor their progress.

Negotiations between the EU and Bulgaria and Romania were completed on 14 December 2004,[1] and the European Council accepted the Commission's recommendations that they should join in 2007 (Council of the European Union 2005, pp. 2, 3) and called for the Accession Treaty to be signed in April 2005. However, in a change from previous enlargements, the EU institutions inserted a caveat that should either country fail to prepare adequately for membership, its accession could be postponed by a year. Agreeing to implement the *acquis* would no longer be enough, states would thenceforth have to demonstrate their commitment as well. The Commission adopted a favourable opinion on 22 February 2005, and the European Parliament gave its assent to the Treaty on 13 April 2005, paving the way for the Bulgaria and Romania to sign their Accession Treaty on 25 April 2005.

Croatia submitted its application for EU membership in February 2003, expressing its hope to join the Union at the same time as Bulgaria and Romania in 2007. The election in 2000 of a left-wing pro-European government and President had put Croatia on an apparently fast path to Europe (Commission, 2004a, p. 6). By 2004, the Commission could give a favourable opinion to the application and, in June, the European Council agreed that Croatia should become a candidate state and commence negotiations in early 2005.

Yet, there was one part of Croatia's past, and present, that rendered progress difficult. In 2001 it had signed a stabilization and association agreement with the Union, the provisions of which included regional co-operation and 'co-operation with the International Criminal Tribunal for the Former Yugoslavia (ICTY)' (Commission, 2004a, p. 5). Continued co-operation with the ICTY was made a condition of opening accession negotiations (Council of the European Union 2005, p. 4). The issue for the EU was that the last indicted Croatian war crimes suspect, General Ante Gotovina, should be extradicted to The Hague. The Croatians denied that he was in their country and the EU postponed the opening of accession negotiations, which were due to begin on 17 March 2005.

The Former Yugoslav Republic of Macedonia (FYROM) submitted its application to the Union on 22 March 2004 and the European Council asked the Commission to produce an opinion on the application.

The country waiting longest to join the European Union is Turkey. Although only formally a candidate state since 1999, Turkey has had an association agreement since 1963. By the late 1990s, however, Member States accepted Turkey's candidature in the belief that an outright rebuff could have negative

[1] For details of the results of the negotiations, see Commission (2005).

consequences, notably a move away from democracy towards Islamic fundamentalism. Despite its considerable economic progress, Turkey did not meet the political Copenhagen criteria, notably with regard to civil–military relations, human rights and attitudes towards minorities. Thus, no date could be set for negotiations to begin.

By October 2004, the European Commission deemed Turkey to have made progress towards meeting the political criteria and at its December meeting the European Council agreed to open negotiations with Turkey in October 2005 (Commission 2004e; Council of the European Communities 2005). Turkish EU membership nevertheless remained a far distant prospect, since the chapters with financial implications could not be opened until the financial perspective for 2014 onwards was agreed (Commission, 2004e, p. 8). Moreover, as the Commission noted, this was 'an open-ended process whose outcome cannot be guaranteed beforehand' (Commission, 2004e, pp. 2–3). In particular, it stressed that political reforms in Turkey must be irreversible, proposed annual reporting, and stated that 'the Commission will recommend the suspension of negotiations in the case of a serious and persistent breach of the principles of liberty, democracy, respect for human rights and fundamental freedoms and the rule of law on which the Union is founded' (Commission, 2004e, p. 6). The European Council accepted this proposal in December 2004. If that were not enough, public and elite opinion on Turkish membership remained deeply divided. By December 2004, Turkey had won the right to start negotiating membership, but its prospects of joining remained uncertain.

References

Commission of the European Communities (2004a) *Communication from the Commission: Opinion on the application of Croatia for membership of the European Union*, Brussels, 20 April 2004, COM(2004) 257 final.

Commission of the European Communities (2004b) *Communication from the Commission to the Council and to the European Parliament: Strategy Paper of the European Commission on progress in the enlargement process*, Brussels, 6 October 2004, COM(2004) 657 final.

Commission of the European Communities (2004c) *2004 Regular Report on Bulgaria's progress towards accession*, Brussels, 6 October 2004, SEC(2004) 1199.

Commission of the European Communities (2004d) *2004 Regular Report on Romania's progress towards accession*, Brussels, 6 October 2004, SEC(2004) 1200.

Commission of the European Communities (2004e) *Communication from the Commission to the Council and to the European Parliament: Recommendation of the European Commission on Turkey's progress towards accession*, Brussels, 6 October 2004, COM(2004) 656 final.

Commission of the European Communities (2005) *Report on the Results of the Negotiations on the Accession of Bulgaria and Romania to the European Union*, DG E1, February 2005.

Council of the European Union (2005) *Presidency Conclusions. Brussels European Council 16/17 December 2004*, CONCL 4, 16238/1/04 REV 1 (Brussels, 1 February 2005).

Justice and Home Affairs

JÖRG MONAR
University of Sussex

Introduction

The end of the transitional period and the deadlines set by the Tampere programme led the Member States to a last-minute rush to agree a number of important measures, especially in the field of asylum policy. In the immigration policy domain, some progress was made on both the external and internal sides. Agreement was reached on the creation of a new electronic data-exchange instrument for visa control, as well as on the establishment of a new border management agency, contributing to the further institutionalization of co-operation. With the creation of a European enforcement order for uncontested claims, an important breakthrough was achieved in the civil law domain. The internal security agenda was largely dominated by the aftermath of the 11 March terrorist attacks in Madrid which led to a new package of anti-terrorism measures. Finally, with the adoption of the 'Hague programme' in November and a major extension of the application of the co-decision procedure in December, the Member States defined important elements of the framework for the future development of the 'area of freedom, security and justice'.

I. Developments in Individual Policy Areas

Asylum

Both the Treaty of Amsterdam and the Tampere programme had provided for Member States to reach agreement on minimum standards on the qualification of third-country nationals as refugees and on minimum standards on procedures for granting or withdrawing refugee status within the transitional period of five years which ended on 30 April. This put considerable pressure on the Council to adopt the so-called 'qualifications' and 'procedures' directives in time for this deadline, and the JHA Council only just managed in a meeting on 29–30 April to achieve a breakthrough on both of these crucial building-blocks for a common EU asylum policy.

As regards qualification for refugee status, the Member States had earlier reached a compromise on the rights to be granted to beneficiaries of refugee status, but there were continuing differences on the minimum level of rights to be granted to the beneficiaries of subsidiary protection status. While in June 2003 a compromise text had found the support of a broad majority, Germany maintained reservations on the recognition of non-state actors of persecution and on the level of rights and benefits accorded to beneficiaries of subsidiary protection, especially in relation to access to the labour market. In the end, Directive 2004/83/EC on minimum standards for the qualification and status of third-country nationals or stateless persons as refugees (the so-called 'qualifications' directive) could be adopted only after Germany finally agreed to remove its reservation on the recognition of non-state actors and other Member States agreed to changes that further lowered the level of minimum rights for beneficiaries of subsidiary protection and allowed a wider margin of discretion to Member States in their recognition of refugee status.

The 'qualifications' directive provides for the minimum harmonization of the qualification elements for the status of refugee as defined – rather vaguely – by the 1951 Geneva Convention. It goes beyond the wording of the convention by recognizing persecution from non-state actors (Article 6) and child-specific and gender-specific forms of persecution (Article 9), by establishing an obligation for Member States to grant subsidiary forms of protection (Article 15) and by providing specifically for the rights and needs of unaccompanied minors (Article 30). Yet, during protracted compromise-building in the Council, some of the substance of the original Commission proposal was considerably watered down. One example is the recognition in Article 9(2)(e) of prosecution for evasion of military service as an act of persecution. While the Commission had proposed a wider definition of conscientious objection based on deeply held moral, religious or political convictions, the directive limits the qualification to cases where persons are required to commit war crimes or other serious crimes as part of their military service. There are also substantial derogation possibilities granted to Member States as regards the rights of beneficiaries of subsidiary protection. It should also be mentioned that Article 14 of the directive allows Member States to deny or revoke refugee status on national security grounds, a ground for exclusion not provided for by the Geneva Convention whose introduction into the directive has clearly been inspired by the perceptions of post-September 11 terrorist threat.

The negotiations on the directive on common minimum standards on procedures for the granting and withdrawing of refugee status were no less difficult. The Member States were in the end able to reach political agreement on 29 April 2004 on the substance of the directive. This defines minimum standards for asylum procedures (access to asylum process, right to interview, access to interpretation and legal assistance, detention, appeals, etc.) and appeals procedures. It also defines the controversial concepts, heavily criticized by the UNHCR and NGOs, of 'safe country of origin' (which allows the consideration of applications of nationals of this country as 'unfounded', and making it subject to an 'accelerated' procedure) and of 'safe third country' (which allows the transfer of responsibility for the processing of an asylum application to countries through which the asylum-seeker has entered the EU). Yet, the draft text was then subject to several national parliamentary scrutiny reservations, and Member States also failed to reach agreement on the common list of 'safe countries of origin' required by the draft directive (Council Document 14203/04). In November, the Council decided to postpone the adoption of the list to 2005, and, by the end of the year, the directive was still not formally adopted, making this a rather blatant case of missing a formal deadline defined in the EC Treaty.

Immigration

In the field of immigration policy, the EU continued to place a major focus on the external side of the management of migratory flows. On 10 March, Parliament and Council adopted Regulation (EC) 491/2004 establishing a programme for financial and technical assistance to third countries in the areas of migration and asylum (*Aeneas*). The programme reflects the growing emphasis placed by the EU on the incorporation of migration-related objectives into EU external relations in general and the programming of aid and development policy instruments in particular. Aeneas allows for the funding of a wide range of measures aimed at reducing immigration pressure on the EU through co-operation with third countries. These measures include: information campaigns in countries of origin on the consequences of illegal immigration, trafficking in human beings and smuggling of migrants, and clandestine employment in the EU; contributions to 'capacity-building' of countries of origin in the areas of asylum and migration legislation; the fight against organized crime and corruption in migration-related areas and external border controls, and support for enhancing the security of travel documents and visas, the observation and analysis of migratory movements for the purposes of identifying their root causes and improvement in reception conditions for asylum-seekers and the durable reintegration of returnees. One of the main purposes of *Aeneas*, which has a budget of €250 million for the period 2004–08, is to support and provide financial incentives for third countries which are actively engaged in preparing or implementing a readmission agreement with the EU. Yet the negotiations of such agreements – which for obvious reasons are less attractive to third countries than the EU – made only slow progress during the year, with only one new agreement – with Macao – being formally concluded in April.

In order to reinforce the monitoring of migratory flows in third countries and co-operation between Member States, the Council adopted on 19 February Regulation No. 377/2004 on the creation of an immigration liaison officers' network. The provisions of this regulation were based on experience already acquired by the Member States in co-operation between immigration liaison officers (ILOs) posted in third countries, such as the Belgian-led ILO network in the Balkans. The regulation defines the tasks of immigration liaison officers abroad in terms of the collection of both operational and strategic information which may be of use in the fight against illegal immigration or the management of legal immigration. It also enables liaison officers to build local or regional co-operation networks with each other with the aim of exchanging information, adopting common approaches to the collecting and reporting of strategically relevant information (including risk assessments) and the drawing-up of bi-annual reports on their activities and the situation in the host country as regards illegal immigration. The ILOs, who are normally posted to national consular authorities, can also share tasks and take care of the interests of other Member States (which may not be represented in the respective host country). The creation of the ILO network can be regarded as a small step towards a common external service arm of the EU's immigration policy.

As regards legal immigration, no progress was made on the crucial directive on the conditions of entry and residence of third-country nationals for the purpose of paid employment and self-employed economic activities (proposed by the Commission in July 2001), as a result of which the Commission decided to draw up a Green Book on managing economic migration where different options for a new proposal for a directive would be outlined for consultation. On 30 March, political agreement was reached in Council on the directive on conditions of admission of third-country nationals for the purposes of study, pupil exchange, unremunerated training or voluntary service (2004/114/EC) which was finally adopted on 13 December after the lifting of parliamentary scrutiny reservations. The directive, whose adoption was made easier by the fact that it has very limited implications for national labour markets, defines minimum admission conditions for third-country nationals falling within the above categories (valid travel documents and sickness insurance, paid fees and parental authorization if applicable, and public security exceptions) and provides for a number of specific framework rules for each of the categories. As regards students from third countries, for instance, the directive makes a contribution to student mobility within the EU by opening up the possibility for continuing or complementing studies already started in one Member State in another Member State (Article 8), and by providing for the entitlement of students to be employed or engage in self-employed activity (Article 17). However, any employment must be outside study time and subject to labour market conditions in the host country. With the implementation of most of the provisions being made dependent on existing national legal provisions, this directive constitutes an other example of 'minimalist' harmonization in the immigration policy domain.

On 19 November, the Council adopted conclusions on the establishment of common principles for immigrant integration policy in the EU (Council Document 14776/04). While these 'conclusions' do not have any legal status, they nevertheless establish for the first time a broad common framework for integration policy. Some of the principles go clearly in the direction of strengthening the status of immigrants in areas where many Member States still pursue rather restrictive approaches. The conclusions recognize, for instance, that employment is a key part of the integration process and central to the participation and social recognition of immigrants in the host societies, and that the participation of immigrants in the democratic process and in the formulation of integration policies and measures, especially at local level, is an important part of integration. The conclusions also reflect the stronger emphasis which some Member States – such as Germany and the United Kingdom – have recently placed on elements of assimilation as part of integration policy. This is particularly obvious in the fourth 'principle' that states that a basic knowledge of the host society's language, history and institutions is indispensable to integration. The absence of any more precise guidelines, or indeed plans, for common framework legislation in this text indicated, however, that the Member States intend to continue to leave this sensitive area largely to domestic policy-making.

Visa Policy

Improving information exchange and security in the issuing and control of visas had been defined as a top priority in the fight against illegal immigration by the Seville European Council in 2002. After considerable preparatory work, also on the technical and data protection issues, the Council adopted, on 8 June, a decision establishing a system for the exchange of visa data between the Member States (VIS) enabling authorized national authorities to enter and update visa data and to consult these data electronically. The architecture of VIS, which is established as part of the Schengen system, has been designed in a way partly similar to that of the Schengen information system. It consists of a 'central visa information system' (CS-VIS), a 'national interface' (NI-VIS) in each Member State, which provides a connection to the relevant central national authority of the respective Member State, and the communication infrastructure between the central visa information system and the national interfaces. Whereas Member States will have to develop and adapt national infrastructures accordingly, responsibility for developing the centralized architecture was given to the Commission. The decision also provides for the development of security requirements, including biometric aspects.

In an earlier text adopted on 19 February (Council Document 6535/04), the Council had defined the basic functionality of the visa information system which is to include both Schengen uniform visas and national visas and to comprise information on visa status (requested, issued, refused, annulled, extended, etc.), personal data allowing for the identification of the visa holder (including digitized or original photographs), grounds for visa refusals, cancellation or extensions and even records of persons issuing invitations and liable to pay board and lodging costs for visa holders. Regarded by the Council as an essential instrument for reducing visa fraud and also an instrument in the fight against terrorism, civil liberty organizations have expressed concern about VIS adding to the storage of personal data, the erosion of privacy and the surveillance of the movements of persons within the EU. According to Commission estimates, the setting-up of VIS, which is expected to become operational in 2007, will cost at least €130 million, meaning another substantial investment in an EU database internal security instrument.

External Border Management

Improving the management of EU external borders remained an issue high on the Council's agenda and, on 26 October, the Member States reached final agreement on Council Regulation (EC) 2007/2004 establishing an agency for the management of operational co-operation at the external borders. The main tasks of the agency are: the co-ordination of operational co-operation of Member States in the field of external border controls; providing assistance to Member States in the training of national border guards (including the establishment of common training standards); carrying out risk analyses; developing research relevant for the control and surveillance of external borders; and providing assistance to Member States in circumstances requiring increased technical and operational assistance at external borders, as well as the necessary support in organizing joint return operations of rejected asylum-seekers and illegal immigrants.

The agency, which was due to come into operation on 1 May 2005 and will be mainly funded from the EC budget, has been vested with quite substantial operational powers which go distinctly beyond those of other agencies in the justice and home affairs domain, such as Europol and Eurojust. According to Article 2 of the regulation, it will not only evaluate but also approve and co-ordinate proposals for joint operations and pilot projects started by Member States. It can also, in agreement with the Member State(s) concerned, launch initiatives for joint operations and pilot projects. In cases in which individual Member States are faced with particular difficulties at external borders requiring increased technical and operational assistance, the agency can organize this assistance by co-ordinating the support provided by other Member States and deploying its own experts (Article 8). It can also decide to put its technical equipment at the disposal of Member States participating in the joint operations or pilot projects.

A particular feature of the agency is that it can, on the basis of a decision of its management board, and subject to the consent of the Member States concerned, decide on the setting up of 'specialized branches' in the Member States which will normally be already established operational and training centres specializing in the different aspects of control and surveillance of the land, air and maritime borders respectively (Article 16). The agency's 'specialized branches' will have the task of developing best practice with regard to the particular types of external borders for which they are responsible, and it will ensure the coherence and uniformity of such best practices. The national 'branches' can also be used by the agency for the practical organization of joint operations and external borders and pilot projects.

Finally, the agency has also been vested with an important monitoring and evaluation function: it has formal responsibility for evaluating the results of the joint operations and pilot projects and making a comprehensive comparative analysis of those results with a view to enhancing the quality, coherence and efficiency of future operations and projects.

Having regard to these substantial functions and powers, it is not surprising that the Member States have made sure that they retain tight control over the agency's activities through its management board which consists of one representative of each Member State (and two representatives from the Commission). The board not only appoints the executive director and decides on the budget, but also holds a number of important decision-making powers, such as on the annual programme of work and establishment of the 'specialized branches' (see above). Well aware that unanimity could mean paralysis for an agency vested with major operational powers, the Member States agreed on most decisions being taken by absolute majority only.

The establishment of the new border management agency must be regarded as an important step towards the more integrated and 'institutionalized' management of external borders. An important element of progress is the solidarity dimension introduced by the possibility of emergency support provided by Article 8 of the regulation (see above), and the 'promotion of solidarity' between the Member States is actually mentioned amongst the reasons for its establishment in Article 1. While the agency clearly does not constitute a 'European border guard' as such, it certainly creates some sort of a co-ordinating command structure and – through the 'specialized branches' – gives the agency a direct reach into national border guard forces that could, at a later stage, considerably facilitate the build-up of European border guard structures. Having regard to its well-known position on maintaining full national control over external borders, it is not surprising that the United Kingdom – and *nolens volens* also Ireland – do not participate in the agency.

Judicial Co-operation

In the domain of civil and commercial law, a significant step forward was taken in the implementation of the principle of mutual recognition, with the adoption by Parliament and Council, on 21 April, of Regulation (EC) 805/2004 creating a European enforcement order for uncontested claims. The regulation applies to all situations in which a creditor, given the verified absence of any dispute by the debtor as to the nature or extent of a pecuniary claim, has obtained in one Member State either a court decision against that debtor or an enforceable document that requires the debtor's express consent, either of which needs to be enforced in another Member State. Of central importance is the abolition of the *exequatur* requirement for such 'uncontested claims' in Article 5, which provides that a judgment which has been certified as a European enforcement order in the Member State of origin shall be recognized and enforced in other Member States without the need for a declaration of enforceability and with no possibility of opposing its recognition. This means that a judgment which has been certified as an European enforcement order by the court of origin is to be treated as if it had been delivered in the Member State in which enforcement is sought. If a number of basic requirements are met, the regulation provides that a judgment on an uncontested claim delivered in a Member State should at any time on application to the court of origin be certified as a European enforcement order, upon which the certificate can be used by the creditor to seek enforcement by the competent authorities of another Member State, the only additional hurdle being that the creditor may have to provide a certified translation of the enforcement order certificate.

This first European enforcement order regulation has some serious limitations. One is the restriction to 'uncontested claims' – as a large number of claims are normally contested – and another the restriction to pecuniary claims which excludes, for instance, claims to property. Nevertheless, it marks an important breakthrough for the free circulation of judgments across the EU which has an 'in principle' importance in the civil and commercial field which may be compared to that of the European arrest warrant in the criminal law field.

The Tampere European Council of 1999 had earlier emphasized the importance of increasing the access to justice of crime victims in cross-border situations. After protracted negotiations, the Member States were able to agree, on 29 April, on Directive 2004/80/EC relating to compensation of crime victims. It sets up a system of co-operation to facilitate access to compensation by victims of violent crime in cross-border situations, which operates on the basis of Member States' schemes on compensation to victims of violent crime, committed in their respective territories. It has a limited harmonization effect as it obliges also those (few) Member States which have not already established such compensation schemes to put them into place.

The directive is of considerable practical importance as crime victims are often not able to obtain compensation from the offender – who may lack the necessary means to satisfy a judgment on damages – or because the offender cannot be identified or prosecuted. The directive establishes the principle that compensation in cross-border situations shall be paid by the competent authority of the Member State on whose territory the crime was committed in accordance with its national compensation regime. The Member States must ensure that where a violent crime has been committed in a Member State other than the EU country where the victim is habitually resident, the victim has the right to submit the application to an authority in the Member State of actual residence. For this purpose, each Member State has to designate one or more national 'assisting authorities' which have to provide crime victims with guidance on how to complete applications for compensation (including supporting documentation), take care of any necessary translation work and transmit the application as soon as possible to the deciding authority in the other Member State. While the directive does not harmonize in any way the compensation levels and does not provide for deadlines for the settlement of compensation claims it, nevertheless, constitutes a step forward for a 'European area of justice' where citizens' rights do not stop at national borders.

In the criminal justice field, some progress was made with the minimum harmonization of substantive criminal law through the adoption on 25 October of framework decision 2004/757/JHA laying down minimum provisions on the constituent elements of criminal acts in the field of drug trafficking. Negotiations on this framework decision had been complicated, *inter alia*, by the efforts of the Dutch government to protect the lawful sale of soft drugs (such as cannabis) in the controlled Dutch 'coffee shops' which were strongly opposed, in particular, by France and Sweden who were advocating tough sanctions even for minor offences. The framework decision provides that offences relating to the production, manufacture, extraction, preparation, sale, distribution, delivery, dispatch, transport, importation or exportation of drugs (including precursors) shall be punishable by criminal penalties of a maximum of at least 1–3 years of imprisonment. If the offence involves large quantities of drugs or if it either involves those drugs which cause the most harm to health, or has resulted in significant damage to the health of a number of persons, the level of criminal penalties is to be raised to a maximum of at least 5–10 years' imprisonment. Yet – as a concession to the Dutch position in particular – the above offences remain excluded from the scope of the framework decision if they are perpetrated for 'personal consumption' only. The definition of 'personal consumption' remains the responsibility of each Member State, an exemption from the scope of the framework decision that has been justified in the preamble by a reference to the principle of subsidiarity – a justification that did little to reduce French and Swedish concerns.

Police Co-operation

The work of Europol, which saw a further growth in its staff numbers because of EU enlargement, was overshadowed by a rather bitter and at times undignified struggle between the Member States over the appointment of its new director. The renewal of the contract of Jürgen Storbeck, who had been in charge of the police organization since its establishment, was opposed by France, while Germany staunchly backed the renewal almost up to the last minute. As a result, Storbeck was finally informed that he had to leave only a few days before the end of his contract – a rather poor reward for years of dedicated work for the institution – and Europol had to be headed by an interim director from July onwards. By the end of the year, the Member States were still at pains in deciding between a French, a Spanish, an Italian and another German candidate, providing just another example of how difficult it is to proceed with senior appointments on the basis of unanimity amongst 25 Member States.

Although the supply of information to Europol by national authorities had improved over the last year, the Dutch Presidency felt it still necessary in September to remind Member States of their obligation to make 'good-quality' information available to the European police organization. It also emphasized that Europol assessments should henceforth focus on expected threats, rather than on descriptions of crime trends in recent years, with Europol threat assessment then forming the basis for the strategic priorities to be set by the Council (Council Document 12687/04).

Inter-agency co-operation was strengthened through the signing on 9 June of a co-operation agreement between Europol and Eurojust aimed at increasing the effectiveness of both institutions in combating serious forms of international crime and to avoid duplication of work. The agreement provides for the exchange of operational, strategic and technical information, as well as the co-ordination of activities and the development of complementary priorities and strategies. Quite innovative is the provision in Article 5 allowing Eurojust to provide Europol with information for the purpose of its analysis work files, or even to present requests to Europol for opening an analysis work file. During the negotiations on the agreement, some members of the Europol management board had expressed some unease about this provision potentially putting Europol in a subordinate position *vis-à-vis* Eurojust. Europol can also supply analytical data and results to Eurojust that may be required for the tasks of Eurojust. According to Article 6, both institutions can also participate in the setting-up of joint investigation teams, and the agreement also provides for the sharing of personal data between Eurojust and Europol. This has given rise to some concern, although the agreement also establishes the right for individuals to have access to data concerning them which are transmitted between the two institutions.

Fight against Terrorism

While the terrorist attacks in Madrid on 11 March sent shock waves across Europe, they were not totally unexpected by anti-terrorist experts in the EU. Especially after the participation of the UK, Spain and several other European countries in the US-led intervention in Iraq, there had been repeated warnings about a heightened risk of large-scale attacks in Europe which, as a result of the war, had potentially come into the firing line of Muslim extremists.

The first problem which the attacks brought to the fore were persisting deficits in the implementation of the September 2001 EU action plan to combat terrorism. The much vaunted European arrest warrant, for instance, had been fully implemented by mid-March by only ten of the (then) 15 Member States. Three Member States had not even yet reported implementation of the crucial framework decision on combating terrorism of June 2002. These and a range of other deficits were clearly identified in a Commission memorandum to the Council on 18 March (Memo/04/63) that was followed by another memorandum (Memo/04/66) proposing tight action on implementation, as well as several new measures. These were discussed at a special meeting of the EU's Justice and Home Affairs Council on 19 March, a meeting which was not without tensions: some ministers had felt misled by the Spanish Aznar government who, in order not to lose the Spanish general elections, had tried almost to the last minute to link the Madrid attacks to ETA terrorists, in spite of mounting evidence of Al-Qaeda involvement. German Minister Otto Schily was particularly outspoken in his criticisms in this respect. The ministers agreed, however, on the need to tackle existing implementation problems and deficits in co-operation between the relevant security services, as well as a number of new measures. On this basis on 22 March the General Affairs Council finalized a draft 'declaration on combating terrorism' which was then formally adopted with few changes by the heads of state and government during the European Council meeting in Brussels on 25 March 2004. The declaration provided for a substantial package of measures which were laid out in detail in a revised version of the EU action plan on combating terrorism adopted by the Council on 15 June 2004 (Council Document 10586/04) and updated on 14 December (Council Document 16090/04). In the end, the total package amounted to over 150 individual measures that will certainly accelerate the 'securitization' of the 'area of freedom, security and justice'.

One of the priorities of the revised action plan was the improved implementation of existing measures. On the legislative side this was still far from satisfactory by the end of the year. While the declaration had set the end of June 2004 as a deadline for the full implementation of key legislative acts of relevance in the fight against terrorism, nine Member States had, by the time of the December update, still not fully implemented the framework decision on combating terrorism. In addition, nine (partly different) EU countries had not implemented the legislation on joint investigation teams and one Member State (Italy) had still parliamentary ratification problems with the European arrest warrant, to give only a few examples (Council Document 16090/04). On the operational side, the picture looked slightly better: Member States, for instance, took the necessary steps to reactivate Europol's counter-terrorism task force (which had become largely obsolete as a result of limited input by the national authorities); a mutual evaluation process was put into place to ensure the supply of counter-terrorism intelligence to Europol and Eurojust; and strategic and ad hoc meetings were organized between anti-terrorist magistrates.

As regards new anti-terrorism measures, the Council adopted, on 29 April, Directive 2004/82/EC on the obligation of carriers to communicate air passenger data (defining a framework for the transmission of data to destination countries after check-in), and negotiations were started on a draft framework decision on the retention of telecommunications data by service providers (such as mobile phone companies) and on the establishment of a European register of convictions and disqualifications. On 13 December, the Council also adopted Regulation EC 2252/2004 on security features and biometrics in passports, providing that newly-issued passports, which must be fully machine-readable, shall include digital facial images (within 18 months) and fingerprints (within three years). The Commission was invited to present proposals on the protection of witnesses in terrorist cases, the facilitation of cross-border hot pursuit, the exchange of personal information (DNA, fingerprints and visas) for the purpose of combating terrorism, the use of passenger data for border and aviation security and for an integrated system for the exchange of information on stolen and lost passports (to be in place by the end of 2005).

In order to arrive at a new quality of intelligence-sharing, Secretary-General/High Representative Javier Solana was asked to integrate within the Council Secretariat an intelligence capacity on all aspects of terrorist threats in Europe. This has been done by adding internal security experts to the external intelligence experts from the Member States working in the Council's 'joint situation centre' (SitCEN). This came about as a compromise between those Member States who had advocated the creation of a new permanent intelligence agency on terrorism and those who had instead favoured the enhanced used of existing informal networks. This move towards the centralization of anti-terrorism intelligence tasks created the problem of a potential overlap with Europol's task in the field.

The most 'visible' innovation brought by the updated anti-terrorism package was the appointment in March of a 'counter-terrorism co-ordinator' in charge of co-ordinating all relevant activities within the Council and monitoring their implementation, this under the authority of the Secretary-General of the Council (Solana). The appointment of the former President of the Liberal Group in the European Parliament and former Dutch junior Minister of Interior Gijs de Vries came as a surprise to some observers as he had no specific credentials in the anti-terrorism field. Yet, de Vries brought with him a reputation as a skilled negotiator able to smooth relations between a variety of actors and putting progress on the substance before personal profile. By the end of the year, it was still unclear to what extent the new co-ordinator would be able to make a real difference, as he was vested with no substantial or even clearly defined powers. Nonetheless, first evidence suggested that de Vries had already assumed an active role in critically assessing national implementation of EU anti-terrorism measures – which is likely to remain a major challenge for the Union.

II. Defining the Framework for Future Development

The Intergovernmental Conference negotiations, which ended in June 2004 with agreement on the EU Constitutional Treaty, resulted in no fundamental changes to the provisions the European Convention had proposed regarding the 'area of freedom, security and justice' (see *Annual Review 2003/04*, pp. 129–32). Nevertheless, some of the few changes were significant enough, and this especially in the domain of judicial co-operation in criminal matters. Mainly in order to accommodate British concerns, the initial remit of the European public prosecutor's office (whose establishment is subject to a unanimous decision of the European Council) was limited to crimes affecting the financial interests of the Union, making an extension of its mandate to all serious crime having cross-border implications dependent on a later unanimous decision by the JHA Council (Article III-274). Also, primarily in response to

British demands, a clause was introduced providing that any minimum rules adopted in the criminal procedure domain shall take into account the differences between the legal traditions and systems of the Member States (Article III-270(2)). Provision was also made for an 'emergency brake' which can be applied to legislation in the fields of procedural and substantive criminal law. This allows a Member State who considers that a draft European framework law in these areas is likely to affect 'fundamental aspects of its criminal justice system' to refer this draft legislative act to the European Council. This has the effect of suspending the normal legislative procedure and giving the European Council a decisive role on the outcome of the legislative process. All these provisions could mean that – if the Constitutional Treaty enters into force – other Member States might well prefer at some stage to use the 'enhanced co-operation' instrument to by-pass the extensive veto possibilities that have thus been maintained in the criminal justice domain.

    With the entry into force of the new Treaty still in the more distant future, if at all, the Union had to address the more immediate question of priorities for the next few years. The end of the transitional five-year period also meant the end of the so-called 'Tampere programme' defined by the European Council in October 1999, although not all of its objectives had been achieved. In its evaluation of the Tampere programme (COM(2004)401) the Commission drew up a broadly positive balance-sheet of what had been achieved. It also highlighted, however, major obstacles to further progress such as the predominance (until then) of unanimity in the Council and serious problems in ensuring the effective implementation of adopted measures by the Member States. The Commission used this occasion also to make a number of detailed proposals for a follow-on programme which, after an extensive consultation exercise and subsequent intense negotiations in the Council, became the basis of the so-called 'Hague programme' (Council Document 16054/04) which the Dutch Presidency successfully steered through to final approval by the European Council on 5 November.

    Being very much a follow-up to the ambitious Tampere programme – which was also in a position to set objectives in areas until then largely untouched by EU measures – the 'Hague programme' could hardly be expected to match its predecessor in terms of originality. Even so, it must be said it has few innovative elements, giving preference to continuity in policy development, placing the main emphasis on completing existing measures and avoiding any potentially controversial issues. Rather significantly, for instance, the establishment of a European public prosecutor's office – which was mentioned as an objective in earlier drafts – was completely removed from the final version of the document. Nevertheless, some deadline-linked commitments were made by the Member States, such as: the development of a common European asylum system with a common asylum procedure and a uniform status for those who are granted asylum or protection by 2010; the establishment of a European return fund by 2007; putting into place the Schengen information system II by 2007; the establishment of a Community border management by 2006; the provision by Europol of regular crime 'threat assessments' from 2006 onwards; the adoption of a framework decision on the European evidence warrant by the end of 2005; and several mutual recognition instruments in the fields of family and succession law, these with the remote deadline of 2011. There are a number of other new elements, such as the creation of common visa application centres and the organization of joint meetings between the chairpersons of the senior Council committees and representatives from the Commission, Europol, Eurojust, the Police Chief's Task Force and the Council's SitCEN, in view of the later setting up of the Committee on Internal Security provided for by Article III-261 of the Constitutional Treaty. Yet the 'Hague programme' is rather vague in its objectives for a number of fields, especially those of legal immigration and criminal justice co-operation.

Of immediate practical consequence for the future development of the 'area of freedom, security and justice' will be a change in the voting rules in the Council provided for by the Hague programme and on which the Member States finally agreed in December 2004. It may be recalled that the Treaty of Amsterdam had brought no immediate breakthrough towards majority voting in the JHA domain, initially maintaining unanimity for the five-year transitional period. The Treaty of Nice had then provided for the use of qualified majority voting in the area of asylum policy – subject to a previous unanimous agreement on 'common rules and basic principles' in this field – from 1 May onwards. This gradual opening towards majority voting was then completed by Decision 2004/927/EC, adopted by the Council on 22 December 2004, to apply the co-decision procedure to all communitarized JHA areas under Title IV TEC, with the exception of measures relating to legal immigration and to family law from 1 January 2005 onwards. As a result, the Council will now decide by qualified majority on asylum, matters of illegal immigration, external border controls and civil law co-operation issues (with the above mentioned exception of family law), and this on the basis of an exclusive right of initiative by the Commission in co-decision with the European Parliament – a major strengthening of both the 'Community method' and parliamentary control in these areas. In the remaining third pillar areas (police and judicial co-operation in criminal matters), however, unanimity will continue to prevail as before.

References

Commission of the European Communities (2004a) 'Communication ... Area of Freedom, Security and Justice: Assessment of the Tampere programme and future orientations'. COM(2004)401.

Council of the European Union (2004a) 'Council Directive 2004/83/EC ... on minimum standards for the qualification and status of third country nationals or stateless persons as refugees or as persons who otherwise need international protection and the content of the protection granted'. OJ L 304, 30 September.

Council of the European Union (2004b) 'Council Regulation (EC) No 377/2004 ... on the creation of an immigration liaison officers network'. OJ L 64, 2 March.

Council of the European Union (2004c) 'Council Directive 2004/114/EC ... on the conditions of admission of third-country nationals for the purposes of studies, pupil exchange, unremunerated training or voluntary service'. OJ L 375, 23 December.

Council of the European Union (2004d) 'Council Decision ... establishing the Visa Information System (VIS)'. OJ L 213, 15 June.

Council of the European Union (2004e) 'Council Regulation (EC) No 2007/2004 ... establishing a European Agency for the Management of Operational Co-operation at the External Borders of the Member States of the European Union'. OJ L 349, 25 November.

Council of the European Union (2004f) 'Council Directive 2004/80/EC ... relating to compensation to crime victims'. L 261, 6 August.

Council of the European Union (2004g) 'Council Framework Decision 2004/757/JHA... laying down minimum provisions on the constituent elements of criminal acts and penalties in the field of illicit drug trafficking'. OJ L 335, 11 November.

Council of the European Union (2004h) 'Council Directive 2004/82/EC ... on the obligation of carriers to communicate passenger data'. OJ L 261, 6 August.

Council of the European Union (2004i) 'Council regulation (EC) No 2252/2004 ... on standards for security features and biometrics in passports and travel documents issued by Member States'. OJ L 385, 29 December.

Council of the European Union (2004j) 'Council Decision 2004/927/EC ... providing for certain areas covered by Title IV of Part Three of the Treaty establishing the European Community to be governed by the procedure laid down in Article 251 of that Treaty '. OJ L 396, 31 December.

European Parliament and Council of the European Union (2004a) 'Directive (EC) 491/2004 ... establishing a programme for financial and technical assistance to third countries in the areas of migration and asylum (AENEAS). OJ L 80, 18 March.

European Parliament and Council of the European Union (2004b) 'Regulation (EC) No 805/2004 of the European Parliament and of the Council of 21 April 2004 creating a European Enforcement Order for uncontested claims'. OJ L 143, 30 April.

Europol (2004a) 'Agreement between Eurojust and Europol'. Available at «http://www.europol.eu.int/legal/agreements/Agreements/17374.pdf».

JCMS 2005 Volume 43. Annual Review pp. 147–62

Developments in the 'Old' Member States*

MICHAEL BRUTER
London School of Economics and Political Science

Introduction

By any account, 2003 was a relatively quiet electoral year for the (then) EU-15. After the electoral shocks of 2002, the future of no large European Union (EU) country's government was to be decided at the polls that year and, in most of the Member States that held a general election, the incumbent government managed to retain at least part of its electoral power.

By contrast, 2004 was expected to be a 'dangerous' year for many European Union leaders, at least in electoral terms. First of all, a new cycle of general or local elections promised to be difficult for some governments in power. At the start of 2004, the incumbent parties were expected to do well in Spain and Greece, even if their electoral support had clearly diminished. Important local elections in France promised a rough ride for the dominant *Union pour la Majorité Présidentielle* (UMP) that was still finding it hard to convince the French electorate after its 2003 Presidential Pyrrhic victory, despite an apparently convalescent opposition. Finally, there were the direct elections to the European Parliament, scheduled for June, that were traditionally conceived as 'second order elections'. These were dreaded by many an unpopular government in Europe, as most of them lived in fear of a mid-term effect which could prove a worrying – if not, in some cases, disastrous – sign of democratic illegitimacy that could impede their action.

---

* This chapter will focus exclusively on the 15 pre-May 2004 'old' Member States. The ten new Member States that joined the Union in May 2004 are covered in a later chapter.

Other important elections in the 'old' Member States included the presidential elections in Austria in April, local elections in the United Kingdom in June, and general elections in Luxembourg, also in June.

I. Elections in the 'Old' Member States

A Greek Half-Surprise?

Throughout Europe, commentators witnessed an amazing achievement in the success of Costas Simitis in improving the state of the Greek economy such that it enabled the country to meet the convergence criteria and join the third stage of economic and monetary union (EMU) so soon after it was launched. However, if Simitis's management of the Greek economy impressed his European neighbours and allowed the Socialist Party, Pasok, to get rid of a long-standing reputation for economic incompetence, the Greek Prime Minister lost popularity in his own country in his second mandate. Greece's economic progress was impressive and the prospect of organizing the Olympic games in the summer of 2004 was a source of national pride, but soon the austere Prime Minister was criticized by his own party. As a result, it was only a 'half-surprise' to see Pasok announce, just a few weeks before the vote, that there was to be a change in the lead candidate for the 2004 election. Simitis quietly stepped down, and Foreign Minister George Papandreou became president of Pasok and lead candidate of a party that, despite its two mandates in power, decided to campaign on the theme of change. The fact that Papandreou was the son of the historical leader of Greece and founder of Pasok, Andreas Papandreou, gave rise to rather diverse domestic reactions. However, despite the party's attempts to modify the direction of the campaign, the left never overcame its handicap in the pre-election poll. On 7 March, Greece, as the first EU country to hold its general election in 2004, returned power to a conservative-led majority. A swing

Table 1: Results of the Greek General Election

	Score	% Change Since 2000	Seats
New Democracy (Conservative)	45.4	+2.7	165
Pasok (Socialist)	40.6	−3.1	117
KKE (Communist)	5.9	+0.4	12
SYN (Extreme left)	3.3	+0.1	6
Laos (Extreme right)	2.2	+2.2	0
Dikki (Left)	1.8	−0.9	0

Source: Bruter and Deloye (2006).

of less than three percentage points for New Democracy was enough for the party and its chief, Konstantinos Karamalis, to confirm that the two main Greek parties were now equally likely to win national elections (see Table 1).

The new government pledged to continue its effort to improve and stabilize the country's economy and to further Greek participation in the process of European integration.

Spain in Mourning

Compared to Greece, Spain was expecting a relatively quiet campaign for its 2004 general election, which was held a week later. As in Greece, however, the party in power, the conservative Partido Popular was to campaign under a new party leader, as the Prime Minister, José Maria Aznar – perhaps surprisingly by the standards of European politics – stuck to his original promise to step down after two consecutive mandates and leave room for a new generation of leaders. This decision, announced at the very beginning of his first mandate, was clearly personal and unprovoked. The conservative government, which had lost some of its popularity over its support for Spanish participation in the war in Iraq, against the wishes of over 80 per cent of the Spanish population, still seemed attractive to voters in part thanks to a good record of economic management.

The continuing row between the Spanish government and most European Union governments over the proposed Constitutional Treaty partly damaged Aznar's reputation as the leader that had helped to make Spain one of the 'major'

Table 2: Results of the Spanish General Election

	Score	% Change Since 2000	Seats
PSOE (Socialist)	42.6	+8.4	164
PP (Conservative)	37.7	−6.8	148
CiU (Catalan)	3.2	−1.0	10
ERC (Catalan left)	2.5	+1.7	8
EAJ/PNV (Basque)	1.6	+0.1	7
IU (Left)	5.1	−0.3	5
CC (Canaries)	0.9	−0.2	3
BNG (Gallician)	0.8	−0.5	2
ChA (Aragon)	0.4	+0.1	1
EA (Basque)	0.3	−0.1	1
Na-Bai (Navarra)	0.2	–	1

Source: Bruter and Deloye (2006).

European nations. Yet, the Spanish public did not seem to mind. In fact, all the opinion polls that were published up to the beginning of March confirmed that a somewhat less electorally popular Partido Popular was expected to retain its parliamentary majority for a third consecutive term, under the new leadership of Mariano Rajoy, a relatively new face in Spanish politics.

However, a dull campaign was to be broken by a most tragic event. On 11 March, three days before the election, a dreadful series of terrorist attacks against the central station of Atocha in Madrid, where workers were arriving in the early morning, caused the deaths of 192 people. Soon after the massacre, the government blamed ETA, the Basque terrorist group despite the unusual and continuous denial by that group. Soon, however, the police started to express serious doubts about this theory and the Interior Minister and Prime Minister alike conceded that the attack had instead been carried out by radical Muslim groups related to the international terrorist organization Al-Qaeda. It is not really in doubt that a significant portion of the Spanish public felt manipulated by the government's early declarations. Moreover, there were claims by several journalists that they had been the victims of direct interference from government officials asking them to publicize the ETA theory when rumours of a more likely radical Muslim attack were already prevalent. This clearly affected the credibility of the Conservatives. All main parties agreed to suspend the electoral campaign between 11 March and an election day marred by sadness. Yet, almost immediately, opinion polls showed a sharp decline in support for the Partido Popular and gains for the Socialist Party, the PSOE, led by José Luis Rodriguez Zapatero. On the day of the election, the victory by the left, with 42.6 per cent of the votes (see Table 2) was hardly celebrated by the winners, but clearly marked an important change in the European political landscape.

The return of a socialist majority in Spain, eight years after Felipe Gonzalez lost power and was accused of corruption and mismanagement, represented the second change of majority in a Member State after just two elections. It was hardly a very reassuring start to the year for the other EU heads of state and government, some of whom faced difficult electoral tests in the following weeks.

The Regional and Local Elections in France: An Impossible Test for Chirac?

If the Spanish change of government came as a surprise to many, the French government did not expect anything good whatsoever to come from regional and local elections in March 2004 that would be regarded by many as a 'midterm' judgement on its performance. After some difficult negotiations, the left (Socialist Party and Greens in most regions, Communist Party in some) fought under joint lists. The centrist UDF, however, chose to present separate lists from the 'Chiraquien' UMP in most regions, except in a few where there was a clear danger of success for the National Front (for example, Provence-Alpes-Côte d'Azur, Alsace and Rhône-Alpes). Most pre-election surveys predicted a relative victory by the left which could, for the first time since the introduction of regional elections in 1982, win a majority in more regions than the right.

Before the vote, the left, which did well in the last regional elections in 1998, controlled the executives of eight of the 22 metropolitan regions of France. It could be threatened in Languedoc-Roussillon, and mostly in Île de France (the Paris region, and the largest in the country), which the UMP hoped to reconquer in order to compensate, with panache, for its expected losses in many other regions. It is unlikely, however, that Prime Minister Jean-Pierre Raffarin or President Jacques Chirac, expected the full extent of the electoral catastrophe the government was about to suffer.

With a new electoral system, the first round was to establish who could run in the final, second ballot. Table 3 shows that the left performed much better than the right in general. Moreover, if the UMP always managed to out-perform its centre-right rival, the UDF, the latter strongly progressed within the right and came only a few votes behind the UMP in many regions, such as Île de France (16.1 per cent), Aquitaine (16.1 per cent). The National Front, traditionally very strong in regional elections, had disappointing results in many regions, including Provence-Alpes-Côte d'Azur, which it hoped to win (22.9 per cent) and Île de France, where Le Pen's daughter, Marine was leading the party's list (12.2 per cent).

Following the election and the very disappointing result for the ruling party, the UMP, talks focused on whether or not President Chirac would replace Prime Minister Jean-Pierre Raffarin, in an attempt to add strength to his majority. While the prospect of resignation originally seemed highly likely to most

Table 3: Results of the French Regional Elections

Party Family	Result 2004	No. of Regions 2004	Evolution No. of Regions 2004/1999
Extreme Left (LCR, Lutte Ouvrière, other)	5.0	0	–
Left (PS, PCF, Greens, other)	40.2	20	+12
Right (UMP, UDF, other)	34.5	2	–12
Extreme Right (FN, other)	16.1	0	–
Other (CPNT, Regionalist, other)	4.2	0	–
Total	100.0	22	

Source: Ministry of Interior (2004).

observers, the French President quickly gave assurances that the Prime Minister would remain in office at least until after the June 2004 direct elections to the European Parliament, and the Prime Minister himself said that he expected still to lead the country in the autumn. This was largely seen as an admission that, whoever was Prime Minister, the President and government alike believed that the right would not do well in the forthcoming European elections. It was also interpreted as evidence of growing tensions between President Chirac and his arch-rival within the UMP, Nicolas Sarkozy.

Presidential Elections in Austria

Since the Conservatives of the ÖVP entered a coalition government with the extreme right FPÖ in 1998, for many Austrians, President Thomas Klestil represented the moral fight against the extreme right. Although a member of the Conservative party, the President never tried to hide his antipathy for the FPÖ or his disapproval of the strategic and moral choices of his own co-party member and Austrian Chancellor, Wolfgang Schüssel. President Klestil openly expressed his rejection of the ideology of the extreme right and obliged the new government of Chancellor Schüssel to sign a document recognizing, for the first time in the country's history, the responsibility of Austria in the Second World War and in the horrors of the Shoah. The Chancellor complied, even though he showed little sympathy for the document and, since that time, Klestil remained one of the symbols of the fight against the extreme right, more widely supported by his international partners and by the social-democrat opposition SPD than by his own party, the ÖVP.

With the second mandate of the President coming to an end, it was difficult to know who would succeed him. In a way, the social democratic candidate, Heinz Fischer, appeared to represent a closer choice to Klestil than the new candidate of the ÖVP, Benita Ferrero-Waldner, the controversial Foreign Minister of the Conservative–extreme-right coalition government. It was she who faced the direct opposition of the rest of the European Union when the EU carried out a partial political boycott of Austria in protest against the presence of the extreme right in the Austrian government.

Ferrero-Waldner entered the competition with some significant advantage. She would be the first woman President of Austria. She represented the 'pride' of Austria when a large part of the country felt unfairly treated by the rest of the European Union. Her party remained the most popular in the country and largely 'won' the 2002 elections, while the simultaneously low score of the FPÖ reinforced the Austrian Chancellor's claim that his strategy had been successful. By contrast the SPD candidate, Heinz Fischer, was a man of relatively low profile. A former professor of political science at Innsbruck University, and a former science minister in the 1990s, he wanted to represent a certain form of political consensus in a society largely divided over the past decade by ideological and political questions.

On 25 April, Heinz Fischer won the election with 52.4 per cent of the vote. Two days before he was due to leave office, President Klestil died, leaving Chancellor Schüssel to ensure functioning in the interim and swear in the new President.

A Difficult Test for Tony Blair

While the entire European Union prepared for a 25-country European Parliament election in June, several Member States were also organizing other national or sub-national elections. In Britain, for example, the European Parliament elections were held at the same time as a number of local elections in England and Wales, and the London mayoral and council elections. In all types of voting, the Prime Minister's Labour Party was expected to suffer significant losses in an atmosphere of public defiance towards the government's policy on Iraq, New Labour's decision to increase university tuition fees, and various other problems. The main opposition party, the Conservatives, were largely expected to profit from Prime Minister Tony Blair's declining popularity and the launch of the Conservative Party's pre-campaign, one year before the expected general election.

The election campaigns reflected the difficulties confronted by a less politically comfortable government. The divided opposition, from the far left to the far right, tried to capitalize on this fragility. The Conservatives, leaders of the British right, tried to end years of unpopularity by, once again, changing party leader. In order to try to refresh their tarnished image as the party of Margaret Thatcher's ultra-conservatism, and to alleviate internal party divisions, a veteran of Conservative politics, Michael Howard, was appointed unopposed as party leader, in the hope that his political maturity would be attractive to British voters. Since his election in autumn 2003, Howard has launched attacks on the Labour government and on Tony Blair personally. The 2004 multiple elections were considered an important test of electoral support for the Conservatives' more aggressive strategy before the next general election, widely expected in 2005, where Blair would seek a historic third consecutive mandate for Labour. The Conservative campaign made extensive use of its traditional euroscepticism to try to persuade a disillusioned electorate. The themes favoured by the Conservatives included opposition to the euro, to the new Constitutional Treaty, and to 'Brussels' and 'federalism' alike.

Nevertheless, as in the past election, the Conservatives were accompanied on the right of the political spectrum by an even more ferociously eurosceptic, populist, and occasionally xenophobic campaign by the United Kingdom Independence Party (UKIP). The party, which advocates British withdrawal from the European Union, enlisted several popular entertainment stars, such as its campaign leader Robert Kilroy-Silk (a former Labour parliamentary candidate and BBC TV presenter who was sacked from the public channel for making comments against Islam) and, in a less prominent way, actress Joan Collins. Further to the extreme right, the xenophobic British National Party (BNP) tried, as usual, to focus its energy on local elections where tradition-ally it had had more success, even though the party also drew up lists for the European Parliament elections.

The third national party, the centrist Liberal Democrats defended its more EU progressive positions in the local elections, and competed in the European elections with a very pro-European agenda by British standards. It hoped to reinforce its positions in cities such as Liverpool, Sheffield, Newcastle and Birmingham, and convince dissatisfied and anti-Iraq war Labour voters to vote Liberal Democrat. The Green Party is traditionally almost absent from the local politics, except in London. Yet, the Greens sought to retain their representa-tives in Strasbourg without realistically being able to achieve the level of their historical success in the 1989 European Parliament elections (14.9 per cent).

As regards the results of the 2004 local elections, they confirmed the worst fears of Labour and the best hopes of the Conservatives. On the whole, Labour remained the main party in those councils up for re-election, and Ken Living-stone, mayor of London, won a second consecutive term in office. However, it was the Conservatives who made the biggest gains (see Table 4). The Liberal Democrats also gained seats and, while they lost two councils, on balance, they won key ones such as Newcastle, and reinforced their position against Labour in Leeds and Hull. John Prescott, the Labour Deputy Prime Minister, admitted that the electorate had given his party 'a kicking'.

Table 4: The 2004 Local Elections in Britain

Party	Seats	Change Seats	Councils	Change Councils
Labour	2250	−479	39	−8
Conservatives	1714	+283	51	+13
Liberal Democrats	1283	+137	9	−2
Plaid Cymru	172	−28	1	−2
Others	625	+13	66	−1

Source: Bruter (2005).
Note: Results are only for the councils at stake in the 2004 elections.

Table 5: General Elections in Luxembourg

Party	Score	Change Since 1999
CSV (Christian Democrat)	36.1	+6.0
LSAP (Socialist)	23.4	–0.1
DP (Liberal)	16.1	–6.0
G (Greens)	11.6	+4.0
ADR (Pensioners' Party)	9.9	–0.6

Source: www.electionworld.org.

General Elections in Luxembourg

Another country of the 'old' Member States to hold national (this time general) elections at the same time as the European Parliament vote was Luxembourg. In this particular case, the right-wing Prime Minister Jean-Claude Juncker hoped to repeat his previous electoral success and obtain a third consecutive term in office. He managed not only to win the election, but also to extend the lead of his Christian Democratic Party (CSV) (see Table 5).

II. European Direct Elections: A Tale of 25 Tests?

Direct elections to the European Parliament are often feared by incumbent governments. The 'second order election' phenomenon does, indeed, suggest that they are likely to be used by voters to express their discontent with the performance of existing national governments, or an occasion to vote for smaller parties that the majority of the electorate would not normally support in a general election, or to abstain altogether. Similarly, the traditional forms of aligned behaviour once expected in 'first order' elections and based on cleavage politics are even less present for European Parliament elections than for general elections in a more electorally volatile contemporary Europe.

The various exit polls conducted after the direct elections proved, once more, that an evolution towards less predictable and more protest-motivated voters could be seen in the context of the 2004 European elections. This, of course, did not mean that no trace of cleavages could be found in the voting patterns of European citizens. For example, social class remained a relatively important predictor of the vote in Germany, Sweden and Spain, while religion continues to play a role in Italy and Northern Ireland. On the other hand, France, the Netherlands and the UK all illustrate the decline of class-based politics. This was seen particularly in Britain, where the working class turned out to be the primary reservoir of UKIP votes, while the middle class was split between Conservative, Labour and the Liberal Democrats and, in smaller numbers, UKIP and the Greens. At the same time, France and Britain are also symptomatic of the new and increasing European dimension of European elections. In both countries, the parties that campaigned on European – rather than national – issues did particularly well. In France, for example, the pro-European UDF and Greens received an electoral 'bonus'. As for the British case, these outcomes illustrate well the specificity of these elections, and even more so when compared to the local elections that were held at the same time (see Table 6).

Indeed, while the local elections turned out to be an impressive success for the Conservatives and, to a lesser extent, for the Liberal Democrats, the European Parliament election could be called a catastrophe for the former, who obtained their worst ever result in a national election. The score of the Conservatives, a very disappointing 26.7 per cent, meant that the party's share of the vote declined by a full 9 percentage points since 1999. This, the Conservatives' worst result ever in a national election is only partly explained by the success of UKIP, which ended up as the third most successful party in this set of elections (with 16.1 per cent). Nevertheless, their poor electoral performance further damaged the Tories' prospect of winning the 2005 general election. UKIP, with a swing of 9.2 points from 1999, confirmed, together with the pro-EU Liberal Democrats, that parties campaigning on European questions enjoyed a clear bonus from voters. At the same time, the Labour Party retained second place in the contest, as in 1999, with 22.6 per cent of the vote. Labour, which lost 5.4 percentage points in five years, could only rejoice at having suffered less of a setback than the Conservatives this time. The 2004 results, however, confirmed the use of the direct elections by voters as a 'second order' vote that allowed them the chance to send a noticeable, yet relatively painless warning to their unpopular incumbent government.

Table 6: The 2004 European Parliament Elections in the UK

Party	% 2004	Change	Seats 2004	Change
Conservative	26.7	–9.0	27	–8
Labour	22.6	–5.4	19	–6
UKIP	16.1	+9.2	12	+10
Liberal Democrat	14.9	+2.3	12	+2
Green	6.3	–	2	–
BNP	4.9	+3.9	0	–
Respect (Centre Left)	1.5	+1.5	0	–
SNP	1.4	–1.3	2	–
Plaid Cymru	1.0	+0.9	1	–

Source: Bruter and Deloye (2006).

As already mentioned, the eurosceptic UKIP obtained an unprecedented high score, which attracted enormous media attention and somehow undermined perceptions of the progress of other parties. In particular, the very pro-European Liberal Democrats saw their score rise by 2.3 points. They kept their 12 representatives in the Parliament with 14.9 per cent of the vote and a much greater swing than in the local and London elections. The Greens remained absolutely stable and gained 6.3 per cent of the votes and two MEPs with, once again, a strong pro-European agenda. In that sense, the pro-Europeans and anti-Europeans alike benefited from the conjuncture of the election and swallowing whole chunks of the Conservative and Labour electorates. Other small parties, such as the BNP, an extreme-right movement, also did particularly well (in the case of the BNP, 4.9 per cent, up 3.9 percentage points from 1999, and their highest score in a national election), except for the Scottish and Welsh nationalist parties (SNP and Plaid Cymru) that declined significantly.

The same pattern was, in different ways, observed throughout the European Union. In many cases, as in the United Kingdom, turnout actually went up rather than down in a way that was completely opposite to what happened in the new Member States (see Figure 1 and Table 7). Figure 1 even indicates that the decline in turnout for European Parliament direct elections has, in fact, been less significant than for national elections over the past 30 years.

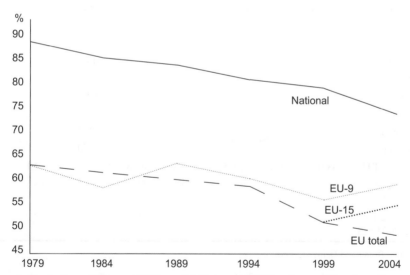

Figure 1: Evolution of Turnout Differential Between EP Election and Previous General Election, 1979–2004

Source: Bruter and Deloye (2006).

Note: EU- 9 represents the evolution of the average turnout in the 9 pre-1981 Member States, EU-15 represents the evolution of the average turnout in the 15 pre-2004 Member States.

Table 7: Turnout in European Parliament Elections: 1979–2004

Member States	1979	1984	1989	1994	1999	2004	Change 1999–2004
Germany	65.7	56.8	62.3	60.0	45.2	43.0	−2.2
France	60.7	56.7	48.7	52.7	46.8	42.8	−4.0
Belgium	91.4	92.2	90.7	90.7	91.0	90.8	−0.2
Italy	84.9	83.4	81.5	74.8	70.8	73.1	+2.3
Luxembourg	88.9	88.8	87.4	88.5	87.3	89.0	+1.7
Netherlands	57.8	50.6	47.2	35.6	30.0	39.3	+9.3
UK	32.2	32.6	36.2	36.4	24.0	38.9	+14.9
Ireland	63.6	47.6	68.3	44.0	50.2	58.8	+8.6
Denmark	47.8	52.4	46.2	52.9	50.5	47.9	−2.6
Greece	–	77.2	79.9	71.2	75.3	63.3	−12.0
Spain	–	–	54.6	59.1	63.0	45.1	−17.9
Portugal	–	–	51.2	35.5	40.0	38.6	−1.4
Sweden	–	–	–	–	38.8	37.8	−1.0
Austria	–	–	–	–	49.4	42.5	−6.9
Finland	–	–	–	–	31.4	39.4	+8.0
Czech Rep.	–	–	–	–	–	28.4	–
Estonia	–	–	–	–	–	26.9	–
Cyprus	–	–	–	–	–	71.2	–
Latvia	–	–	–	–	–	41.4	–
Lithuania	–	–	–	–	–	48.4	–
Hungary	–	–	–	–	–	38.5	–
Malta	–	–	–	–	–	82.4	–
Poland	–	–	–	–	–	20.9	–
Slovenia	–	–	–	–	–	28.3	–
Slovakia	–	–	–	–	–	17.0	–
Average EU	63.0	61.0	58.5	56.8	49.8	45.7	−4.1
Average 9 pre-1981 MS	63.0	59.2	63.2	59.5	55.1	58.2	+3.1
Average 15 pre-2004 MS	63.0	61.0	58.5	56.8	49.8	52.7	+2.9

Source: Bruter and Deloye (2006).

Table 8: Government Parties' Losses in the 2004 EP Elections

Country	Differential EP Election–Last Election	Country	Differential EP Election–Last Election
Estonia	−43.1	Cyprus	−11.0
Poland	−31.7	Denmark	−9.7
Latvia	−29.2	Netherlands	−8.8
Czech Republic	−27.1	Slovenia	−7.7
United Kingdom	−18.4	Belgium	−6.2
France	−17.1	Hungary	−5.6
Ireland	−16.0	Italy	−5.0
Sweden	−15.0	Greece	−2.3
Potugal	−14.9	Finland	−2.1
LithuaniaI	−13.8	Luxembourg	−0.2
Germany	−13.7	Spain	+0.6
Austria	−13.2	Slovakia	+3.9
Malta	−11.8	Average	−12.8

Source: Bruter and Deloye (2006).
Note: Scores are the difference between the total share of the vote of all government parties in the 2004 European Parliament election and the last general elections.

Comparison of Turnout for National and EP Elections for EU, EU-15, EU-9

Table 8 also confirms the global pattern of government losses in the European second order elections. We can see that across EU countries, and with only two exceptions (only one of which concerns the 'old 15' covered in this chapter), national government parties were punished by voters and lost a significant proportion of their vote in the last general election of the country. In countries such as the UK, France, Ireland, Sweden, Portugal, Germany and Austria, these losses exceeded 10 percentage points, and were sufficient to worry the parties in government when it came to assessing their national future.

In terms of voters' motivations, the results available confirm that the de-alignment hypothesis remains more persuasive in explaining voting behaviour in the European elections than cleavage-based models. Voters make up their mind according to their ideology, specific issues such as European integration and government approval, rather than according to their stance on important cleavage dimensions. Partisan identification, on the other hand, continues to decrease and was significant in only a few specific cases, while elsewhere a significant proportion of voters seemed to cast their vote easily in favour of some parties they do not usually support in national elections.

Small party families and the parties on the extremes of the political spectrum did particularly well in the 2004 direct elections. Both the extreme right and the extreme left did well in several countries although, interestingly enough, they rarely did so simultaneously in the same nation. The extreme left did well, for example, in the Czech Republic and Cyprus, while the extreme right performed well in Belgium, the UK and Denmark. Both party families significantly increased their representation in Strasbourg although this was largely due to their results in the new Member States.

As for the moderate parties, the Conservatives overwhelmingly dominated the political scene in the centre of the continent (Germany and Austria, for instance), the socialists and social democrats progressed in Europe's south west (Spain, Portugal, France), while the liberals made strong gains in Italy, Belgium and Finland.

Conclusion

The results of the European Parliament election came as a 'severe weather warning' for almost all governments in the European Union. Perhaps for this reason, many rejoiced over finding agreement on a Constitutional Treaty only a few days after the vote. It was hoped that this would give Member State governments and the European Union a better image among the public. Following the signature of the Constitutional Treaty, countries became divided between those committed to holding a referendum on the new Treaty and those using parliamentary channels only. By the end of 2004, France, the UK, Spain, Denmark, Portugal, Ireland, the Czech Republic, Poland, the Netherlands and Luxembourg looked set to hold a popular vote on the project, while the other Member States would use parliamentary ratification (see Table 9).

It is not completely unimportant to note that the list of referendum countries includes, by and large, many of the most eurosceptic countries in Europe, raising fears of possible rejection in at least one of the ten, despite the overall support of the European population for the new Constitutional Treaty.

Table 10 shows that support for an EU constitution is not only high but has also clearly risen in most Member States when compared to 2003. Of the 15 'old' Member States, only four saw a drop in levels of support between 2003 and 2004 (Sweden, Greece, Denmark and Italy), and four again a drop in the level of net support (the difference between supporters and opponents: Greece, Italy, the UK and Austria). Support for the Constitutional Treaty increased considerably in countries such as Belgium, Germany, Spain and Finland, but remained quite volatile in most of the referendum countries where the 'no' campaigners often proved more dynamic than the supporters of the new Treaty in most Member States. In France, for example, the socialist party had to organize an internal referendum on the question, although the victory of the

Table 9: Mode of Ratification of the EU Constitutional Treaty

Country	Method	Date
Austria	Parliament	Early 2005
Belgium	Parliament	2005
Cyprus	Parliament	March 2005
Czech Republic	Referendum	June 2006
Denmark	Referendum	Autumn 2005
Estonia	Parliament	First half of 2005
Finland	Parliament	Late 2005
France	Referendum	29 May 2005
Germany	Parliament	May-June 2005
Greece	Parliament	Early 2005
Hungary	Parliament	Ratified on 20 December 2004
Ireland	Referendum	Late 2005 or early 2006
Italy	Parliament	Early 2005
Latvia	Parliament	Early 2005
Lithuania	Parliament	Ratified on 11 November 2004
Luxembourg	Referendum	10 July 2005
Malta	Parliament	Mid-2005 or later
Netherlands	Referendum	1 June 2005
Poland	Referendum	Second half of 2005
Portugal	Referendum	April 2005?
Slovakia	Parliament	First half of 2005
Slovenia	Parliament	1 February 2005
Spain	Referendum	20 February 2005
Sweden	Parliament	December 2005
United Kingdom	Referendum	May or June 2006

Source: Bruter and Deloye (2006).

'yes' camp, with 59 per cent of the vote on a turnout of 80 per cent of party members, surprised even the optimists.

After the first European direct elections for the enlarged EU-25 in June 2004, it was, therefore, the Constitutional Treaty that attracted the attention of all the Member States on the eve of 2005. After the parliamentary ratification in Lithuania and Hungary in autumn 2004, Spain was the first country to hold a referendum (and approve) the new EU Treaty on 20 February 2005. If no EU country rejects the Treaty, at least six other countries were expected to vote on the Treaty in 2005, sometimes under conditions of extreme suspense.

Table 10: Support for a European Constitution

Country	In Favour	Change 2004/2003	Net Support (Pro–Against)	Change 2004/2003
Belgium	81	+13	+68	+15
Germany	79	+16	+66	+12
Luxembourg	77	+11	+63	+6
Italy	73	−1	+59	−10
Netherlands	73	+6	+53	+2
Spain	72	+7	+59	+2
France	70	+10	+52	+0
Greece	69	−5	+49	−15
European Union [a]	68	+6	+51	−1
Austria	67	+3	+52	−6
Portugal	61	+6	+50	+4
Ireland	61	+8	+48	+1
Finland	58	+9	+23	+7
Sweden	50	−13	+25	+25
United Kingdom	49	+1	+20	−14
Denmark	44	−2	+8	+5

Source: Eurobarometer.
Note: [a] The figures for the European Union include all 25 Member States in 2004 and only 15 in 2003. They are not, therefore, directly comparable as many of the new Member States have particularly high levels of opposition.

References

Bruter, M. (2005) 'Voting Behaviour in European Capital Regions: The Case of London'. In Vanaclocha, F.J. (ed.) *Voting Behaviour in European Capital Regions* (New York: Dykinson) (forthcoming).

Bruter, M. and Deloye, Y. (eds) (2006) *Encyclopaedia of European Elections* (Basingstoke: Palgrave), forthcoming.

Developments in the New Member States and Applicant Countries

KAREN HENDERSON
University of Leicester

Introduction

On 1 May 2004 ten candidate countries changed their status to that of new Member States. Eight of them – the Czech Republic, Estonia, Hungary, Latvia, Lithuania, Poland, Slovakia and Slovenia – had been communist regimes only 15 years previously. However, although they had mastered rapid and radical transformation in order to consolidate democracy and a 'return to Europe', their domestic political systems still showed signs of instability that distinguished them from the 'old' Member States. Half of them changed Prime Minister during the course of 2004 without having a parliamentary election, and their first European Parliament elections in June demonstrated some marked discontinuities in party systems.

Four candidate states remained after the first wave of eastern enlargement – Bulgaria, Croatia, Romania and Turkey – and Macedonia also applied in March 2004 to join. In these countries, the pressure of the EU accession process on the domestic political scene was more explicit than it had been in the central European states, where the entire economic and political reform project of the early post-communist years had coincided with the drive to join the EU. By 2004, the external rules of the game for aspiring members with democratic weaknesses were well established, and thereby fixed the parameters within which politicians and parties could act at home.

I. European Parliament Elections in the New Member States

Coming the month after accession, the European Parliament elections allowed the citizens of the new Member States their first opportunity to contribute to the EU's decision-making procedures. They also confirmed how the politicians of post-communist states would fit into the EP transnational party groups and, as so often in the old Member States, they gave a useful snapshot of domestic public opinion, which was particularly interesting given the still mobile party systems in central and eastern Europe.

The biggest shock of the EP elections was the low turnout in the new Member States. Even Malta's 82.4 per cent was not as impressive as it seemed, as its national election turnout is usually above 95 per cent, and its EU accession referendum turnout of 90.9 per cent the year before had been considered disappointing. Cyprus's 71.2 per cent was achieved by compulsory voting, and the only other new Member State to achieve a turnout above the EU-25 average of 45.5 per cent – Lithuania, with 48.4 per cent – had held presidential elections on the same day (see below). Slovakia, which the year before had achieved a record high 93.7 per cent 'yes' vote for EU membership in the accession referendum, managed in 2004 to break another record by achieving the all-time low EP election turnout of 17 per cent.

Various reasons were put forward to explain this low turnout. Some emphasize that citizens did not understand the European institutions and lacked sufficient information about the function of the European Parliament. The EU remained to some extent an elite project. Yet the EU had a high profile in the new Member States, since there had been accession referendums in nine of them the year before, and the 1 May accession date had been celebrated with huge firework displays throughout Europe. On the other hand, the EP elections

Table 1: European Parliament Elections, June 2005: Turnout in the New Member States

State	Turnout %
Malta	82.4
Cyprus	71.2
Lithuania	48.4
Latvia	41.3
Hungary	38.5
Czech Republic	28.3
Slovenia	28.3
Estonia	26.8
Poland	20.9
Slovakia	17.0
EU average	45.5

Source: European Parliament «http://www.elections2004.eu.int/ep-election/sites/en/results1306/turnout_ep/index.html».

were certainly 'second order' elections, and largely dominated by domestic political arguments between the competing parties. Where European themes were emphasized, eurosceptic tones crept into the campaign, with parties of many differing political complexions promising to promote their country's national interests in Brussels. Given the subordinate role of the candidate states during the lengthy accession negotiations, and widespread annoyance at the continuing restrictions on the free movement of labour, finally having equal decision-making rights with other Member States gave the notion of pursuing national interests a certain popular appeal. In February 2004, the Hungarian Prime Minister Péter Medgyessy even went as far as suggesting that all parties should join forces and nominate a single list of Hungarian MEP candidates, thereby indicating that it was not just the voting public that was hazy about the EP's purpose. What 'national interests' were was rarely clear, and the fact that domestic political competition frequently involved radically different opinions on the subject was overlooked. However, at the same time as promising to defend their countries in the EP, candidates also boasted of their experience in European affairs and, where appropriate, emphasized their membership in the large transnational political groups in the EP.

The low turnout may also have been a true reflection of the fact that the outcome of the European Parliament elections did not, objectively, matter very much to citizens. They had taken the key decision on EU membership in the previous year's referendums, and over the past decade and a half they had experienced a plethora of other elections that had been crucial turning points in the democratic and economic development of their countries, as well as influencing their chances of EU membership. Politicians and parties had not emerged from this experience with a very high status, and disillusionment with politics in general was widespread. In addition, the new Member States were mostly small countries where the national parliament and government were not geographically very distant, and the number of MEPs they were electing to the distant European Parliament was small – sometimes less than 1 per cent of the total of 732 MEPs. Their countries had a proportionally stronger voice in intergovernmental decision-making. And yet even Poland, with 54 MEPs, managed a turnout of only 20.9 per cent – the second lowest in the entire EU.

Despite the low turnouts, and the accompanying danger that the elections failed to reflect accurately the balance of domestic political forces in the states concerned, the distribution of party preferences in the new Member States is interesting. The presence of observers from the accession states in the European Parliament during the previous year had given a clear indication of the groups that the MEPs from most new Member States parties would join, and it was expected both that the right-of-centre European People's Party-European Democrats (EPP-ED) would be – at least numerically – the main beneficiary of enlargement, and that the EPP-ED and Party of European Socialists (PES) would gain proportionally more members than the smaller groups.

These predictions proved partly justified, and reflected domestic developments in the new Member States. To be centre-right was more fashionable than socialism or social democracy in post-communist states, and most of the new Member States contributed MEPs of more than one party to the EPP-ED, so that it obtained a quarter of the new MEPs although they comprised only 22.1 per cent of the total. Half the new Member States chose at least half their MEPs from parties linked to EPP-ED and, in the case of Slovakia, not only did the eight of 14 MEPs who came from the governing parties join the EPP-ED, but another three, from Vladimír Mečiar's Movement for a Democratic Slovakia, aspired to EPP-ED membership, and became Independents in the EP purely because the party's past made it unacceptable to the mainstream centre-right.

The only possible disadvantage of this expansion for the EPP-ED was the increase in its heterogeneity. The largest of the three Czech parties that became members, the Civic Democratic Party (ODS) formerly led by the current Czech President Václav Klaus, joined the British Conservatives and Unionists in the smaller European Democrats part of the group, where they remained free to express their hostility to the EU Constitutional Treaty. Even some new

Table 2: Political Groups of New Member States MEPs, July 2004

State	EPP-ED	PES	ALDE EFA	Greens/ NGL	EUL/ DEM	IND/	UEN	NA	Total
Poland	19	10	4	0	0	10	7	4	54
Czech Rep.	14	2	0	0	6	1	0	1	24
Hungary	13	9	2	0	0	0	0	0	24
Slovakia	8	3	0	0	0	0	0	3	14
Lithuania	2	2	7	0	0	0	2	0	13
Latvia	3	0	1	1	0	0	4	0	9
Cyprus	3	0	1	0	2	0	0	0	6
Estonia	1	3	2	0	0	0	0	0	6
Slovenia	4	1	2	0	0	0	0	0	7
Malta	2	3	0	0	0	0	0	0	5
% MEPs of new MSs	25.0	15.5	21.6	2.4	19.5	29.7	48.1	34.5	22.1

Source: Calculated from data of European Parliament, «http://www.elections2004.eu.int/ep-election/sites/en/results1306/parties.html».

Notes: EPP-ED = European People's Party-European Democrats; PES = Party of European Socialists; ALDE = Alliance of Liberals and Democrats for Europe; Greens/EFA = Greens/European Free Alliance; EUL/NGL = European United Left/Nordic Green Left; IND/DEM = Independence/Democracy; UEN = Union for Europe of the Nations; NA= Non-attached.

members who shared the EPP's Christian Democratic orientation, such as the ruling Christian Democratic Movement (KDH) from Slovakia, held eurosceptic views that were alien to MEPs from founding Member States.

The PES did less well, in part because the timing of the EP elections was particularly disadvantageous in terms of domestic electoral cycles. Incumbency was an especial handicap in the post-communist world, where fretful voters rarely re-elected a government, and had been known to catapult the leader of a new party straight into the premiership as soon as it entered parliament. In 2004, the three largest new Member States, who had nearly twice as many MEPs as the other seven together, all had Social Democratic governments suffering from mid-term unpopularity.

This was not so serious in Hungary, where the Hungarian Socialist Party at least remained clearly one of the country's two major parties, gaining more than one-third of the vote and EP mandates. When Prime Minister Medgyessy subsequently resigned in August, it was because of pressure within his own coalition relating to a plethora of domestic political issues rather than the party's EP election performance. In Poland, however, both the popularity of the main government party, the post-communist Democratic Left Alliance, and of Prime Minister Leszek Miller, had slumped to the point where Miller announced in March 2004 that he would resign the day after Poland joined the EU, and a new party, Polish Social Democracy, was formed from breakaway parliamentary deputies. The Democratic Left Alliance garnered less than 10 per cent of the EP election vote, compared to more than 40 per cent in the 2001 parliamentary election, and gained only five EP mandates from Poland's 54. The breakaway formation, Polish Social Democracy, established itself electorally by gaining 5 per cent of the vote, and contributed a further three MEPs to the PES.

The EP elections were also a disaster for the ruling Czech Social Democrats, who – unlike their Hungarian and Polish counterparts – were not a post-communist party. Their vote sunk from 30 per cent in the 2002 parliamentary election to below 9 per cent, giving them (and the PES) just two of the 24 Czech EP seats. This was the strongest factor leading to the resignation of the Social Democrat Prime Minister, Vladimír Špidla, and his replacement by the Social Democrats' deputy Prime Minister, Stanislav Gross.

Compared to the PES, the Alliance of Liberals and Democrats for Europe (ALDE) did better from the addition of new Member States, who returned Liberal MEPs in approximately the same proportion as old Member States. The Greens were the real losers of enlargement, obtaining only a single MEP from a new Member State, Latvia, where there had been a Green Prime Minister at the beginning of 2004 (one of three Latvian Prime Ministers in the course of the year). The far left European United Left-Nordic Green Left EP group, which had been inherently unlikely to gain from enlargement because of the widespread aversion to communism in most of the new Member States, fared proportionally much better. This was largely because it was a beneficiary of the Social Democrats' misfortune in the Czech Republic: the unreformed Communist Party of Bohemia and Moravia, which had been a significant un-coalitionable presence in all Czech parliaments since the fall of communism, gained over 20 per cent of the vote in a nationwide Czech election for the first time in the EP election, and returned six MEPs – one-quarter of the entire Czech contingent.

The most marked presence of MEPs from new Member States was to be found, however, among the more eurosceptic EP groups: the Union for Europe of the Nations (UEN), the openly anti-EU Independence/Democracy group, and the 'Non-Attached' MEPs. This was partly due to the strength of eurosceptic parties in the only large new Member State, Poland, where three parliamentary parties – the League of Polish Families (LPR), Law and Justice (PiS) and Self-Defence (SO) – returned MEPs who joined Independence/Democracy, the UEN and the Non-Attached respectively. However, the Czech Republic, Latvia, Lithuania and Slovakia also contributed to the pool of MEPs who did not belong to an established programmatic group. Such MEPs should not be seen merely as evidence of growing hostility to the EU in the new Member States now that accession has taken place and the public is free to express their views without fear of exclusion from 'Europe'. They also reflect a more general protest vote, and an unconsolidated party landscape that allows new parties and politicians to penetrate the political scene. In the Czech Republic, nearly 20 per cent of the vote went to 'independent' associations (although one was pro-EU and its MEPs joined the EPP-ED). Additionally, those politicians in small post-communist states who are not adept at the complex political game of compromise and consensus-building fit more easily into smaller groups where idiosyncratic stances (often hidden behind a rhetoric of 'sovereignty') are less problematic.

However, the instability of post-communist party systems should not be overemphasized. Some states, such as Estonia, Hungary and Slovakia, returned only established parliamentary parties to the EP, and avoided the election of any extremists on the right and left. Furthermore, the fact that domestic politics predominated in the EP election campaign and the voters used the EP elections to register a protest vote against incumbent governments, rather than primarily to express views on the EU, indicates convergence with electoral behaviour in the 'old' EU.

II. National Elections in the New Member States

Only two of the smaller new Member States – Slovenia and Lithuania – held national parliamentary elections during 2004, and only the Slovenian parliamentary elections led to clear alternation of government and a change of Prime Minister. Most of the rearrangement of governments that took place during the year was due to Prime Ministers falling, once in the Czech Republic, Hungary and Poland (see above), and twice in the case of Latvia, where the party composition of the government also changed. In addition, both Slovakia and Lithuania held direct elections to the Presidency. Such elections give an interesting insight into public opinion and party constellations, even though in both cases the Presidency is largely a ceremonial office. In the post-communist world popular election of the President is not necessarily linked with enhanced executive powers.

Slovakia

Slovaks had begun to elect their President directly only in 1999, following more than a year without a President after a deeply polarized parliament proved incapable of garnering the 60 per cent majority necessary to choose a successor to the republic's first President at the end of his term in office. The opposition parties had supported the introduction of direct presidential elections to break this gridlock and, when they gained power in the 1998 elections, they felt obliged to keep their promise to change the constitution and give the power to the people, notwithstanding the fact that they now had more than 60 per cent of parliamentary deputies and could have chosen a President straightaway by the existing method. Ironically, in the April 2004 presidential elections, it was

Table 3: Slovak Presidential Elections, 3 and 17 April 2004

Candidate	Party	% of Vote (First Round)	% of Vote (Second Round)
Ivan Gašparovič	Movement for Democracy (HZD)	22.3	59.9
Vladimír Mečiar	Movement for a Democratic Slovakia (HZDS)	32.7	40.1
Eduard Kukan	Slovak Democratic and Christian Union (SDKÚ)	22.1	–
Rudolf Schuster		7.4	–
František Mikloško	Christian Democratic Movement (KDH)	6.5	–
Martin Bútora		6.5	–
Others (5)		2.3	–

Source: Statistical Office of the Slovak Republic, «www.statistics.sk/prezident2004».

precisely those parties that had pushed so strongly for direct election who suffered from its unpredictable effects.

The expected outcome was an easy victory for Foreign Minister Eduard Kukan, who had guided the country to EU and Nato membership and who represented the largest of the four parties in the ruling centre-right coalition. It was also predicted that his opponent in the second round run-off would be former Prime Minister Vladimír Mečiar, who had presided over Slovakia's exclusion by the EU and Nato in 1997, and led the more nationalist opposition party in parliament, the Movement for a Democratic Slovakia (HZDS). While Mečiar had very solid core support from about a quarter of the electorate, he was loathed by too many of the rest ever to obtain more than 50 per cent in a run-off (one reason why his party had always opposed direct presidential elections). In the event, however, direct election of the President depolarized political competition and the eventual victor, Ivan Gašparovič, was the choice of the political middle ground, despite the fact that he was a former ally of Mečiar.

The explanation for Kukan's unexpectedly coming third in the first round was twofold. Firstly, the four-party governing coalition, and Prime Minister Dzurinda who, like Kukan, belonged to the Slovak Christian Democratic Union (SDKÚ), made a fundamental mistake in failing to agree a single candidate. One of SDKÚ's coalition partners backed Kukan, the other two supported the Christian Democrat candidate, while part of the liberal electorate opted for an independent candidate. SDKÚ was also affected adversely by several short-term events before the elections. Secondly, Gašparovič was fortunate in gaining the endorsement of Robert Fico, whose centre-left Smer party was the other large opposition party in parliament apart from HZDS.

Slovak government supporters therefore ended up with an uncomfortable choice in the second round, forced either to choose one of two men closely associated with the negative political developments in the mid-1990s, or to abstain. In the end, the strength of anti-Mečiar sentiment prevailed, and Gašparovič more than doubled his vote on a lower turnout to win an easy victory. Despite the reservations many Slovaks had about their new President, he had the unusual advantage of being genuinely independent from the three largest parties in the country.

Lithuania

2004 was a difficult year in Lithuania, since the early months were occupied with the impeachment of President Rolandas Paksas. The Seimas (parliament) voted in February to recommend his impeachment, and at the end of March the Constitutional Court ruled that he had breached the constitution and his oath of office on three of six counts raised against him. These related largely to his links to a Russian businessman. The Seimas finally voted for his removal on these grounds by an overwhelming majority on 6 April. New presidential elections were called, with the first round scheduled for 13 June, to coincide with the European Parliament elections. The parliamentary election was called for 19 September (although it was later delayed by three weeks until 10 October).

The Paksas affair continued to sow confusion because his Liberal Democratic Party nominated him for the repeat presidential elections, and the Central Electoral Commission was unsure whether he was excluded on the grounds of his impeachment. The matter was finely settled in May by a parliamentary amendment to the electoral law that disqualified impeached presidents from standing again, and by a Constitutional Court ruling to the same effect.

The presidential election was won in the second round by Valdus Adamkus, a 77-year old who had already served one term in office before being defeated by Paksas in January 2003. He defeated the first Prime Minister of independent Lithuania, Kazimiera Prunskiene, in a second round run-off. Adamkus, technically an independent, had lived in the US until 1997, was pro-western and had centre-right support, and also gained centre-left support from the defeated candidates of the governing coalition in the second round. This was more acerbic and polarized than the first round, and attracted a slightly higher turnout (52.5 per cent as opposed to 48.4 per cent), with the excluded Paksas's supporters rallying behind Prunskiene. The second round result was close, and might have swung in Prunskiene's favour had she gained clear support from the most successful party in the EP elections, the new Labour Party that had been formed by Viktor Uspaskich, a businessman of Russian origin, in 2003.

The Labour Party's success was repeated in the parliamentary election in October, when it fell just short of the 30 per cent of the vote obtained in the EP elections. The governing Lithuanian Social Democratic Party and New Union-

Table 4: Lithuanian Presidential Elections, 13 and 27 June 2004

Candidate	Party	% of Vote (First Round)	% of Vote (Second Round)
Valdus Adamkus	Independent	31.1	52.6
Kazimiera Prunskiene	Farmers and New Democracy Union (VNDPS)	21.3	47.4
Petras Austrevicius	Independent	19.3	–
Vilija Blinkeviciute	New Union-Social Liberals (NS-SL)	16.4	–
Ceslovas Jursenas	Lithuanian Social Democratic Party (LSDP)	11.9	–

Source: Keesing's Record of World Events, June 2004, p. 46075.

Table 5: Lithuanian Parliamentary Election, 10 and 24 October 2004

Party	First Round % of Vote	Party Lists Seats	Total Seats
Labour Party (DP)	28.4	22	39
'Working for Lithuania' (UDL)	20.6	16	
Lithuanian Social Democratic Party (LSDP)			20
New Union-Social Liberals (NS-SL)			11
Homeland Union (TS)	14.8	11	25
Liberal and Centre Union (LCS)	9.2	7	18
Liberal Democratic Party (LDP)	11.4	9	10
Farmers and New Democracy Party Union (VNDPS)	6.6	5	10
Independents			6
Lithuanian Poles' Electoral Action (LLRA)	3.8	0	2
Others	5.2	0	0

Sources: Central Electoral Committee of the Republic of Lithuania, «http://www.vrk.lt/rinkimai/2004/seimas/rezultatai/rez_e_20.htm»; «http://www.vrk.lt/rinkimai/2004/seimas/rezultatai/rez_pgl_part_e_20.htm».

Social Liberals stood together for the list vote, and lost heavily compared to their performance in October 2000, when they had gained a parliamentary majority. However, Prime Minister Algirdas Brazauskas of the Lithuanian Social Democratic Party managed to remain in power by forming a coalition with the Labour Party, whose leader Uspaskich took the economics portfolio, and with the Farmers and New Democracy Union.

Slovenia

Slovenia's first parliamentary elections after joining the EU produced an unexpected and significant result which led to a clear alternation of government. Liberal Democracy of Slovenia (LDS), whose leader Anton Rop had replaced long-standing Prime Minister Janez Drnovšek when the latter was elected President at the end of 2002, was finally ousted from power, and the centre-left government was replaced by one that was clearly right of centre.

There had been indications throughout the year that the governing parties might do badly in the elections. In April 2004, 95 per cent of voters participating in a referendum had rejected a government-backed bill restoring residence rights to 'erased persons' – non-Slovenes who had been erased from official records in 1992 for failing to apply for Slovenian citizenship or permanent residence by the required date. The result of the referendum was not binding, and the turnout was only 31.5 per cent, partly because leading political figures such as the Prime Minister, President and former President had called on citizens

Table 6: Slovenian Parliament Elections, 3 October 2004

Party	% of Votes	Seats
Slovenian Democratic Party (SDS)	29.1	29
Liberal Democracy of Slovenia (LDS)	22.8	23
United List of Social Democrats (ZLSD)	10.2	10
New Slovenia – Christian People's Party (NSi)	9.0	9
Slovene People's Party (SLS)	6.8	7
Slovenian National Party (SNS)	6.3	6
Democratic Party of Pensioners of Slovenia (DeSUS)	4.0	4
Others	11.7	0
National communities (Hungarian and Italian)	2	

Sources: Keesing's Record of World Events, October 2004, p. 46268; National Electoral Commission/ Government Centre for Informatics,«http://volitve.gov.si/dz2004/en/html/rez_si.htm».

to abstain. Nevertheless, the entire affair bolstered the standing and nationalist credentials of the opposition parties, and also contributed to the departure of the small Slovene People's Party from the government.

LDS also fared badly in the European Parliament elections, where the New Slovenia party, with 23.6 per cent of the vote, did better than LDS and the Democratic Party of Pensioners of Slovenia (DeSUS) who, together, obtained 21.9 per cent, while the rightist Slovenian Democratic Party (SDS) gained 17.6 per cent. However, in the parliamentary election it was SDS which topped the poll with 29.1 per cent, thereby nearly doubling its vote in the previous parliamentary election in 2000. It was clear that the SDS leader Janez Janša would become Prime Minister, but the composition of the government initially remained uncertain since the SDS, together with New Slovenia and the Slovene People's Party, only just held half the parliament's 90 seats and really required a fourth coalition member. The Slovene National Party was a possible candidate, but one likely to cause concern abroad. Eventually, it was the pensioners' party DeSUS who became the fourth party in the government approved by parliament in December 2004.

Although Slovenia had some long-standing border disputes with Croatia, and Prime Minister Rop had even indicated that Slovenia, now in the EU, might obstruct Croatia's application to join, the advent of a more right-wing government did not exacerbate Slovenia's relations with its neighbour, and Janša's government has continued to support Croatia's EU membership bid.

III. Developments in the Applicant Countries

By the end of 2004, there were five remaining applicant states seeking EU membership. These fell into four separate categories, indicating that further eastward enlargement is likely to be a rolling affair and another 'big bang' enlargement is unlikely. Domestic political stability was important for all five states in pursuing their integration ambitions. Bulgaria and Romania, who completed negotiations in December 2004 and were scheduled to join on 1 January 2007, needed to continue implementing reforms in order to achieve membership by that date, and were subject to continuing annual progress reports prior to accession. Croatia, which was due to start negotiations on 17 March 2005, was required to demonstrate full co-operation with the International Criminal Tribunal for the Former Yugoslavia, and the seriousness of this international pressure was made clear when the March date eventually had to be moved back because of Croatia's failure to apprehend indicted war crimes suspect Ante Gotovina. Turkey's date for the start of accession negotiations was set as 3 October 2005, with caveats relating to the implementation of recently adopted legislation relating to human rights, and its recognition of the EU Member State the Republic of Cyprus. Macedonia, which applied to join in March 2004 but was still awaiting an opinion from the European Commission and the formal status of a candidate state, continued to be taxed by problems of co-operation between the ethnic Macedonians and Albanians among its citizenry. Finally, in a category of its own was the Turkish Republic of Northern Cyprus, whose chances of joining the EU depended on agreement with its Greek Cypriot neighbours.

Against this background, parliamentary elections, presidential elections and referendums in the applicant states had acute importance, and the EU dimension was rarely far from the concerns of political elites.

Northern Cyprus

Whether or not Turkish Cypriots would join the EU on 1 May 2004 was finally decided only on 24 April, when a referendum was held throughout Cyprus on a United Nations plan for reunifying the island that had been accepted by the Presidents of both the Republic of Cyprus and the Turkish Republic of Northern Cyprus in February 2004. Turnout was high in both parts of the island, at 87 per cent in the Turkish north and 89 per cent in the Greek south. However, the results differed widely, with 64.9 per cent in favour in the north and 77.8 per cent against in the south. The Greek Cypriot government was generally blamed for the rejection, since President Papadopoulos had eventually urged the electorate to vote against the plan. As the Turkish Cypriots were not responsible for the referendum's negative result and their consequent exclusion from the

EU, they were rewarded by the EU's lifting of the economic embargo on the north that had led to it being accessible only from Turkey.

Given the north's uncertain European future, domestic political developments were particularly important. The results of the December 2003 parliamentary elections had been indecisive, and new elections held on 20 February 2005 showed a shift in support towards the pro-reunification Republican Turkish Party. Presidential elections on 17 April 2005, when the Prime Minister, Mehmet Ali Talat, would attempt to replace long-standing President Rauf Denktash, were likely to prove even more crucial for the future of Cyprus.

Macedonia

Macedonia's attempts to join the EU had the most inauspicious start possible. In February 2004 President Boris Trajkovski was killed in a plane crash in Bosnia-Herzegovina on the very day when Prime Minister Branko Crvenkovski was due to submit Macedonia's application for EU membership to the Irish Presidency. Crvenkovski immediately returned home, and the application was submitted a month later. Presidential elections to choose a replacement for Trajkovski were held in April.

The presidential elections proved controversial. There was, predictably, no first-round winner since the election law required a victor to obtain the endorsement of at least 50 per cent of all registered voters. In the second round run-off between the two leading candidates, only 50 per cent support from the voters who actually took part was required, providing there was a 50 per cent turnout. This meant that the candidate best able to gain the vote of the

Table 7: Macedonian Presidential Election, 14 and 28 April 2004

Candidate	Party	% of Vote (First Round)	% of Vote (Second Round)
Branko Crvenkovski	Social Democratic Alliance of Macedonia (SDSM)	42.5	62.6
Sashko Kedev	Internal Macedonian Revolutionary Organisation– Democratic Party for Macedonian National Unity (VMRO-DPMNE)	34.1	37.4
Gëzim Ostreni	Democratic Union for Integration (BDI)	14.8	–
Zudi Xhelili	Democratic Party of Albanians (PDSh)	8.6	–

Sources: Keesing's Record of World Events, April 2004, p. 45794; Macedonian Information Agency, «http://www.mia.com.mk/IzboriPI2004/en/index.asp; OSCE/ODIHR»; «http://unpan1.un.org/intradoc/groups/public/documents/UNTC/UNPAN018344.pdf».

country's 23 per cent Albanian minority was most likely to win the election. The defeated candidate, Sashko Kedev of the opposition VMRO-DPMNE (from which Trajkovski had originally come), alleged widespread fraud, and the OSCE's report commented on ballot box stuffing and other irregularities. The results from five polling stations were annulled by the Supreme Court but, given Crvenskovski's convincing margin over Kedev, it is unlikely that electoral irregularities affected the election result.

Since the winning candidate was the sitting Prime Minister, the government required a new leader, and interior minister Hari Kostov was approved by the parliament at the beginning of June. In November, his government had to face a referendum challenging its reforms of the country's territorial districts, and although the referendum failed through low turnout, Kostov resigned in response to disagreements with his party's Albanian coalition partner, the Albanian Union for Integration (BDI), whom he accused of corruption. He was replaced in December by Vlado Buckovski, also from the Social Democratic Alliance of Macedonia.

Romania

In November 2004 Romania embarked on presidential and parliamentary elections for the second time since EU accession negotiations had begun. It was the last time that the two elections would be held simultaneously, since a constitutional amendment in 2003 had extended the President's term of office – previously four years, like that of the parliament – to five years. Romania is one of the more semi-presidential post-communist political systems, and the President is not only directly elected but also has a measure of power and influence. This is partly due to the fact the post was won by Ion Iliescu, the dominant political figure in post-communist Romania, in three of the four elections held since the overthrow of Ceauşescu's communist regime in 1989. Consequently, when in future the two elections are held at different times, Romania is far more likely to experience 'cohabitation', where the President and the Prime Minister, who needs a parliamentary majority, come from different parties. In the event, this situation nearly arose at the end of 2004, thereby presenting an interesting test for Romanian democracy.

For the previous four years, President Iliescu's Social Democrats had ruled under Prime Minister Adrian Năstase with a minority government assisted heavily by votes from the Hungarian Democratic Union of Romania (UDMR) and other ethnic minority deputies. For the 2004 elections, the Social Democratic Party (PSD) ran together with the small Humanist Party of Romania (PUR) and marginally increased the vote of around 37 per cent that it had obtained in the elections to both chambers of parliament in the 2000 elections. However, the National Liberal Party (PNL) and the Democrat Party (PD), who stood together as the Justice and Truth Alliance, took votes from both the nationalist Greater Romania Party (PRM) and a number of smaller parties. They thereby markedly improved on their 2000 performance when the electorate had ousted them from power after four years of less than impressive domestic performance in government, where progress towards European integration had been one of their few achievements.

Since the Social Democrats were the largest single party in both chambers of parliament, they began coalition negotiations, hoping that the Hungarian UDMR would join them in government. These calculations were upset by the second round run-off of the presidential elections held in mid-December, where Traian Băsescu, the current Mayor of Bucharest who was standing for the Justice and Truth Alliance, faced Prime Minister Adrian Năstase for the Social Democrats. The opposition had asked the Constitutional Court to annul the results of both the parliamentary and first round presidential elections on the grounds of widespread fraud, but the court refused, arguing in the case of the presidential ballot that fraud had not been sufficiently widespread to affect which two candidates progressed into the run-off. When the second round took place, Băsescu came from behind and narrowly defeated Năstase. This was particularly surprising because it had been assumed that the PRM voters of the third-placed candidate Corneliu Vadim Tudor would opt for the Social Democrats. In fact, after Băsescu performed impressively in a live television debate with Năstase, more of them voted with the opposition. Opportunities for electoral fraud were also lessened in the second round due to the considerable publicity given to the issue after the first round of voting.

Table 8: Romanian Parliamentary Election, 29 November 2004

| Party | Chamber of Deputies | | Senate | |
	% of Votes	Seats	% of Votes	Seats
National Union	36.8		37.2	
Social Democratic Party (PSD)		113		46
Humanist Party of Romania (PUR)		19		11
Justice and Truth Alliance	31.5		31.8	
National Liberal Party (PNL)		64		28
Democratic Party (PD)		48		21
Greater Romania Party (PRM)	13.0	48	13.6	21
Hungarian Democratic Union of Romania (UDMR)	6.2	22	6.2	10
National minority lists	2.9	18	0.2	0
Others	9.6	0	11.0	0

Source: OSCE/ODIHR, «http://www.osce.org/documents/odihr/2005/02/4281_en.pdf».

Table 9: Romanian Presidential Elections, 29 November and 13 December 2004

Candidate	Party	% of Vote (First Round)	% of Vote (Second Round)
Traian Băsescu	Justice and Truth Alliance (PNL and PD)	33.9	51.2
Adrian Năstase	National Union (PSD and PUR)	40.9	48.8
Corneliu Vadim Tudor	Greater Romania Party (PRM)	12.6	–
Markó Béla	Hungarian Democratic Union of Romania (UDMR)	5.1	–
Others (8)		7.5	–

Source: OSCE/ODIHR, «http://www.osce.org/documents/odihr/2005/02/4281_en.pdf».

The cohabitation scenario therefore appeared likely. However, Băsescu, who came from the Democratic Party, had made it clear that he would nominate the leader of his liberal coalition partners, Calin Popescu-Tăriceanu, as Prime Minister if he won. The outgoing President Iliescu also encouraged the idea of a grand coalition of the two largest parties as an effective way of securing Romania's path to the EU. However, it was the new President Băsescu's desire that prevailed: the UDMR was persuaded to change its mind and enter a coalition with the Justice and Truth Alliance, and so too was the Social Democrats' own electoral partner, the small Humanist Party of Romania. The implication of this was that in the Romanian political system, the holder of the presidential office is key in determining the complexion of the government.

While Popescu-Tăriceanu's government does not have a large majority, the election placed Romania favourably for completing integration into the EU, which both the government and President emphasized as a priority. Part of their electoral success was due to attacking the outgoing government for corruption, which has long been a concern of the EU in negotiating Romania's accession.

IV. Public Opinion in the New Member States and Applicant Countries

Shifts in public opinion towards the EU in the new Member States and the applicant countries in the course of 2004 were of particular interest. They can throw some light on the initial popular reactions to the realities of membership, and are important because some of the hurdles of EU membership – joining the euro area and the Schengen zone – have yet to be crossed. In the case of applicant states, it was likely that the accession of near neighbours would reinforce the perception that there was no option to joining the EU.

Yet the EU's own *Eurobarometer* polls are not entirely conclusive about opinion in the new Member States. With the exception of Malta – which had been by far the most divided candidate state in the EU accession referendums of 2003 – samples taken in February-March and in October-November 2004 showed a marked increase in the percentage of citizens who thought EU membership was a 'good thing'. However, support had also increased in the old Member States during the same period, and the number of new EU citizens who had no view either way, answering either 'neither good nor bad' or 'don't know', remained high, exceeding 40 per cent in Latvia, the Czech Republic, Slovenia, Poland and Hungary. Positive endorsement of EU membership was also below the EU-25 average in all new members except Lithuania and Slovakia. Likewise, only in Slovenia, Lithuania and Cyprus did a higher percentage of citizens have a more positive image of the EU than the average for the EU-25.

Of the candidate countries, Romania, Bulgaria and Turkey had more positive images of the EU than existing members, underlining a long-term trend whereby the EU is regarded more positively by states who are furthest from achieving membership. In this light, it is notable that only 36 per cent of Croats had a positive image of the EU in 2004. This gives credence to Croatian government warnings that EU intransigence on the issue of insisting on 'full co-operation' in delivering Gotovina to The Hague may fuel euroscepticism in Croatia.

Despite apparently lukewarm feelings towards the EU in general, the new Member States demonstrated fairly positive attitudes on individual aspects of EU policy. Their most marked enthusiasm was for further enlargement of the EU, where all ten new members ranked above the EU-25 average. This can be attributed to self-interest as much as solidarity: support was particularly high in Poland, Lithuania and Slovenia, who had problematic external EU borders, and among old Member States, support was high in Spain, Greece and Italy, who are also affected by geographical proximity to the less stable regions. There was strong support among new Member States for a common defence and security policy as well. Interestingly, however, the 'old Europe' versus 'new Europe' divide was marked in attitudes towards the role of the United States' contribution to 'peace in the world' and 'the fight against terrorism': with the exception of Cyprus, pro-American views were notably stronger in the new Member States.

The most crucial issue for the immediate development of the EU, however, is the attitude of the new Member States towards the future Constitutional Treaty. *Eurobarometers* showed that support tended to be highest in states such as Lithuania, Slovakia and Slovenia where attitudes to EU membership were also the most positive. Yet knowledge of the contents of the Constitutional Treaty was patchy. Lack of awareness was most marked in Cyprus, presumably a side-effect of citizens' preoccupation with their own island's pressing constitutional problems with reunification.

Most of the new Member State governments, having recently given their citizens a voice on the EU in the 2003 accession referendums, have opted for parliamentary ratification of the Constitutional Treaty, acutely aware among other issues of the problems of mobilizing a representative turnout in popular referendums, with the attendant risk that a vocal but unrepresentative minority may 'kidnap' referendum results. By February 2005, Lithuania, Hungary and Slovenia had become the first three EU Member States to ratify the Constitutional Treaty. Only in Poland, where euroscepticism and concerns about national sovereignty were potent domestic political issues, was there a general consensus that a referendum should be held in the second half of 2005, probably at the same time as the presidential election due in September. While the chances of a 'yes' vote were good, the consequences of a 'no' vote in Poland would be more serious for the EU than elsewhere in the new Member States because Poland is by far the largest new member, containing over half of all the new EU citizens. The Czech Republic, where there is also politically significant euroscepticism, had yet to exclude a referendum in early 2005, but prospects that politicians could agree a referendum law and a referendum date appeared so slim that parliamentary ratification was more probable.

In general, while public perception of the EU in the new Member States is prone to fluctuation, it is probably less volatile than in the old Member States. Having recently succeeded in fulfilling their aspirations for European integration, there is more of a sense that belonging to the EU, and the existence of a united Europe, is linked to the long-term destiny of their country.

Conclusion

2004 was an exceptional year in witnessing the largest ever enlargement of the European Union. It also represented the Union's greatest achievement ever in assisting democratic consolidation in Europe. Despite the continuing instability in the party systems of the new Member States, and the greater fragility of their coalition governments, their politicians showed an encouraging degree of adaptability to the institutions of the EU, both in the European Parliament and at European Council meetings. This positive experience of the first wave of eastern enlargement to the post-communist world, together with the new Member States' personal commitment to further widening of the Union, make further expansion of the European Union and its democratic standards appear a realistically attainable goal.

JCMS 2005 Volume 43. Annual Review pp. 181–97

Developments in the Economies of the 'Fifteen'*

NIGEL GRIMWADE
London South Bank University

I. Overview

For the members of the euro area and, to a lesser extent, the EU-15, 2004 was a year of two halves. The first half saw the recovery which had begun in 2003 gain momentum, aided by strong growth in the world economy. However, the second half witnessed an unexpected deceleration in economic activity, which was again largely the result of external factors. The rise in oil prices and the strengthening of the euro were the most influential factors. Although the year as a whole saw a much better economic performance, 2004 ended with some uncertainty. The prospects for oil prices and serious economic imbalances in the global economy added to concern about the domestic outlook.

In the *Annual Review 2003/04*, the forecast of the European Commission was for output growth in 2004 of 1.7 per cent in the euro area and 2 per cent the EU as a whole, a significant improvement on the previous year. By the autumn, the Commission had raised its forecasts to 2.1 per cent in the euro area and to 2.5 per cent for the EU as a whole (Commission, 2004). The upward revision was a response to the sharp acceleration in the level of economic activity that occurred in the first half of the year. The distinguishing feature of this process was the role played by exports, as the EU benefited from expansion in other regions of the world. Despite the problems caused by the appreciation of the euro, EU exporters gained from one of the best years for world trade

---

* For the purposes of this article, the EU economies are taken to be the 15 states belonging to the EU on 1 January 2004, except where otherwise stated. These are also referred to elsewhere as the 'old' Member States to distinguish them from the ten 'new' Member States that joined the EU in May 2004.

in several decades. Over the year as a whole, world trade grew by 10 per cent (Commission, 2005).

The IMF estimated that, between mid-2003 and mid-2004, global GDP growth averaged 5 per cent a year (IMF, 2004). This was the highest for nearly three decades. The global recovery was driven by strong output growth in the United States and rapid expansion in the emerging economies, especially China. Despite the pick-up in the euro area, Europe continued to lag behind these regions. By the second quarter, however, the momentum was already slackening, due mainly to rising oil prices. A combination of surging demand and concerns about supply in several oil-exporting countries (Iraq, Russia and Venezuela) were the main factors causing this, while a shortage of spare capacity in the world combined with speculative buying made the situation worse. By 19 August, oil prices had reached $44.71 a barrel. Although, in subsequent months, the price fell back, this was followed in the autumn by another rise to a peak of over $50 a barrel. Although this still left oil prices well below the levels of the 1970s in real terms, the rise in the nominal price was sufficient to hit consumer and business confidence and to make a significant dent in world economic growth.

As global output grew more slowly, the pace of the recovery weakened in Europe. After increasing at a rate of 0.7 per cent and 0.5 per cent in the first and second quarters respectively, GDP in the euro area grew by only 0.2 per cent in each of the third and fourth quarters (Commission, 2005). Forecasts for the first quarter of 2005 were revised downwards and talk of recession even crept into the parlance of some private forecasters (see Atkins, 2004). The main problem for Europe was over-reliance on exports for growth in the first half of the year. In the second half, export growth was outpaced by the increase in imports. However, private domestic demand, especially household consumption, failed to take up the slack. Although private investment spending held up well, households responded to rising oil prices and structural reforms in several of the largest Member States by increasing their savings. Only in the final quarter were there signs that household consumption might pick up.

II. Main Economic Indicators

Economic Growth

In its *World Economic Outlook* in November, the IMF estimated the annual average rate of growth at 2.2 per cent for the euro area (IMF, 2004). Although this compared favourably with 0.5 per cent in 2003, it was well below the expansion enjoyed by other industrialized countries. For example, the IMF estimates showed that GDP grew by 4.3 per cent in the United States and 4.4

per cent in Japan over the same period, while in developing Asia output grew by 7.6 per cent. In its December *Economic Outlook*, the OECD estimated GDP growth for 2004 at only 1.8 per cent for the euro area, compared with 4.4 per cent in the United States and 4 per cent in Japan (OECD, 2004). Of particular concern was the performance of the largest economies in the euro area. The OECD's estimates for output growth in 2004 were only 1.2 per cent for Germany and 2.1 per cent for France. By way of contrast, growth was noticeably stronger in the EU Member States that were not part of the euro area. For example, the IMF and OECD, respectively, estimated UK GDP growth at 3.4 per cent and 3.2 per cent for the year as a whole. Growth was also strong in the Nordic countries.

Table 1 sets out the latest estimates of the European Commission for GDP growth in the euro area plus the UK, Sweden and Denmark (i.e. omitting the ten new Member States) and the forecast for 2005.

Table 1: Annual Average % Change in Gross Domestic Product (GDP) at Constant Prices for the EU-15, 1996-2005

	1996 to 2000	2000	2001	2002	2003	2004 Estimate	2005 Forecast
Euro area Member States:							
Belgium	2.7	3.9	0.7	0.9	1.3	2.7	2.2
Germany	1.8	2.9	0.8	0.1	−0.1	1.6	0.8
Greece	3.4	4.5	4.3	3.8	4.7	4.2	2.9
Spain	3.9	4.4	2.8	2.2	2.5	2.7	2.7
France	2.7	3.8	2.1	1.2	0.5	2.5	2.0
Ireland	9.8	9.9	6.0	6.1	3.7	5.4	4.9
Italy	1.9	3.0	1.8	0.4	0.3	1.2	1.2
Luxembourg	7.1	9.0	1.5	2.5	2.9	4.2	3.8
Netherlands	3.7	3.5	1.4	0.6	−0.9	1.3	1.0
Austria	2.9	3.4	0.7	1.2	0.8	2.0	2.1
Portugal	3.9	3.4	1.7	0.4	−1.1	1.0	1.1
Finland	4.7	5.1	1.1	2.2	2.4	3.7	3.3
Euro area	2.6	3.5	1.6	0.9	0.6	2.0	1.6
Non-euro area Member States:							
Denmark	2.7	2.8	1.6	1.0	0.4	2.0	2.3
Sweden	3.2	4.3	1.0	2.0	1.5	3.5	3.0
UK	3.2	3.9	2.3	1.8	2.2	3.1	2.8
EU-15	2.7	3.6	1.7	1.1	0.9	2.3	1.9

Source: Commission (2005).

While growth was higher in the three non-euro area countries than the euro area average, Belgium, France, Greece, Spain, Ireland, Luxembourg and Finland achieved a similar output performance or better. By way of contrast, Germany, Italy, the Netherlands and Portugal all performed poorly, albeit better than in the previous year.

As discussed above, the major contribution to growth on the demand side in the first half of the year came from exports, which grew at an average rate of 2 per cent quarter-on-quarter (Commission, 2005). This was despite the fact that the euro had risen by more than 50 per cent against the US dollar over three years. However, with only 16 per cent of euro area exports going to America, and with the euro's trade-weighted value rising by much less, the appreciation of the exchange rate had less of an effect on euro area exports than might be expected. In the face of an appreciating exchange rate, some exporters in the euro area placed more emphasis on non-price factors, while others were content to allow profit margins to decline. Changes in the composition of world import demand (e.g. booming demand for investment equipment) may also have favoured EU exporters (Commission, 2004). Private domestic demand, however, was weak. Private consumption grew by only 1.3 per cent in the euro area, although by more in the UK, Sweden and Denmark. In Germany, it fell by 0.4 per cent over the year as a whole. Although private investment grew more strongly, it was affected by declining construction investment in Germany. The rise in oil prices also had a dampening effect on investment, by reducing the future profitability of investment projects.

More recently, there has been much discussion of the failure of the EU to realize the objectives set at the famous Lisbon summit of 2000. As part of the so-called Lisbon agenda, the EU set itself the aim of becoming 'the most competitive and knowledge-based economy in the world' by 2010. One aspect of this was the commitment by heads of state to raise the EU's average rate of economic growth from 2 to 3 per cent, closer to that achieved by the United States. The fact that the growth rate for both the euro area and the EU as a whole remained well below this level in 2004 has become a source of concern. However, as is now well established, a large part of the explanation for the higher growth rate of the US economy is a much faster population growth rate. The latter has grown by 1.2 per cent a year over the past decade compared with 0.4 per cent for the EU as a whole (Groom, 2005). When growth is expressed in terms of GDP per head, the gap between the US and the EU is much smaller, with growth in the EU at 1.8 per cent a year compared with 1.9 per cent in the US. Although productivity as measured by output per man hour has grown more slowly in the EU, adjusting for differences in the economic cycle shows that the EU may even have done better than the US (*The Economist,* 19 June 2004).

Employment

The buoyancy of the EU economy in the first half of the year contributed to a more rapid growth in employment. In 2004, employment grew by 0.6 per cent in both the euro area and the EU-15, compared with 0.2 and 0.3 per cent respectively in 2003. However, this was not sufficient to prevent the rate of unemployment from rising to 8.8 per cent in the euro area and 8 per cent in the EU-15. Employment rose a little more slowly than at the same stage of the cycle on previous occasions, just as it was slower to fall in the preceding downturn. The European Commission sees this as reflecting a greater tendency than in previous cycles for employers to hoard labour rather than sack workers when output turned down (Commission, 2004).

Table 2 shows the percentage of the civilian labour force that was unemployed in the euro area plus the UK, Sweden and Denmark between 1996 and 2004, with the forecast for 2005.

Table 2: % Share of the Civilian Labour Force Unemployed in the EU-15, 1996–2005

	1996– 2000	2000	2001	2002	2003	2004 Estimate	2005 Forecast
Euro area Member States:							
Belgium	8.7	6.9	6.7	7.3	8.0	7.8	7.7
Germany	8.3	7.2	7.4	8.2	9.0	9.5	9.7
Greece	10.7	11.3	10.8	10.3	9.7	10.3	10.5
Spain	14.9	11.3	10.6	11.3	11.3	10.8	10.4
France	10.8	9.1	8.4	8.9	9.5	9.6	9.4
Ireland	7.8	4.3	3.9	4.3	4.6	4.5	4.6
Italy	11.0	10.1	9.1	8.6	8.4	8.0	7.9
Luxembourg	2.6	2.3	2.1	2.8	3.7	4.2	4.6
Netherlands	4.2	2.9	2.5	2.7	3.8	4.7	5.2
Austria	4.2	3.7	3.6	4.2	4.3	4.5	4.1
Portugal	5.6	4.1	4.0	5.0	6.3	6.7	7.0
Finland	11.7	9.8	9.1	9.1	9.0	8.8	8.4
Euro area	9.7	8.2	7.8	8.2	8.7	8.8	8.8
Non-euro area Member States:							
Denmark	5.1	4.4	4.3	4.6	5.6	5.4	4.9
Sweden	8.0	5.6	4.9	4.9	5.6	6.3	5.9
UK	6.5	5.4	5.0	5.1	4.9	4.7	4.7
EU-15	9.1	7.6	7.2	7.6	7.9	8.0	8.0

Source: Commission (2005).

A big disparity continued to exist between the different members of the euro area. Germany, Spain, France and Greece had relatively high unemployment rates, while Ireland, Luxembourg, the Netherlands and Austria all enjoyed relatively low unemployment. Outside the euro area, the UK also enjoyed a relatively low level of unemployment. Of particular concern was the continuing rise in the numbers unemployed in Germany, as the biggest economy in the euro area. Although some of the increase was a delayed response to the cyclical downturn of 2003, a further factor was the labour market reforms introduced by the government as part of a programme to boost competitiveness. The effect of such measures in the short term was to encourage employers to shed labour in the face of declining demand, while encouraging households to cut consumption and save more. In the long term, however, the movement towards more flexible labour contracts and cuts in the tax burden of labour can be expected to increase employment.

Although unemployment has been slow to fall as the EU economy has recovered from the downturn of the previous year, the employment rate (defined as the share of the employed in the total population of the 15–64 age group) has continued to rise. In 2004, this rose in the EU-15 from 62.4 per cent in 2003 to 64.7 per cent, and is forecast to rise further to 65 per cent in 2005 (Commission, 2004). However, this is still below the intermediate target of 67 per cent for 2005 set as part of the Lisbon agenda. To achieve the Lisbon target of 70 per cent by 2010, the employment rate will, therefore, need to rise by five percentage points in the second half of the current decade or by an annual average of 1 per cent a year (assuming an unchanged working-age population). Such an increase has not been achieved by the members of the euro area since 2001 and will, therefore, prove difficult to realize.

Inflation

As measured by the Harmonized Index of Consumer Prices (HICP), inflation fell below 2 per cent in the early part of the year, in line with forecasts. However, in March, the rate accelerated, reaching 2.3 per cent by August. After dipping to 2.1 per cent in September, inflation rose again to 2.2 per cent in November (Commission, 2004). This was above the European Central Bank's target of 'close to-but below-2 per cent', leaving no scope for any reduction in the lending rate. A similar trend was apparent in other advanced industrialized countries, driven mainly by higher commodity prices.[1] In the first six months of the year, oil prices rose by 27 per cent and non-oil commodity prices by 9 per cent (IMF, 2004). By the autumn, oil prices had risen to approximately $50 a barrel. However, core inflation (the HICP excluding energy and unprocessed

[1] See IMF (2004) for a discussion of this.

food) was more subdued, with the index rising from 1.9 per cent in January to 2.2 per cent in August, before declining to 2 per cent in September (Commission, 2004). A rise in the prices of processed food in the early part of the year, due to a rise in indirect taxes on tobacco in some Member States, and a rise in administrative prices in the service sector were the main cause of this (Commission, 2004). Wage increases, however, remained moderate, with compensation per employee in the euro area growing by a modest 2.1 per cent and unit labour costs by only 0.7 per cent (Commission, 2004). Further downward pressure on inflation was brought about by the lagged effect on import prices of the appreciation of the euro.

Table 3 shows the estimated annual percentage changes in the HICP for the members of the euro area plus the United Kingdom, Denmark and Sweden, including the Commission's forecasts for 2005.

Within the euro area, a broad dispersion of inflation rates continued to prevail, with Greece, Spain and Luxembourg above 3 per cent and Belgium,

Table 3: % Change in the Harmonized Index of Consumer Prices in the EU-15, 1996–2005

	1996–2000	2000	2001	2002	2003	2004 Estimate	2005 Forecast
Euro area Member States:							
Belgium	1.6	2.7	2.4	1.6	1.5	1.9	2.0
Germany	1.1	1.4	1.9	1.3	1.0	1.8	1.3
Greece	4.6	2.9	3.7	3.9	3.4	3.0	3.2
Spain	2.6	3.5	2.8	3.6	3.1	3.1	2.9
France	1.3	1.8	1.8	1.9	2.2	2.3	1.9
Ireland	2.6	5.3	4.0	4.7	4.0	2.3	2.1
Italy	2.4	2.6	2.3	2.6	2.8	2.3	2.0
Luxembourg	1.7	3.8	2.4	2.1	2.5	3.2	3.1
Netherlands	1.9	2.3	5.1	3.9	2.2	1.4	1.3
Austria	1.2	2.0	2.3	1.7	1.3	2.0	2.3
Portugal	2.4	2.8	4.4	3.7	3.3	2.5	2.3
Finland	1.6	3.0	2.7	2.0	1.3	0.1	1.1
Euro area	1.7	2.1	2.4	2.3	2.1	2.1	1.9
Non-euro area Member States:							
Denmark	2.0	2.7	2.3	2.4	2.0	0.9	1.4
Sweden	1.1	1.3	2.7	2.0	2.3	1.0	0.4
UK	1.6	0.8	1.2	1.3	1.4	1.3	1.7
EU-15	1.7	1.9	2.2	2.1	2.0	2.0	1.8

Source: Commission (2005).

Germany, the Netherlands and Finland all below 2 per cent. All three of the non-euro area countries enjoyed relatively low inflation. It follows that the operation of a single 'one-size-fits-all' monetary policy for the euro area continued to exert a relatively greater deflationary effect on the countries with the lowest inflation rates in the euro area. Two of these, Germany and the Netherlands, were also countries that experienced the slowest growth rates.

Despite hints in the earlier part of the year from the President of the ECB that interest rates might be cut to boost domestic consumption in the face of evidence that growth was slackening, the ECB kept its lending rate unchanged at 2 per cent throughout the year. Evidence of a more rapid growth in the money supply (rising at an annual rate of about 6 per cent towards the end of the year) appears to have been one concern of the ECB. Household borrowing also grew strongly, with lending to consumers for house purchase rising at an annual rate of 10 per cent in the last two months of the year (*Financial Times*, 29–30 January 2005). House price inflation continued at a rapid rate in a number of Member States, with France followed by Spain, the UK and Ireland topping the table. By way of contrast, the housing market in Germany remained depressed. While the fear of encouraging asset price inflation may have constrained the ECB in lowering rates, the strength of the euro was an additional factor constraining the ECB in raising rates.

Public Finances

During 2004, members of the euro area ran general government deficits equivalent to 2.7 per cent of GDP, as against 2.8 per cent in the previous year. However, the cyclically adjusted balance was unchanged on the previous year at 2.4 per cent of GDP (Commission, 2005). This suggests that fiscal policy was broadly neutral over the year as whole. Over the same period, the output gap (the deviation of actual from potential output) fell from –1.1 per cent to –0.9 per cent of potential output (Commission, 2005). However, concern remained about the continuing state of the public finances of several Member States. In 2004, three countries in the euro area – Germany, Greece and France – ran deficits that exceeded the 3 per cent limit permitted under the rules of the Stability and Growth Pact (SGP). The decision of the Council of Finance Ministers (Ecofin) in November 2003 not to impose sanctions on countries that had breached the 3 per cent limit for two years in succession left the Pact in limbo throughout 2004. A further concern remains the long-term fiscal situation of several countries, resulting from the ageing of their populations. In the euro area alone, the ratio of government debt to GDP stood at 71.3 per cent in 2004, up from 70.8 per cent in 2003 (Commission, 2004). In addition, seven countries had debt to GDP ratios in excess of 60 per cent. In its December *World Economic Outlook*, the IMF argued for stronger action on the part of these countries to consolidate public finances to meet these long-term challenges and to allow sufficient room in the future to use fiscal policy as a stabilization measure (IMF, 2004).

Table 4 sets out the net lending/borrowing of Member State governments expressed as a percentage of GDP for the period from 1996 to 2004 plus the European Commission's forecast for 2005.

All of the three countries in the euro area – Germany, France and Greece – with deficits in excess of 3 per cent did so for the fourth successive year. Of these, only France made some significant progress in reducing the deficit, thanks largely to faster than expected growth, and is forecast to meet the requirements of the SGP in 2005. The Greek deficit was the outcome of a series of successive revisions, after it was revealed in September that budget data had been significantly under-reported for several years in a row. Furthermore, the Greek deficit for 2004 was the highest ever recorded by a member of the euro area

Table 4: Net Lending (+) or Net Borrowing (–) as a % of GDP in EU-15, 1996 –2005

	1996–2000	2000	2001	2002	2003	2004 Estimate	2005 Forecast
Euro area Member States:							
Belgium	–1.3	0.2	0.6	0.1	0.4	0.1	–0.2
Germany	–1.7	1.3	–2.8	–3.7	–3.8	–3.7	–3.3
Greece	–5.2	4.1	–3.6	–4.1	–5.2	–6.1	–4.5
Spain	–2.6	–0.9	–0.5	–0.3	0.3	–0.3	0.0
France	–2.6	–1.4	–1.5	–3.2	–4.2	–3.7	–3.0
Ireland	2.1	4.4	0.9	–0.4	0.2	1.3	–0.6
Italy	–3.0	–0.6	–3.0	–2.6	–2.9	–3.0	–3.6
Luxembourg	3.5	6.2	6.2	2.3	0.5	–1.1	–1.5
Netherlands	–0.2	2.2	–0.1	–1.9	–3.2	–2.5	–2.0
Austria	–2.4	–1.5	0.3	–0.2	–1.1	–1.3	–2.0
Portugal	–3.4	–2.8	–4.4	–2.7	–2.9	–2.9	–4.9
Finland	1.3	7.1	5.2	4.3	2.5	2.1	1.7
Euro area	–2.1	0.1	–1.7	–2.4	–2.8	–2.7	–2.6
Non-euro area Member States:							
Denmark	1.3	2.6	3.2	1.7	1.2	2.8	2.1
Sweden	1.1	5.0	2.5	–0.3	0.2	1.4	0.8
UK	–0.3	3.8	0.7	–1.7	–3.4	–3.2	–3.0
EU-15	–1.6	1.0	–1.1	–2.2	–2.8	–2.6	–2.5

Source: Commission (2005).

since the start of the SGP. Two other countries – Italy and Portugal – narrowly missed exceeding the limit, but are predicted to do so in 2005. Outside the euro area, the UK also exceeded the limit for the second year in succession, but is projected to reduce its deficit below the ceiling in the next two years.

III. Economic Developments Inside the Euro Area

Germany

After enjoying a relatively good start to the year with output growing by 0.5 and 0.4 per cent (quarter-on-quarter) in the first and second quarters respectively, growth came to a dramatic halt in the third quarter. In the fourth quarter, GDP actually fell by 0.2 per cent. The expansion in the first half of the year was based entirely on export demand, especially exports of investment goods. Germany's exports have been the one bright spot in the country in recent years, reflecting the success achieved by German business in boosting productivity and cutting costs. In the past five years, German exports have grown three times faster than American exports, making Germany the only G-7 country to increase its share of world exports (*The Economist*, 19 February 2005). In the third quarter, however, the growth in exports faltered, as world economic growth was hit by rising oil prices. Although opinions are mixed, a view held by some is that the decline in export growth was a lagged response to the appreciation of the euro (*Financial Times*, 8 December 2004).

However, Germany's main problem was that booming export demand in the first half of the year failed to pass through into domestic demand, which fell in both of the first two quarters. Private investment fell, despite rising company profits and a booming stock market, with construction falling especially severely. Private consumption also fell, as households reacted to low wage increases and rising unemployment. Fears among workers of losing their jobs and of future cuts in welfare benefits served to damage consumer confidence. As a result, the ratio of private sector savings to GDP rose to 22.7 per cent, higher than any other country in the euro area (Commission, 2005). As a result, unemployment rose to 4.48 million workers in December or 10.8 per cent of the active population. In part, however, the rise reflected a statistical change, as changes to social benefit eligibility criteria required an estimated 200,000 persons to register as unemployed to continue receiving benefits (Commission, 2004). In the long run, it is hoped that labour market reforms (the so-called Hartz IV) will create more jobs by lowering labour costs and increasing labour market flexibility.

In 2004, Germany exceeded the borrowing limit under the SGP for the fourth successive year. The outcome was mainly the result of declining fiscal revenues, with public expenditure unchanged in nominal terms (Commission, 2004). While slow growth contributed greatly to the fall in government revenues, a cut in income tax rates equivalent to 0.7 per cent of GDP implemented at the beginning of 2004 was an added factor. Revenues from indirect taxes were also affected by low consumption spending. In cyclically adjusted terms, the fiscal deficit played a marginally expansionary role in 2004, although the constraints of the SGP left little room for any discretionary expansion. With inflation rising from 1 to 1.8 per cent, real short-term interest rates fell over the year, but by too little to have any impact on final demand.

France

As with Germany, the French economy enjoyed a strong recovery in the first half of the year with GDP growing at a (quarter-on-quarter) rate of 0.7 per cent in the first two quarters. Unlike Germany, the main factor driving the recovery was private domestic demand, especially private consumption. Encouraged by rising equity and house prices, households reduced their savings and spent more. In 2004, France had the highest rate of house price inflation of any country in Europe. In the second half of the year, however, the recovery faded such that, over the year as a whole, GDP grew by only 2 per cent (Commission, 2005).

The deceleration in the second half of the year resulted from a decline in private investment, as firms reacted to the uncertainty created by rising oil prices. Private consumption also grew less rapidly, as employment fell despite the rise in output in the first half of the year. Over the year as a whole, employment fell by 0.2 per cent and unemployment rose to 9.6 per cent, the third highest rate in the euro area (Commission, 2005). The continuing high level of unemployment led to internal pressure on the government to look for alternatives to the 35-hour week as a policy for creating more jobs. Proposals included amending the 35-hour week law to allow workers to work for longer hours where employers and workers were in agreement, and deregulation of protected markets, especially in the service sector (see Thornhill, 2005).

For the fourth year in succession, France, like Germany, ran a budget deficit in excess of the 3 per cent ceiling under the SGP. However, the deficit did fall from 4.2 per cent in 2003 to 3.7 per cent, and is forecast to fall to within the ceiling in 2005. The improvement in the fiscal situation largely resulted from a better macroeconomic performance over the year as a whole than had originally been forecast. As result, tax revenues rose faster than expected and public expenditure grew less rapidly than output.

Italy

In 2004, Italy had the second lowest growth rate of any country in the euro area. Over the year as whole, GDP grew by only 1.2 per cent, an improvement on last year's derisory 0. 3 per cent, but well below the official forecast of 2.1 per cent. Even in the first half of the year when the recovery was at its strongest, the Italian economy was growing more slowly than other euro area countries. In the final quarter of the year, Italy's GDP contracted by 0.3 per cent (*Financial Times*, 16 February 2005). Supply-side measures by the Berlusconi administration to stimulate growth achieved only limited success. In 2003, labour market reforms were introduced to raise employment. In July of last year, pension reforms were pushed through in the face of trade union opposition to raise the retirement age. Towards the end of the year, the government announced a budget for 2005 that includes sizeable income tax cuts.

However, there was much concern about the state of Italy's public finances. With a debt to GDP ratio of 106 per cent, Italy was the second most indebted country in the euro area. Last year, Italy just succeeded in running a fiscal deficit within the 3 per cent ceiling of the SGP. However, this was largely achieved by a series of one-off measures, estimated by the European Commission as amounting to around 1.5 percentage points of GDP (Commission, 2004). With the government making sizeable tax cuts, other offsetting measures will be required if the fiscal deficit is to be kept below 3 per cent in 2005.

A continuing concern remains Italy's competitiveness in the global economy. Exports grew by only 3.2 per cent over the year, one of the slowest of any country in the euro area, although this exceeded the rise in imports of 2.5 per cent (Commission, 2005). While Italy continues to do well in a number of industrial sectors in which the country has always been strong, global competition in some of the more traditional sectors such as textiles and furniture is increasing. Moreover, a much smaller proportion of Italy's exports is concentrated in fast-growing sectors, such as ICT, than in other Member States. Some observers have argued that Italy's large number of small, family-owned businesses are a factor contributing to the country's relatively low level of investment in research and development and low rate of innovation (Barber, 2005).

Spain

In 2004, Spain grew a fraction more quickly than in the previous year and a rate more than half a percentage point higher than the average for the euro area. However, this otherwise impressive growth performance concealed two major concerns. The first was the heavy reliance of the expansion on private consumption and building. Private consumption grew by 3.5 per cent and construction by 4.4 per cent, both encouraged by relatively low real interest rates (Commission, 2005). With inflation at 3.1 per cent, short-term interest rates were, once again, negative in real terms. During the year, house prices rose at the second fastest rate of any country in the euro area, and household indebtedness expressed as a percentage of disposable incomes rose quickly. The second concern was the performance of the external sector. In 2004, Spain ran a current account deficit of 5 per cent of GDP, as imports increased by 7.2 per cent and exports by only 6.9 per cent (Commission, 2005). A relatively high rate of inflation meant an erosion of competitiveness in both the euro area and abroad.

Spain's other major problem was unemployment which, in 2004, remained over 10 per cent, a little down on the previous year but still the highest in the euro area. In addition, 30 per cent of those in work were estimated to be on short-term contracts (Grimond, 2004). Despite the fact that employment has been rising at a steady rate for several years, unemployment has fall only marginally. One reason was the relatively rapid increase in the active population, stimulated by immigration and a rising female participation rate. A relatively rapid rate of increase in wages may also have contributed. In 2004, compensation per person employed rose by 4 per cent a year, compared with 4.3 per cent in the previous year, while labour productivity rose by only 0.6 per cent (Commission, 2005).

On the fiscal front, Spain ran a small budget deficit in 2004 of 0.3 per cent of GDP, after being in surplus to the tune of 0.3 per cent of GDP in 2003. However, with a positive output gap (i.e. actual output exceeding potential output) of 0.1 per cent, Spain might have hoped for a stronger fiscal position (Commission, 2005). Nevertheless, the deficit is forecast to disappear in 2005. In the long run, however, in line with other countries in the euro area, Spain will need to create room in the public finances for increased spending on pensions, as life expectancy increases and fertility rates among women fall (Grimond, 2004).

Other Members of the Euro Area

Belgium experienced strong economic growth in 2004, although, in line with developments in the world economy, the pace of growth slackened in the final quarter. Over the year as a whole, GDP grew by 2.7 per cent, compared with 1.3 per cent in the previous year. On the demand side, the biggest contribution came from household spending and government spending, although investment spending also performed well. Employment grew for the first time in three years, bringing Belgium's unemployment rate down to 7.8 per cent.

With a growth rate of 4.2 per cent, *Luxembourg* was, with Greece, the second-fastest growing economy in the euro area with manufacturing, especially the steel sector, and construction making the major contribution.

By way of contrast, the *Netherlands* remained sluggish. GDP grew by only 1.3 per cent, after declining by 0.9 per cent in 2003. Between 2000 and 2003, the Dutch economy has grown by only 0.2 per cent, compared with 3.5 per cent between 1994 and 2000 (Munchau, 2004). From being one of the fastest growing economies in the EU, the Netherlands has become one of the worst performers. As a result, employment fell by 1.6 per cent in 2004, bringing the unemployment rate to 4.7 per cent. With an inflation rate of only 1.4 per cent, short-term interest rates of 2 per cent in the euro area have exerted a negative effect on demand. At the same time, with a budget deficit of 2.5 per cent of GDP, little scope remained for using fiscal policy to stimulate demand. Exports were the one bright spot in the economy, growing by 8.5 per cent after several years of near stagnation (Commission, 2005).

After growing at a rate of 4.7 per cent in 2003, economic activity in *Greece* slackened a little in 2004, with GDP growing by 4.2 per cent. However, this still left Greece, with Luxembourg, the second fastest growing economy in the euro area. Some slowing down of the economy was to be expected as the construction boom associated with the Olympic Games ceased to benefit the economy. However, with the pace of growth still strong, inflation was a concern. In the two-year wage agreement signed in May, nominal pay was raised by 6 per cent with a further 5.5 per cent to follow in 2005, well in excess of productivity increases. A second difficulty arose from the revelation that, due to gross under-reporting of budget data, Greece has broken its deficit limit for every year since 2000. In 2004, the deficit stood at 6.1 per cent of GDP or 7.1 per cent in cyclically adjusted terms.

After growth faltered in 2003, *Ireland,* the 'Celtic tiger', roared again with a growth rate of 5.4 per cent. While this compares poorly with an average growth rate of between 9 and 10 per cent in the second half of the 1990s, it still meant that Ireland was yet again the fastest growing economy in the euro area. However, as is well known, growth measured in GDP terms tends to overstate the actual expansion of the economy. GNP is a better measure of Ireland's national income, as it excludes profits remitted abroad, which are a major factor in the Irish economy due to the high level of foreign investment and low corporate taxes. As profit outflows grew in 2004, growth in GNP terms was somewhat smaller (Commission, 2004). Ireland's major concern remains inflation, although the HICP rose by only 2.3 per cent in 2004, down from 4 per cent in the previous year. However, property prices have continued rising at a faster rate and the economy remains vulnerable to any collapse in the housing market (see Peet, 2004).

Of the remaining members of the euro area, *Finland* enjoyed strong growth, with GDP growing by 3.7 per cent compared with 2.4 per cent in the previous year. Growth picked up in *Austria*, with GDP growing by 2 per cent compared with 0.8 per cent in the previous year. In *Portugal*, GDP grew by a very poor 1 per cent, after falling by 1.1 per cent in the previous year. This was not sufficient to prevent unemployment rising further to 6.7 per cent.

IV. Economic Developments in the UK, Sweden and Denmark

Outside the euro area, both the United Kingdom and the Scandinavian countries enjoyed relatively strong economic growth. The European Commission estimated *United Kingdom* economic growth at 3.1 per cent for the year, a little lower than the estimates of the IMF and OECD (Commission, 2005). This compared with 2.2 per cent in 2003. The main driving force was domestic demand. Private consumption grew strongly in response to rising incomes and rising house wealth. Capital investment was also strong as corporate profitability rose and government spending (especially on health and education) played an important supporting role. While inflation remained relatively low (1.3 per cent over the year as whole), the prospect of inflation rising above the Bank of England's 2 per cent symmetric target prompted the Monetary Policy Committee to make a series of upward adjustments to interest rates. Interest rates were raised by 0.25 percentage points on four occasions during the year to bring the rate to 4.75 per cent by the end of the year, with most forecasters predicting a further increase to 5 per cent in 2005.

Given the high levels of household indebtedness, a major concern throughout the year was the risk of an abrupt adjustment in property prices, leading to a sharp fall in household consumption. Although housing inflation moderated during the year, the fear that prices might fall did not materialize. In 2004, the UK's fiscal deficit stood at 3.2 per cent of GDP, after reaching 3.4 per cent in 2003. In its fiscal policy, New Labour applies the so-called 'golden rule' that, over the course of the business cycle, it will borrow only to meet the costs of capital spending. However, with public spending rising quickly and tax revenues not as buoyant as the Treasury had expected, the risk remains that the government could breach the golden rule at some stage in the future.

Among the Scandinavian countries, *Sweden* enjoyed a growth rate of 3.5 per cent in 2004, compared with 1.5 per cent in the previous year. A key factor was the expansion of exports, which grew at a rate of 10.2 per cent over the year as whole. Domestic demand also grew strongly, assisted by cuts in the Riksbank's lending rate of 0.75 percentage points over the year as whole. Despite the rapid growth of the economy, inflation remained modest at 1.0 per cent. In *Denmark,* GDP grew by 2 per cent in 2004, compared with only 0.4 per cent in the previous year. Although exports grew rapidly, this was more than offset by increased imports. Instead, the main boost to growth on the demand side came from private consumption, stimulated by rising incomes and tax cuts. As in Sweden, inflation remained subdued throughout the year with the HICP rising only 0.9 per cent.

Conclusion

Both the IMF and the European Commission in their twice-yearly forecasts have adopted a cautious view of the prospects for the EU-15 in the current year. IMF projections that were published in November point to unchanged growth in the euro area. The most recent forecasts of the Commission, however, expect growth to be slower. The basis for this relatively pessimistic forecast is the uncertainty about developments in the global economy. In particular, the likelihood that oil prices will remain high and volatile is expected to exert a dampening effect on economic growth in all countries of the world. For members of the euro area, a further concern must be the future course of the euro. The large United States current account deficit and the consequent build-up of dollar balances in the rest of the world carries the risk of another sharp fall in the external value of the US dollar. If, at the same time, the Asian countries prefer to keep their exchange rates fixed against the dollar, the danger is of another upward shift in the euro, further hitting EU exports and cutting growth.

In this situation, there is little that the euro area can do to stimulate domestic demand. With inflation likely to remain high due to oil prices, the scope for using monetary policy to generate more demand will be limited. At the same time, fiscal policy is likely to be constrained by the already large fiscal deficits of several Member States and the need to consolidate public finances to prepare for the long-term effects of an ageing population. This places much of the policy burden on structural measures to boost competitiveness and raise the EU's long-term growth potential.

References

Atkins, R. (2004) '"Flirting with Recession": Weak Demand in the Eurozone Baffles the Economists'. *Financial Times*, 8 December.

Barber, T. (2005) 'Worries over Loss of Competitivenes'. Special Report on Italy, *Financial Times*, 15 March.

Commission of the European Communities (2004) *Economic Forecasts, Autumn 2004*. Directorate-General for Economic and Financial Affairs, Brussels.

Commission of the European Communities (2005) *Economic Forecasts, Spring 2005*. Directorate-General for Economic and Financial Affairs, Brussels.

Grimond, J. (2004) 'The Second Transition, A Survey of Spain'. *The Economist*, 26 June.

Groom, B. (2005) 'Fit to Compete? The EU Renews Efforts to get its Economy Moving More Swiftly'. *Financial Times,* 7 March.

IMF (2004) *World Economic Outlook 2004* (Washington D.C.: International Monetary Fund), November.

Munchau, W. (2004) 'The Dutch Model's Decline is a Lesson for Europe'. *Financial Times,* 11 November.

OECD (2004) *Economic Outlook* (Paris: Organization for Economic Cooperation and Development).

Peet, J. (2004) 'The Luck of the Irish, A Survey of Ireland'. *The Economist,* 16 October.

Thornhill, J. (2005) 'Back to Work: France Finds Little Reward in the Costly Leisure of its 35-hour Week'. *Financial Times,* 15 February.

JCMS 2005 Volume 43. Annual Review pp. 199–214

Developments in the Economies of the New Member States and the Candidate Countries

DEBRA JOHNSON
University of Hull

I. Context

Accession took place on 1 May 2004 against a more positive external economic background. The tentative world economic recovery that began in late 2003 became well established and more broadly based across many of the world's regions in 2004. Growth peaked in early 2004, easing back slightly thereafter. However, growth remained robust and reached 5 per cent for 2004 as a whole – the fastest global growth rate since the 1970s.

The outlook remains positive, but key risks remain. A feature of 2004 was the increase in both fuel and non-fuel commodity prices. The former were driven by strong demand, especially as a result of surging growth in emerging Asia, and supply concerns. Oil price uncertainty contributed to the moderation of economy activity in the second half of 2004 and could do so more drastically in the future.

A second global risk is the perseverance of the twin deficits of the US – the budget and trade deficits. Nevertheless, the US performed relatively strongly in 2004; persistent macroeconomic imbalances could, however, restrain future US growth. Elsewhere, Japan's economic performance showed its most marked improvement for some years. China's economic boom continued with growth reaching almost 10 per cent in 2004, accompanied by strong growth elsewhere in emerging Asia. The post-2002 recovery in Latin America gathered pace in 2004 with the return of investor confidence and strong external demand. African growth of 4.5 per cent, although below the world average, exceeded its recent performance. Russia and other hydrocarbon rich CIS members prospered as a result of high fuel prices.

Growth in 2004 in both the euro area and the EU-25 was, at 2.1 per cent and 2.5 per cent respectively, significantly below that of the US and other advanced industrialized economies, but was more than satisfactory by recent EU standards. The main factors behind this improved performance were global growth and trade expansion, helped by supportive macroeconomic policies, low inflation and structural reforms. Growth accelerated during the first half of 2004 more quickly than most forecasters anticipated. However, it was not sufficient to bring forth anything but a weak contribution from domestic demand, with investment growth being particularly disappointing. Whilst euro area growth remains dependent on export demand, the region remains particularly vulnerable to further euro appreciation.

II. Preparedness for EU Membership

The new Member States benefited from the cyclical upturn in the global economy that coincided with accession. Moreover, they continued to reap the rewards of their earlier structural reforms and accession to continue to play catch-up with their new EU colleagues. With the exception of Malta, which

Table 1: Real Growth in Gross Domestic Product (GDP), Annual % Change

	1997–01	2003 Outturn	2004 Estimate	2005 Forecast	Real GDP in 2003 [a] (1989=100)
Cyprus	4.2	2.0	3.5	3.9	n/a
Czech Republic	1.0	3.1	3.8	3.8	108
Estonia	5.2	5.1	5.9	6.0	102
Hungary	4.5	3.0	3.9	3.7	115
Latvia	6.1	7.5	7.5	6.7	83
Lithuania	3.6	9.7	7.1	6.4	84
Malta	3.4	0.2	1.0	1.5	n/a
Poland	4.2	3.8	5.8	4.9	135
Slovakia	3.3	4.0	4.9	4.5	114
Slovenia	4.2	2.5	4.0	3.6	120
Bulgaria	2.0	4.3	5.5	6.0	84
Croatia		4.3	3.8	4.0	91
Romania	−1.0	4.9	7.2	5.6	92
Turkey	1.2	5.8	8.5	5.0	n/a
EU-15	2.6	1.0	2.3	2.6	n/a

Sources: Commission (2004); [a] EBRD (2004).

nevertheless improved on its 2003 performance, the growth rates of the new Member States were significantly above the EU-15 average. In most cases, growth accelerated in 2004 with the Baltic States again registering the strongest growth among new Member States. The now much reduced group of candidate countries of Romania, Turkey, Bulgaria and Croatia, having begun seriously to tackle their structural problems, also continued to demonstrate consistent growth rather than the stop–start performance of earlier years.

In all cases, export growth in the new Member States was robust and generally in double figures. However, the stimulus from major export markets was often insufficient to offset the even greater growth of imports set in train by private consumption and investment growth. In several cases, the import content of exports was also high, thereby linking high export demand to high import demand. In short, although the export sectors of the new and candidate Member States performed extremely well, the net contribution of the external sector to overall growth tended to decrease in 2004. Instead, it was domestic demand, especially private consumption and investment, which were the main contributors to growth in the region. Hungary was the main country to buck this trend.

Foreign direct investment (FDI) continues to play an important, albeit changing, role in the new and applicant Member States. Large-scale greenfield investments and investment opportunities from privatization have become less frequent because the best options have already been exploited and investors are encountering difficulties arising from the region's inflexible labour markets. FDI is also becoming more focused on the service sector and involves more small and medium-sized companies. Furthermore, FDI inflows in some new Member States have begun to be partially offset by FDI outflows and by the repatriation of earnings from earlier investments. These factors are more pronounced in more mature economies like Hungary and Slovenia, but such trends will spread to other new Member States and candidate countries.

The buoyant growth of the new members and candidate states would ordinarily give rise to job creation and a fall in unemployment. However, net job creation has been limited and any unemployment reductions have been marginal. This is because growth has taken place within a context of ongoing structural reform, with the result that net job creation was limited by the loss of jobs in sectors undergoing reform. Moreover, growth has been accompanied by productivity improvements stemming from restructuring. Although improved productivity performance is essential for the long-term competitiveness of these countries, it does not help the resolution of unemployment problems in the short term.

The new Member States and candidate countries are also known for labour market inflexibilities such as persistently large differences in regional

Table 2: FDI Net Inflows Recorded in the Balance of Payments (US$ m)

	1990	1995	2000	2003 Est.	2004 Projection	Cumulative FDI Inflows 1989–2003	Cumulative FDI Inflows per Capita 1989–2003
Bulgaria	4	98	1 003	1 398	2 000	6 235	795
Croatia		109	1 085	1 700	1 100	8 204	1 857
Czech Rep.	n.a.	2 526	4 943	2 351	5 000	38 243	3 710
Estonia	n.a.	199	324	743	684	3 246	2 402
Hungary	311	4 410	2 191	874	1 691	33 641	3 364
Latvia	n.a.	245	401	328	365	3 372	1 454
Lithuania	n.a.	72	375	142	500	3 683	1 067
Poland	0	1 134	9 324	3 839	5 000	51 906	1 355
Romania	–18	417	1 051	1 520	2 100	10 536	486
Slovakia	24	194	2 058	549	1 500	10 815	1 894
Slovenia	–2	161	71	–118	–32	3 277	1 647

Source: EBRD (2002, 2003, 2004).

unemployment, even within smaller countries, and in skills mismatches. The situation is exacerbated by limited domestic labour mobility. Better integration and operation of labour markets is required in all new and candidate countries to facilitate macroeconomic and social stability, to ease further integration into the single market and to ensure that eventual euro area membership does not create long-term adjustment problems.

Accession requires a commitment to join the euro area and the acceding states have expressed their intention to do so as soon as possible. This demands compliance with the convergence criteria, and the ease with which they achieve this will vary. The Baltic States and Slovenia will be the first to adopt the euro as they do not have the fiscal problems of the larger new members. Estonia, Lithuania and Slovenia joined ERM II in June 2004, a necessary precursor for euro adoption. Given the need for a minimum two-year period in ERM II, the earliest possible date for admission to the euro area for these countries is June 2006, although it may not occur until January 2007.

Inflation increased significantly in all new Member States in 2004, with the exception of Cyprus, Slovakia and Slovenia. Two general factors underpinned this trend. First, there was an upsurge in both oil and non-oil commodity prices. Secondly, several new members had to increase indirect taxation to bring them into line with the *acquis* – a factor that will drop out of the index by early 2005. In short, there were highly specific and short-term reasons for the surge in inflation in the new Member States in 2004, but the medium-term inflationary outlook is Maastricht compliant. Even if oil prices continue to

Table 3: Indicators of Real and Nominal Convergence, 2004

	Inflation (%)	Long-term Interest Rates (%)	Govt. Balance /GDP	National Debt /GDP	Unemployment (%)	Current Account/ GDP
Cyprus	2.4	5.8	−5.2	72.6	4.2	−4.5
Czech Republic	2.8	5.0	−4.8	37.8	8.3	−6.1
Estonia	3.4	4.5	0.5	4.8	9.7	−13.0
Hungary	6.9	8.4	−5.5	59.7	5.8	−8.7
Latvia	6.8	5.0	−2.0	14.6	9.9	− 9.9
Lithuania	1.2	4.6	−2.6	21.1	11.4	−8.7
Malta	3.7	4.7	−5.1	72.4	8.6	−4.0
Poland	3.5	7.2	−5.6	47.7	19.0	−2.6
Slovakia	7.7	5.1	−3.9	44.2	18.4	−2.9
Slovenia	3.9	4.8	−2.3	30.9	6.3	−0.2

Source: Commission (2004).

increase, they will also impact on euro area economies and push the Maastricht reference point upwards.

Although slight improvements were seen in 2004, the budget deficit criteria pose the biggest threat to the euro aspirations of the larger new Member States, notably Poland, Hungary and the Czech and Slovak Republics. Strong economic growth had a positive effect on revenues. Moreover, indirect tax reforms helped several states reap larger than anticipated revenues. These factors do not release the bigger states from the need to take unpopular decisions regarding their public finances, but they do ease the pressure somewhat especially if, as anticipated, strong economic growth is sustained. Cyprus and Malta also have serious budget problems within the context of euro membership and, unlike the other new members, also breach the national debt criteria to which Hungary also comes perilously close. For other new members, the fiscal criteria pose no problems for euro membership, and reform of the Stability and Growth Pact could ease things further.

III. Economic Developments in Individual States

Poland

Poland's economy is much more robust than two years ago and its outlook continues to improve. Recovery began in 2003 when growth reached 3.8 per cent and accelerated to almost 6 per cent in 2004. Initially, recovery was driven almost equally by net exports and domestic demand but, in 2004, domestic demand became the main contributor to growth. In early 2004, domestic demand was supported by favourable monetary conditions and delays in tightening fiscal policy. However, inflationary pressure resulted in two interest rate hikes during the summer, the first for four years, and aspects of the delayed fiscal recovery plan should finally come into play in 2005.

These less supportive monetary and fiscal policies helped slow economic growth slightly towards the end of 2004, but investment will provide the main push behind domestic demand in the medium term. Investment declined between 2001 and 2003, but began to recover slowly from the end of 2003. During 2004, it grew by 6.5 per cent and should reach double figures in 2005 and 2006. This improvement is founded on EU accession-related opportunities, high levels of corporate profitability and high levels of capacity utilization and emerging output constraints.

Investment has also been boosted by export demand, a trend which continued in 2004, despite the moderate appreciation of the zloty against the euro, and which was helped by the improved performance of Poland's main export markets and manufacturing productivity gains. The overall net contribution of exports to Polish growth is declining however, as a result of the high import content of Polish exports and the resurgence of investment.

Despite positive growth and investment, Poland has still seen only a moderate improvement in its high unemployment rate. Indeed, in 2004 total employment declined slightly. Continuing job losses so far into the recovery reflect ongoing restructuring, especially in heavy industry and agriculture, and productivity improvements. Sustained growth will eventually reverse the trend, but not sufficiently to lead to a rapid improvement in labour markets. In 2004, Polish unemployment averaged 19 per cent of the civilian labour force. By 2006, the European Commission forecasts that unemployment will still be 18.1 per cent.

There was slightly better news in 2004 for Poland's other big economic problem – its public finances. The budget deficit for 2004 was 5.6 per cent, slightly lower than forecast. Improvement stemmed from the stronger than anticipated economic performance which, in turn, translated into higher government revenues. However, the deficit still represented a 1.7 percentage point deterioration on the 2003 deficit. The improved cyclical performance resulted in a downward revision of the forecast for the deficit to 4.1 per cent and 3.1 per cent in 2005 and 2006, respectively. Achievement of the target also depends on implementation of long delayed plans to cut spending, which looks far from certain.

It is the public sector finance issue which ensures that Poland will not be in the first tranche of new Member States to adopt the euro. The second part of 2004 saw inflation accelerate to 3.5 per cent from 0.7 per cent in 2003 as a result of accession-related indirect tax increases, and rising oil and food prices.

Although the outlook for oil prices remains uncertain, favourable developments in other determinants of inflation are such that inflation will not cause problems to Poland's euro ambitions.

Hungary

In 2004, real GDP growth in Hungary reached 3.9 per cent, based on accelerating growth in exports and investment which increased by 12.3 per cent and 10 per cent respectively. This contrasts starkly with 2003 when the 3 per cent growth rate was driven largely by an 8 per cent growth in private consumption. Reduced net disposable income and an increasing savings ratio reduced private consumption growth to 3 per cent in 2004.

Inflation reached a turning point in 2004. Although the annual average annual inflation rate hit 6.9 per cent, more than two percentage points above 2003 levels, disinflation began to take hold in late 2004. The price surges of late 2003 and early 2004 resulted from increases in administered prices, indirect taxes, and food and fuel prices. However, these factors began to fall out of the figures by late 2004. The easing of inflationary pressures was also helped by a stronger and more stable forint, marginal increases in public sector wages and intensification of import competition between tradeable goods resulting from EU accession.

The fight against inflation is not helped by continuing labour market tightness and the notoriously inflexible Hungarian labour markets, which have resulted in the fast growth of real wages, especially in the private sector. Although unemployment is relatively low by European standards, labour market participation rates are low and employment growth has been slow, a factor partly explained by some of the highest labour taxes in the OECD. In September 2004, the government introduced exemptions from 50 per cent of social contributions to small companies hiring staff. These and other measures are needed to prevent labour market bottlenecks and inflexibilities, inhibiting long-term growth and to maximize opportunities from the single market.

Public finances are another troublesome area for Hungary. Despite higher than forecast real GDP growth, shortfalls in tax revenues and expenditure levels above what was planned meant that the budget deficit target was missed. In September cuts and temporary freezes in expenditure were introduced, but these postponed rather than cancelled spending, and will take full effect only in the longer term. Moreover, the revenue side has been adversely affected because cuts in personal income tax have not been fully offset by tax increases elsewhere. Such problems mean that at 59.7 per cent in 2004, the national debt remains perilously close to the Maastricht limit of 60 per cent.

In the medium term, the outlook is relatively positive for Hungary. Economic policy will be guided more and more by the goal of euro entry during 2008–10.

This will not be easy. Although inflation is moving in the right direction, the budget deficit is proving stubborn and will require the strict enforcement of austerity packages, a policy that is not too attractive in the face of an approaching election. Growth will remain solid rather than spectacular, and will be driven by exports and investment, which will grow more slowly than in 2004. However, the effect of any modest slowdown in these two indicators will be compensated for by a moderate increase in private consumption.

Czech Republic

The acceleration of economic growth that began in 2003 continued into 2004, reaching 3.8 per cent for the year as a whole. Growth has become less reliant on private consumption and with a greater contribution from investment and an improved export performance. Enlargement improved access to western European markets and the modest EU recovery benefited Czech exporters. The Czech economy is also starting to reap the competitive benefits of restructuring.

Earlier FDI is now yielding benefits with the result that, in 2004, half of industrial output and 70 per cent of exports originated from foreign-owned companies. Good infrastructure, a location at the heart of Europe and a skilled but relatively cheap labour force underpin the Czech Republic's ability to attract the greatest amount of FDI per capita amongst the new Member States. The automotive and electronics industry have been particularly attractive to foreign investors. As a result of the increasing maturity of the Czech economy, more FDI is occurring in services and research and development which creates higher paid and better quality jobs, and which helps the Czech Republic develop its knowledge economy. Moreover, FDI increasingly includes investments by small and medium-sized companies.

Total FDI inflows are likely to decline, however, in the face of strong competition for investment and the emergence of constraints, of which the persistence of labour market skills mismatches and immobility are the most serious. Unemployment is particularly concentrated in regions like northern Bohemia and northern Moravia, regions which are unattractive to investors because of poor transport links. In regions that have attracted FDI, investors are reporting difficulties finding sufficient skilled workers. Unemployment generally has not responded to the growth of the last few years because of these structural rigidities and because of ongoing industrial restructuring, the impact of which has been greater than that of job creation in new industries.

Despite reaching 2.8 per cent for the year as a whole, following deflation of 0.1 per cent in 2003, inflation is not a major concern for the Czech economy. The price surge stemmed from higher oil prices and one-off indirect tax increases as a result of EU accession. Price increases peaked in the third quarter and, by the end of 2004, inflation was again on a downward trend and in the target range of 2–2.4 per cent. Strong domestic and foreign competition, two interest rate hikes, appreciation of the koruna and lower food prices all helped.

Of more concern, however, is the public deficit. The strong growth of 2004 and indirect tax reforms boosted revenues and helped lower the budget deficit to 4.8 per cent of GDP, a bigger than anticipated fall. However, further progress will require expenditure cuts, cuts which the government appears reluctant to implement in the face of its small parliamentary majority and looming elections. This helps explain the Central Bank's advice that the Czech Republic should not attempt to enter ERM II in 2005. Price and interest rate criteria are currently fulfilled, but 2008 is the official target date for achieving a 3 per cent budget deficit.

Smaller Acceding Countries

In *Slovakia*, real GDP growth accelerated from 4 per cent in 2003 to almost 5 per cent in 2004. Growth in 2003 relied on a 23 per cent growth in real exports, whereas the contribution from domestic demand was non-existent. In 2004, although export performance remained strong at 16 per cent, import growth almost offset it, leading to a much smaller growth contribution from external demand. Consequently, private consumption, benefiting from renewed growth in real personal disposable income, and investment replaced net exports as the main drivers of growth in 2004.

The authorities are aiming for ERM II entry in early 2006, with a view to euro adoption on 1 January 2009. After an inflationary surge in 2003 and 2004, rapid improvements in inflation are expected as the effects of indirect tax increases fall out of the figures. Already by December 2004, inflation had fallen to 5.9 per cent in relation to December 2003, compared to an average of 7.7 per cent for the year as a whole. Attempts to reduce the general government deficit are also yielding gradual results. The deficit was estimated at 3.9 per cent in 2004 and will remain at similar levels in 2005 and 2006, before falling to 3 per cent in 2007.

At 18.4 per cent in 2004, unemployment is not far below the 2001 peak of 19.4 per cent, and remains Slovakia's most serious economic problem. The employment growth of 2003 was reversed in 2004 as economic restructuring continued and unemployment rose again after its strongish fall in 2003, following unemployment benefit reform. Some improvement in labour markets, albeit gradual rather than rapid, is expected in the medium term, but large regional disparities persist.

In 2004, real GDP growth in *Slovenia* bounced back from its ten-year low in 2003 to register 4 per cent on the back of a surge in investment, increases in household expenditure, a significant increase in inventories and a narrowing trade deficit. Slovenia remains on track to adopt the euro by early 2007. In June 2004, the tolar entered ERM II at a rate of 239.64 tolar per euro within a fluctuation band of +/– 15 per cent. Monetary policy had hitherto been directed towards slow depreciation of the currency. Since June, there has been a gradual appreciation in nominal effective exchange rates against the dollar and the pound sterling, but the tolar has remained stable against the euro.

Inflation had been the biggest threat to euro adoption at over 8 per cent in 2001, but it had fallen below 4 per cent by late 2004. Following on the 2003 agreement to reduce public sector wage indexation, it was agreed in May 2004 that private sector wages should lag productivity growth by at least one percentage point. Higher levels of growth and the risk of higher oil prices pose the biggest inflationary threat, but, assuming continuation of anti-inflationary policies and exchange rate stability, the long-term movement of prices should be downwards.

No major problems are anticipated on the fiscal side. A technical revision of accounts has raised the general government deficit by 0.2–0.5 per cent for the period 2000–03 and, although a slight deterioration was forecast for 2004, control of the deficit will be helped by buoyant growth and tight control over expenditure.

Real GDP growth in *Estonia* accelerated to almost 6 per cent in 2004. This resurgence resulted from a combination of improved export performance and buóyant domestic demand. The latter benefited from employment growth, real wage increases and credit expansion. Despite the export recovery and good tourism results, in 2004 Estonia had a current account deficit equivalent to about 13 per cent of GDP. It is this external imbalance, plus future uncertainty over oil prices, which pose the greatest threat to sustained growth in Estonia.

In June 2004, the kroon entered ERM II at a rate of €1 = 15.6466 kroon. During its ERM II membership, Estonia will continue with its currency board arrangement and has stated that it does not intend to use the 15 per cent fluctuation bands. Indeed, for the remainder of 2004, the kroon's value against the euro remained unchanged.

In terms of convergence criteria, Estonia remains well placed. Inflation accelerated to 3.4 per cent in 2004, largely as a result of one-off accession-induced indirect tax increases and rises in administered prices. A gradual decrease in prices is anticipated beyond 2005. Public finances remain in good order: in 2003, the government surplus reached 3.1 per cent of GDP. Although the surplus fell to 0.3 per cent of GDP, modest surpluses are anticipated to continue throughout 2005 and 2006.

In 2004, real GDP growth in *Latvia* was 7.5 per cent, the highest in the EU and 3.5 times the euro area average. Private consumption and investment continue to be the driving force behind growth. The former was boosted by employment growth, sustained increases in real wages and domestic credit growth. Investment was helped by favourable credit conditions and macro-economic stability. Export growth also accelerated in 2004, but imports grew even more quickly, resulting in a negative contribution from external trade and a current account deficit of 9.4 per cent of GDP in 2004.

High growth helped reduce unemployment, albeit slowly, which averaged 10 per cent in 2004. The limited improvement is partly explained by high levels of regional disparities, skills mismatches and continuing job losses from restructuring. Productivity improvements have also soaked up additional demand for labour.

In preparation for ERM II entry, the pegging of the lat shifted from the SDR to the euro at a rate of €1 = 0.702804 lat on 30 December 2004. Latvia comfortably met the Maastricht convergence criteria until inflation (boosted by tax reforms, oil and regulated price increases and lat depreciation) acceler-ated towards the end of 2003, resulting in an annual inflation rate of 6.8 per cent in 2004, the highest for six years. In future, robust demand could lead to overheating. Public finances remain healthy: although public expenditure increased by almost 18 per cent in 2004 revenues, encouraged by strong growth and above target tax collection rates, registered almost 20 per cent growth. Accordingly, the budget deficit for the year remained with the target range of 2 per cent of GDP.

In *Lithuania*, strong credit expansion, higher employment and accession-related invested projects underpinned rapidly growing private consumption and investment, the major contributors to real GDP growth of 7 per cent in 2004. Export growth accelerated to almost 10 per cent but imports grew even faster (13.4 per cent). The widening trade deficit was a major factor in the increase in the current account deficit to almost 9 per cent of GDP.

In June 2004, Lithuania entered ERM II at a rate of €1 to 3.45280 litas. During its sojourn in ERM II, Lithuania's currency board will remain intact. The Central Bank has expressed a preference for 1 January 2007 for full euro area entry, and Lithuania appears well positioned to meet the convergence criteria. Despite a reversal in the deflationary trend of 2002–03 as a result of higher oil, transport and health care prices coupled with tax reform, inflation was only 1.2 per cent in 2004. The 2004 budget deficit increased to 2.6 per cent of GDP in 2004, compared to 1.7 per cent in 2003. Capital projects, pension reform and a rise in public sector wages and welfare benefits pushed the deficit upwards. However, revenue growth remains strong and further deterioration of the deficit is not anticipated. Government debt, at 21 per cent of GDP, remains well within the convergence criteria for euro area entry.

Lithuania's biggest economic problem is unemployment. However, a combination of economic growth and active labour market policies reduced joblessness from its peak of 16.4 per cent of the workforce in 2001 to below 10 per cent by the end of 2004.

Real GDP growth in *Malta* was strong during the first quarter of 2004 but fell back thereafter, reaching 1 per cent for the year as a whole – low by the standards of other new Member States but an improvement on the 0.2 per cent outturn of 2003. This moderate growth increase results from continuing strong, albeit declining, investment growth and higher exports. The external sector has been helped by a recovery in Malta's export markets and sluggish domestic demand that has restrained imports. The relative buoyancy of investment and the external sector were sufficient to offset the continuing stagnation in public and private consumption. Destocking also exercised a negative impact on Maltese growth in 2004.

Despite subdued domestic demand, inflation, largely driven by higher fuel prices and increased VAT rates, more than doubled to reach 3.7 per cent in 2004. Some price moderation is expected in 2005, however, as the effect of the tax increases falls out of the figures. The modest growth of 2004 boosted employment slightly, but has had little effect on unemployment, which has been affected by some manufacturing restructuring. Some recovery in domestic consumption is forecast for 2005–06. This, combined with sustained export demand, will help the labour market in the medium term. Public finances are also improving: the deficit was reduced to 5.1 per cent of GDP in 2004, but gross government debt remains over 70 per cent of GDP.

Cyprus is one of the more prosperous of the new Member States, but is particularly vulnerable to external shocks. Tourism, for example, contributes as much as 15 per cent to GDP, but between 2001 and 2003 tourist arrivals fell significantly as a result of the unstable situation in the Middle East, SARS and low growth in the EU. Tourist arrivals increased by 3 per cent in 2004, but were still only 82 per cent of 2001 levels.

Despite this unfavourable external environment, GDP growth accelerated to 3.5 per cent in 2004 from 2 per cent in 2002 and 2003. Strong investment and private consumption, helped in part by increasing employment, were the main drivers behind growth. Investment was helped by accession, continuing liberalization and restructuring of the utilities sectors. Improvements in EU markets also helped stimulate real export growth which made a smaller, but nonetheless important, contribution, to overall growth.

On 19 October, the Council of Ministers decided in principle to apply for membership of ERM II. Inflation in 2004 fell to 2.4 per cent, tempered by appreciation of the local currency. Interest rates were raised by 1 per cent in April to offset fears of a devaluation sparked off by the 'no' vote in the referendum on the Annan plan on reunification and to reduce the risk of capital outflows following the final capital liberalization prior to accession. The biggest convergence problem for Cyprus lies with public finances. There was some success in 2004 in reducing the budget deficit to 5.2 per cent, down from 6.4 per cent the previous year. It is projected to fall to 3 per cent and 2.4 per cent in 2005 and 2006 respectively. However, general government debt remains above 70 per cent of GDP and will remain above the 60 per cent Maastricht level for some years.

Candidates for Post-2004 Accession

In 2004, real GDP growth in *Bulgaria* was again based on domestic demand and accelerated to 5.5 per cent, compared to 4.3 per cent in 2003, thereby consolidating the recovery underway since 1998. Private consumption in 2004 registered 6 per cent growth, driven by credit expansion, employment increases and real disposable income gains, whereas investment grew by 15 per cent. Strong domestic demand meant that, despite an 11.1 per cent increase in the value of real exports, imports grew even more quickly (13.8 per cent) and net exports made a large negative contribution to GDP.

Having fallen steadily since 2000, inflation accelerated to 6 per cent in 2004 as a result of higher food, administered and oil prices, and indirect tax increases. Resumption of the downward trend is forecast, but wage increases in excess of productivity increases could limit this. Unemployment began to fall in 2002 – a trend that continued into 2004 when joblessness averaged 12.2 per cent. Increases in labour market participation rates and ongoing restructuring prevented the faster fall in unemployment that rapid economic growth would suggest.

The general government balance was in surplus to the equivalent of 0.5 per cent of GDP in 2004 in line with the government's commitment to maintain a balanced budget and to save extra revenues as a bulwark against external shocks. High GDP growth will facilitate continuation of this favourable budgetary position.

Overall, the outlook for the Bulgarian economy is optimistic, considering its basic dysfunctionality less than ten years ago. However, it remains vulnerable in terms of external balance and the danger that real wage increases, if not accompanied by appropriate productivity gains, could undermine Bulgaria's competitiveness and take the brake off inflation.

Romania's strong economic recovery was sustained in 2004 with real GDP growth of over 7 per cent compared to 4.9 per cent in 2003. Recovery continued to be driven almost entirely by domestic demand: household consumption surged 8 per cent as a result of easy credit and higher real wages. Public consumption growth was also the highest for some years and investment, underpinned by a strong construction sector and economic restructuring, accelerated 10 per cent.

However, strong domestic demand has had a negative impact on the external sector. In 2004, despite a 17.9 per cent growth in the real value of exports, real import growth was even higher at 18.9 per cent as the heightened domestic demand growth sucked in imports, leading to trade and current account deficits equivalent to 8.6 per cent and 6 per cent of GDP respectively. Financing of the current account deficit will be facilitated by the increasing remittances from Romanians working abroad and higher levels of FDI inflows.

Reductions in Romania's inflation continued in 2004. Although still high by standards elsewhere in the region, the 12 per cent rise in Romania's consumer price index in 2004 represented a considerable improvement on the 45 per cent plus inflation of 2000. Strong growth has not resulted in overheating because of productivity gains resulting from industrial restructuring. A deceleration of the rate of depreciation of the lei has also helped mitigate price pressure. The main inflationary risk factor remains global energy prices.

Romanian public finances remain healthy. In the summer of 2004, on the back of strong revenue growth, two supplementary budgets were introduced which reduced the general government deficit target for 2004 to 1.6 per cent of GDP, down from 3 per cent. First estimates suggest the target was attained. Strong revenue growth is expected to continue, but the deficit could creep up marginally in 2005 and 2006 as a result of tax cuts.

Unemployment remains stable at around 6.6 per cent. This relatively low and stable unemployment rate has been made possible by the compensatory effect of the growth in private-sector employment relative to the redundancies resulting from restructuring of state-owned companies. If restructuring accelerates as expected, the net effect on Romanian employment may turn negative.

After real GDP growth of 5.2 per cent and 4.3 per cent in 2002 and 2003, respectively, growth in *Croatia* fell to 3.8 per cent in 2004. The EU anticipates that growth will accelerate to 4 per cent in 2005 and 4.5 per cent in 2006 as stronger external demand increasingly begins to compensate for weaker domestic demand which was affected by tight monetary policy and restricted credit growth. Both public and private consumption growth rates fell in 2004, and even though investment grew by 7.3 per cent, this was significantly below the 12 per cent and 16.8 per cent growth of 2002 and 2003, respectively. Further declines in investment growth are forecast for 2005 and 2006.

Croatia's external sector has benefited from lower domestic demand in the form of lower import growth which has helped reduce the trade deficit to 26.9 per cent of GDP (from 27.4 per cent in 2003) and the current account balance to 5.7 per cent from 7 per cent in 2003. However, a gradual increase in import growth is anticipated for 2005 and 2006 in response to the anticipated gradual pick-up in domestic demand and to the relatively high import component of exports, which are expected to grow more strongly over the 2004–06 period.

Croatian growth contributed to employment growth of almost 1 per cent in 2004 but, given continuing industrial restructuring, unemployment crept up to 14.7 per cent from 14.5 per cent the previous year. The anticipated acceleration of GDP growth over the next two years will help reverse the upward movement of unemployment. Inflation accelerated to 2.4 per cent in 2004 from 1.8 per cent in 2003 because of higher fuel, housing and transport costs, but was further contained by the moderation of domestic demand. Public sector reforms and greater financial discipline in public organizations, plus one-off revenue measures helped reduce the government deficit from 6.3 per cent of GDP in 2003 to 4.5 per cent in 2004.

Turkey's economic recovery accelerated in 2004 with growth increasing from 5.8 per cent in 2003 to 8.5 per cent in 2004. Private consumption and investment benefited from greater political and economic stability, and remained the main drivers behind growth. Consumption grew by over 11 per cent in 2004, whereas investment increased by around 40 per cent, bolstered by strenuous modernization initiatives. The European Commission forecasts further strong growth in 2005 and 2006, albeit at a lower level than in 2004, with consumption and investment continuing their pivotal role. A further vote of confidence for Turkey comes from the IMF. In a December 2004 press release, the IMF's managing director spoke of the 'positive results' achieved by Turkey in its current economic programme and his expectations that a new three-year programme, for which it is seeking IMF support, would 'help Turkey create the conditions for sustained growth and enhance the economy's resilience ... It should also allow Turkey to exit from further financial support'.

The fall in inflation has continued to exceed expectations. By the autumn of 2004, inflation had fallen to 10 per cent, compared to 25 per cent for 2003. Wage restraint, a strong lira and a commitment to fiscal discipline have helped contain price increases, a trend that is forecast to continue over the next couple of years. The budget deficit in 2003 was 8.7 per cent and fell to around 7 per cent in 2004 – a major achievement given that the deficit almost reached 30 per cent of GDP as recently as 2001. Strong economic growth made the deficit reduction possible by boosting revenues whilst expenditures were kept within targets. The falling budget deficit has also facilitated declines in general government debt to 83 per cent in 2004 from 105 per cent in 2001.

News is less positive on the unemployment front. Although there was some increase in employment in 2004, the unemployment rate has remained stable at 10–11 per cent since 2002, despite the buoyancy of growth. Part of the explanation for this lies in modernization, which has resulted in labour shedding and increased productivity. Large increases in the labour supply, given the large number of young people set to enter the labour force, make any major inroads on joblessness unlikely in the next couple of years.

Greater domestic demand has also contributed to strains in the external account by sucking in imports. Despite the strength of the lira, export growth has remained robust, but not robust enough to prevent a big increase in the trade deficit. Textile trade liberalization will increase competition for Turkey's most important manufactured export. The current account has also deteriorated (from 2.9 per cent of GDP in 2003 to 4.9 per cent in 2004), but there are hopes that good tourism performance will help offset further external pressures.

Conclusion

Growth in the new and candidate Member States in 2004 benefited from sustained and strong growth in the global economy, unlike the previous year when they faced an unwelcoming external environment. In most cases, buoyant domestic demand, especially of private consumption and investment, was the most important factor in growth and is forecast to continue to perform this role. Improvements in labour markets were disappointing, but this may change as restructuring nears conclusion. The inflationary boost of 2004, apart from the contribution from oil and commodity prices, appears to have been a one-off phenomenon and inflation should abate somewhat in 2005. European Commission forecasts for these economies in 2005 and 2006 suggest a mild slowdown, but growth generally remains strong and at a level which enables the newer Member States to continue the long process of catch-up with pre-2004 members.

References

Commission of the European Communities (2004) 'Economic Forecasts'. *European Economy*, No. 5/2004.
EBRD (2002) *Transition Report 2002: Agriculture and Rural Transition* (London: European Bank for Reconstruction and Development).
EBRD (2003) *Transition Report 2003: Integration and Regional Co-operation* (London: European Bank for Reconstruction and Development).
EBRD (2004) *Transition Report 2004: Infrastructure* (London: European Bank for Reconstruction and Development).

Chronology: The European Union in 2004

LEE MILES
University of Liverpool

At a Glance

Presidencies of the EU Council: Ireland (1 January–30 June) and the Netherlands (1 July–31 December).

Signing of 'Treaty establishing a Constitution for Europe' (TCE – otherwise known as the EU Constitutional Treaty). Beginning of ratification phase.

Accession of ten new countries expands the size of the Union to 25.

January
13   Commission proposes 'Bolkestein Directive' establishing a legal framework for elimination of obstacles to free movement of services between Member States.

21   Commission's First Report on Implementation of 2003–05 Broad Economic Policy Guidelines (BEPG).

February
6   Commission presents mid-term assessment of action plan on skills and mobility.

10   Commission communication on new financial framework – 'Building our common future – Policy challenges and budgetary means of the enlarged Union 2007–13'.

Journal compilation © 2005 Blackwell Publishing Ltd, 9600 Garsington Road, Oxford OX4 2DQ, UK and 350 Main Street, Malden, MA 02148, USA

11   Commission action plan to promote entrepreneurship.

11   Council and Parliament adopt decision on monitoring greenhouse gas emissions, and directives on measuring CO_2 emissions and light commercial vehicles.

19   Council adopts Regulation (377/2004) on immigration liaison officer network.

March

10   Parliament and Council adopt Regulation (EC 491/2004) on programme for financial and technical assistance to third countries on migration and asylum (ARENEAS).

11   Terrorist bombing in Madrid.

22   Former Yugoslav Republic of Macedonia (FYROM) submits full membership application.

24   Commission finds Microsoft guilty of abusing dominant market position and hands out largest fine ever imposed under EU competition policy rules.

24–25 European Council summit in Brussels. Recommend that IGC be re-convened to be concluded by June 2004 and agrees declaration on combating terrorism.

25   Tripartite social summit held in Brussels between social partners.

April

20   Commission communication on 'A Proactive Competition Policy for a Competitive Europe'.

21   Council and Parliament's adoption of directive on environmental liability regarding the 'polluter pays principle' (PPP).

30   Commission publishes Green Paper on EU action on public–private partnerships.

May

1   Accession of ten new countries. EU enlarges to 25.

12   Commission presents strategy paper and country reports as part of European neighbourhood policy (INP).

21   First EU–Russia summit in Moscow. EU pledges support for Russian entry
          into the World Trade Organization.

June

1   Partial introduction of European health card in certain Member States.

1   Commission published first review of Cardiff process.

8   Decision establishing system for exchange of visa data between Member
          States (VIS).

9   Commission action plan on a European environment and health strategy.

10–13   Direct elections to the European Parliament (EP).

16   Commission communication on 'Science and technology, the key to Europe's
          future'.

17–18   European Council summit in Brussels. IGC reconvened. Major agreement on
          EU Constitutional Treaty achieved.

July

5   Council agrees to update Broad Economic Policy Guidelines (BEFG).

7   Commission establishes new guidelines on permissible state aids for rescuing
          and restructuring firms.

12   Commission report on European employment services (EURES).

14   Commission submits proposals for the post-enlargement cohesion policy and
          2007–13 financial perspective.

August

12   Commission communication on results of European social dialogue.

September

3   Commission presents communication on 'Strengthening economic governance
          and clarifying the implementation of the Stability and Growth Pact'.

23   Commission publishes Green Paper on European regulatory framework for
          defence equipment.

23   'Employment in Europe 2004' report published.

29   Commission proposes LIFE+ as EU's sole financial instrument for the environment.

October
26   Council regulation on agency for the management of operational co-operation at external borders.

28   Commission's15th annual report on the implementation of structural funds.

29   Signing of EU Constitutional Treaty in Rome.

November
4–5   European Council summit in The Hague. Approves 'Hague programme' (Council Document 16054/04).

19   Council adopts conclusions on common principles for immigrant integration policy in the EU.

22   Barroso Commission takes office.

25   Second EU–Russia summit in The Hague.

December
8   EU–China summit in The Hague.

12   Commission communication (2004/795) proposes draft action plans under European neighbourhood policy (INP).

15   Council and Parliament agree directive on transparency of European capital markets.

16   European Parliament adopts 2005 budget – the first covering the EU-25.

16–17   European Council summit in Brussels. Confirms Bulgarian and Romanian Accession Treaty can be finalized and opening of accession negotiations with Croatia and Turkey in 2005.

Index

Note: Italicized page references indicate information contained in tables.